ALLEN
VERBATIM

Selected major works by Allen Ginsberg:

HOWL AND OTHER POEMS (1956)
KADDISH AND OTHER POEMS (1961)
EMPTY MIRROR (1961)
REALITY SANDWICHES (1963)
THE YAGE LETTERS (with William Burroughs) (1963)
PLANET NEWS (1968)
INDIAN JOURNALS (1970)
THE GATES OF WRATH (1972)
THE FALL OF AMERICA (1973)

ALLEN VERBATIM LECTURES ON POETRY, POLITICS, CONSCIOUSNESS

by Allen Ginsberg
edited by Gordon Ball

McGRAW-HILL BOOK COMPANY
New York   St. Louis   San Francisco
Düsseldorf   London   Mexico
Sydney   Toronto

Book design: Elaine Gongora

123456789BABA7987654

Library of Congress Cataloging in Publication Data

Ginsberg, Allen, 1926–
    Allen verbatim: lectures on poetry, politics, consciousness.

    1. American poetry—20th century—Collected works.
2. Narcotics, Control of—United States—Collected works. I. Title.
PS3513.I74A69   815'.5'4   73-20079
ISBN 0-07-023285-7

Editor's dedication:

To my mother and father

and to Edward Tyler Urich,
            hermit
            planter
            teacher

Acknowledgments

During the past two years I have become deeply indebted to everyone who has shared time, resources, and optimism with me in the making of this book. I wish to thank first, of course, Allen; and Robert Duncan; and Joyce Johnson at McGraw-Hill, who in lending her acumen to the final version gave much of her personal as well as professional time. All members of my family —mother, father, sister, brother—have been encouraging throughout, and Bob Bertholf at Kent State was always available with advice and help when I needed him.

To friends and mentors at or near the University of North Carolina at Chapel Hill—Carolyn Kizer, Lewis and Mary Warren Leary, Richard Williams, Maggie Ketchum, Joan and Peter Trias, Louise Parrish, Ron Bayes, and Dennis Willigan—goes my gratitude for their sustained and generous helpfulness and patience.

And I wish to thank equally as much: heroic Peter Orlovsky, Denise Mercedes, Leslie Trumbull, Miles, Elva Bishop, Nancy Phillips, Lawrence Ferlinghetti, Joseph Cain III, Molly LaBerge, Janet Greenberg, Don Allen, Jon Sholle, Louis and Edith Ginsberg, Al Caen, Allen DeLoach, Kathy Doble, Ray Mungo, Carolyn and Martin Karcher, Rick Fields, Pattie O'Neill, David Barron, Diana and Tom Robbins, Ann and Harley Beal, Becky, Ann Buchanan, Ettore Sottsas, Donald Schanche, Nadine Reitzel, Alex and Linda McIntire, Lucien Carr, Rosalie Trew, Peter McNamara, Mike Finnegan, William and Keith Trotter, Frances Driver, Beverly and Tom Schwarz, Jon Miller, Peter Teeuwissen, Lou Rogers, Julie Runk, David and Susan Southern, Thomas Fitzsimmons, Gene Kimsey, Juli Tenney, Sara Vogeler, Ann Jones, Joe Gross, Peter Dale Scott, Elsa Dorfman, Michael Aldrich, and Stanley Karnow.

To all, and to all friendly strangers met along the way of this book these last two hard American years, thanks—rest, work and love well, it's over!

G.B.
New York City
August 25, 1973

Contents

Introduction

At the conclusion of three years I spent with Allen and several other friends on an Upstate New York farm, Allen invited me to join him on his cross-country college reading tour in the spring of 1971. He added, jokingly, that I could be his bodyguard. By the beginning of the seventies campus confrontations were at their height, and we were due to visit Kent State eleven months after its massacre.

I had acquired a portable Sony cassette recorder which I used to make various journalistic jottings and sometimes to record musician friends, and I brought it along.

Prior to the college readings, we stayed two weeks in Washington headquartered at the Institute for Policy Studies, where Allen was given a desk (see "Political Opium") next to former Goldwaterite Karl Hess. During that time Allen put the finishing touches on personal research he'd begun over a decade back, research he had shared with me and to which I lent a hand with some of the paperwork. Its purpose, basically, was twofold: to alleviate the "law 'n' order" problem in this country by exposing the bureaucratic shell game, the police masquerade, which has forced over a million citizens afflicted by opiate addiction into a life of crime in lieu of medical treatment; and to help end our military and political involvement in Southeast Asia by uncovering U.S. support of the main opium and heroin traffickers there. Since police state intrusions upon the persons of many of my generation were becoming almost commonplace, the subject of the "Political Opium" section was a matter about which I carried more than tepid feelings. I had heard Allen make these points on numerous occasions, in public discussions and on TV talk shows, and was determined that a record be made.

Moving on to Kent State, we joined fellow poets Robert Duncan and Richard Grossinger, musician Lloyd McNeill, the Bread and Puppet Theater, and other artists for a weeklong Arts Festival. I continued recording. It was early April; the trees were barren, and the ground froze nightly. We retraced some of the steps of May 4, 1970, as the Bread and Puppet Theater enacted a pageant for victims and survivors. With the anniversary of the shootings and massive national antiwar demonstrations less than a month away, anxiety prevailed among many of the students (see "War and Peace: Vietnam and Kent State"). No less anxious was the university administration, which had established a sort of campus crisis center to which all campus "incidents," potential or actual, could be reported by phone. The efficiency of their response was aptly demonstrated while we were there. Poet Gary Snyder, on his way to read at Kenyon College, stopped in at Kent to visit Allen on the one mild sunny day of the week, and together they gave an unscheduled reading in the far corner of an athletic field. Although there was little advance notice, several hundred students and faculty gathered to hear them. Soon after they began chanting "Gaté, Gaté, Para Gaté. . . ," a dispute arose between the sponsors of the reading and a girls' softball class led by their coach, who claimed the territory. Within moments an administration official and several campus security men were on the scene. Allen and Gary asked their group if they would mind moving elsewhere, and everyone reassembled in a new spot.

Enroute to Wisconsin, we spent two days in Cleveland, home of two poets who took their own lives (Hart Crane and d.a. levy) and of Lake Erie, whose waters have been deadened —completely—by industry. The land bordering the highway near the lakefront was spotted with seductive calls such as "Get Away From It All—Come to Treasure Lake!"

From Platteville, Wisconsin, we journeyed by train along the Mississippi River to Minneapolis, then flew to Laramie, Wyoming, for three days that included climbing ancient Amerindian sacred mountains with local brown-power people. The tour concluded at Davis, California, and chapters recorded there ("Identity Gossip" and "Myths Associated with Science") begin and end the book.

Throughout the tour, Allen's energy and interest in people and their situations and environments almost never flagged. Whereas Allen seemed to thrive on the activity, I sometimes felt as if I were sleepwalking from airport to campus to home to dormitory to class to reading to radio or TV station to airport, particularly as the journey wore on. We spent an average of two and a half or three days on each campus, and he would talk, read, or sing on each occasion as long as anyone wished, meeting all scheduled and unscheduled classes and events without fail. A few times in the past he had returned from long tours completely exhausted and sometimes ill, but was in good health in California at this tour's end.

A number of weeks later as we were waiting on the corner of San Francisco's Broadway and Columbus in front of City Lights Bookstore, facing the heart of North Beach and its dozens of topless joints which have now replaced the small bars, coffee shops, and galleries where two decades ago the poems of Ginsberg, Kerouac, Corso, Snyder, McClure, and others were first heard, Allen suggested, "You know, you could make a book from those tapes."

* * *

These chapters are a selection from transcriptions of approximately twenty hours of informal lectures and conversation. In terms of portraying Allen and the range and depth of his multiple interests and attentions, they are by no means comprehensive, as they were generated during one particular and rather short period of time. Nor are they entirely "verbatim," as much was edited (deleted or rephrased or restructured) to reduce repetition and fat normal in conversation but awkward in reading. (Although spoken language has been retained as much as possible.) Notes and introductory material are offered wherever I thought they might be useful, and all such entries should be considered mine except where otherwise indicated.

Gordon Ball

"Gnostic" Consciousness

The message is: Widen the area of consciousness.
—A.G., epigraph to *Kaddish and Other Poems* (San Francisco: City Lights, 1961)

Identity Gossip

1

RAP SESSION: UNIVERSITY OF CALIFORNIA AT DAVIS
April 27, 1971

"Identity Gossip" records the end of a long day at Davis, California. It had begun with a morning address to science students (see pp. 213-223) and was followed by open-air talks and poetry with the rest of the student body and a late-afternoon visit to gentle mouni Hari Dass (teacher of the former Richard Alpert, Baba Ram Dass). As we returned from an evening visit to a prisoners' writing class at Vacaville State Prison (where Dr. Timothy Leary was incarcerated prior to his transfer to and subsequent escape from the State Prison at San Luis Obispo), an impromptu rap session arose in the lounge of the dormitory where we were staying. A cameraman immediately began taking flash pictures, and thus the chapter begins with Allen's response to a question about fame, about being a center of attention.

AG: The problem of being the center of attention, like now, or being famous is an identity problem no different from anybody's identity problem because of the vastness of all of our identity problems: "Who am I," like "Who're you?" What's the actual identity, what's the actual inner person, *is* there even an inner self, is there any identity? Anybody's identity problem is the entire universe, it's as vast as the entire universe. Yours as well as mine. So actually in the grand scale with which we're dealing, my identity problem is not any bigger than yours.

Q: But it seems like you're moving around and surrounded by different people all the time.

AG: So are you. Aren't you? So are you. Now whether or not you relate to them and are conscious of them and they're conscious of you, on a subliminal level everybody's conscious of everybody including the trees, all the time. It's just that usually you don't acknowledge the tree's eyeball or you're not totally "on" in the communication. But in actuality you are moving around and surrounded by people and relating with people, one way or another. A negative relation or a blank relation is nonetheless a choice. So like when you're high on acid you know that you're surrounded by sentient beings all interrelated all the time except that you choose generally not to notice it, but you realize that you could notice it all the time if you wanted, if you were open.

You all know what a Zen koan is? It's like a verbal riddle or conceptual riddle presented to the body, to the meditator, which he meditates on in order to discover his ultimate nature. And one koan is, What is the face you had before you were born? So I find the problem of being stared at by others or being a center of energy or center of consciousness or "fame," like a koan. It presents me constantly with a mystical riddle of identity, to move through continuously and solve in different ways. The alternative would be to get paranoid about it and think of it as a big drag rather than as a karmaic mystic charming problem.

Q: Do you feel that people see you as you see yourself? As you visualize yourself?

AG: Sometimes, amazingly. Often not. I find out later, many years later, sometimes. . . . Like I gave a reading in Lawrence, Kansas, in 1965 and ran into someone here today who was at that reading, who said it freaked him out, freaked him out sort of, not in a bringdown way. He was studying business administration at the time, and I came around with Peter Orlovsky, who seemed a bit mad, and also there was the overt homosexual relation between us, plus Peter's catatonic brother Julius came along, so the "entourage" with me seemed to him completely socially displeasurable or socially out of bounds.

Now the point I was making was that socially out of bounds or not, the people I was running around with were existent, were there, were real at least in my life, so why shut them up in bughouses or something, why suppress it all? I mean it was there. The cat who was then freaked out is now sort of satisfied,

"Oh, it was just there," you know, the people were just there. He was trying to exclude them from reality at the time because he was trying to make it on a short-hair business scene where a schizophrenic catatonic wasn't welcome—though he existed, he wasn't welcome in that universe.

In other words at that time he was not seeing me as I saw myself.

Q: That seems to be a problem right here——

AG: But that's everybody's problem, too, see. I mean do people see you the way you want them to see you? Do they?

Q: No, but most of the people, you know—like when you're on the David Frost show, or something like that, and you start getting letters then you find out how they visualize you in specific terms. . . .

AG: Yeah; I know. But they send you eye glances, they send you all sorts of fan mail in the form of heart throbs, eye glances, little cries, and oo-bop-shebams, and moans in bed. In other words you get a feedback, actually.

Q: Isn't there a difference though in the awareness which you have of your audience and the balance of awareness coming back to you?

AG: Uh, don't know. I assume, actually, that there is one consciousness that we all share on the highest level, that we are all one Self, actually, that we are all one Self with one being, one consciousness.

Q: So the awareness between you and other persons is virtually the same as between me and us?

AG: Yes. When we all address ourselves to the highest awareness possible, to the highest awareness that we can conceive of among ourselves. So in a situation like this I try to address myself to that one consciousness, I try to pay attention or keep it in mind at least, conceptually if not heartwise, as much as possible, try to keep my body in a condition of the highest possibility of awareness, or keep that as the touchstone of the relationship, and so *can't* go wrong—trusting, however, that others do recognize this gleam in themselves.

Q: Then you never try to analyze this highest possibility of awareness?

AG: Yeah, sometimes analyze it in order to explain it for those who feel the hearthrob-gleam-mind-consciousness shared but who don't understand how it can be true.

Q: But for yourself you don't try to analyze something you're conscious of?

AG: No, to the extent that analysis requires the babble of language running like ticker tape through mind consciousness, I try to silence that babble and feel with my body more, exist in the feeling. Because what it is, finally, that highest level of consciousness, is like feeling, really, a feeling-sensation—consciousness. It's a body consciousness as well as a conceptual consciousness. So like in yoga the highest wisdom is centered in the heart.

A yogi today was telling me something I didn't know in yogic terms, that the heart is supposed to be guided by the third eye, or the area here *(points to the center of his forehead)*, the *ajana*, I think they call it, which is like intuition, imagination too. But at any rate the highest awareness of mammal is heart's knowledge.

Q: So the highest awareness doesn't necessarily involve a separation between body and mind.

AG: No. It means a stilling of superficial mind yatter and a sinking of the mind into the heart area. In fact there is a Tibetan mantra that articulates that particular conceptual set that we were just talking about, performed as Om Ah Hūṃ. Body *(points to head)* set in the head, actually, as if the body were just a mind concept that sprang out of mental conception. Body: Om. Ah *(points to larynx):* Speech. Mind *(points to heart):* Hūṃ. It's a very funny idea, the mind in the heart, as they put the body up there in the brain. Om Ah Hūṃ Vajra Guru Padma Siddhi Hūṃ, at least that's how it's done if you're practiced in that yoga, which is Om Ah Hūṃ, already explained. Then, Diamond Teacher—hard teacher, masculine teacher, tough teacher, hard: samsara, maya; hardness *(raps table)*—Vajra Guru. Padma (lotus, feminine, soft) Padma Siddhi: Lotus power, flower power. Why don't I chant that for a couple of minutes, because that's an interesting new addition to the American yoga scene. Since Hare Krishna be-

came a kind of pop mantra, you know, penetrated interestingly, this is as far as I know the second important mantra to hit America in the seventies. *(Chants five minutes)*
Try Om, it's interesting. . . . Close your lips at the end of the "Ooooommm" without clenching your teeth; it gives a funny vibrational massage to the front of your skull. . . *(continues with Om)*. . . you have to straighten your backbone to get enough air in your lungs. . . and breathe in your lower abdomen like natural childbirth breathing. . . straighten your backbone and let your belly hang out. *(Ends with Om Ah Hūṃ)*
   If that's done properly, actually you can get a slight buzz, literal physiologic buzz out of it. It's supposed to be equivalent to *kundalini*, what is called serpent power, or *kundalini* power, which is a bodily sensation, and also a mental sensation of the space of emptiness in a body. So, to conclude the question, finally I feel like a radiant but empty body. So that there is no disturbance in the radiant body which is the same as all body, all consciousness.

Q: What about Leary and his scene—how do you see it?

AG: I got a card from him two days ago, said everything's all right, surprisingly. So I don't know. I like him, I trust him; I think he's done heroic work, like he's taken all the lightning and the anxiety and all the shit for the entire nation's change of consciousness, to the extent that psychedelic drugs have catalyzed it. So I think he deserves like a great big reward and a giant professorship of psychology at the Supreme University of Consciousness in Minneapolis. He's done the best formulations of terminology about set and setting conditioning the Acid experience; he is really the best and most acute and most adept psychologist and the most serious psychologist in this area, of psychedelic psychology, and he obviously is being persecuted for his philosophy and his professional practice. You know—sent to jail for two roaches.
   Now when they sent him to jail, when he was sentenced to ten years in California and in Texas—ten years each, twenty years—and when he was denied bail the judges pronounced that he was being given heavy sentence for small amounts of grass specifically because of his writings and teachings, because his writings and teachings were "a menace to the community." And that's a very important basic fact: he's not in jail for two roaches,

because almost nobody except political prisoners get sent up so long for roaches, particularly not a college professor with a good record who's never been busted. He was sent up ostensibly by the judges for his public philosophizing—if you read the trial sentencing record—and sentenced for his texts, specifically a text in *Playboy*. And fragments of text of his testimony at the Chicago Trial were clipped out of the newspapers by the prosecuting attorney, and given to the judge as appendix material to show him why Leary should be kept in jail and denied bail and be given a long sentence.

So Leary therefore is in the class of a philosopher or professional savant who is being persecuted for his philosophy, his language, rather than any action that was illegal, that they could get him on. So I see him as one of the major scandals of the Academy. In other words, any psychology department in any university which does not ardently desire to have Leary on its faculty is a psychology department betraying its academic responsibility. Any law faculty which is not interested in his case as a case of abuse of constitutional propriety is ignorant of its scholarship responsibilities. Any student body accepting the fake materialistic mechanical science subsidized by Department of Defense grants and ignoring the sciences and arts proposed by Leary is doing itself out of an education. So I see Leary's situation as one of the major academic and legal scandals presently floating in the American karma.

He's the only man I know that no country in the world will have. So that means he couldn't be wrong. No bureaucracy in any country will accept him—which means that he couldn't be all bad. Everybody else can go somewhere—Communist, revolutionary, this one, that one; China, Russia, Korea—but he can't go anywhere, except to Algerian refuge under the aegis of Cleaver and Cleaver's very irritable with him, so Leary must be very uncomfortable. And I don't know what can be done, but sumpin' oughta be done.*

---

*On January 13, 1973, in the Kabul, Afghanistan, airport Dr. Timothy Leary was kidnapped in Watergate style by agents of the U.S. government and returned to the U.S. in violation of international law. Prior to his escape conviction his bail was set at $5 million, the highest for any single person in American history.

In December 1973 Dr. Leary was transferred from Folsom Prison to the California Medical Facility at Vacaville, where he is serving a six-month to ten-year sentence for possession of two roaches. He has also been given a five-year sentence (to be served consecutively, not concurrently) for his escape from San Luis Obispo, and the state of Texas has a ten-year "hold" on him for his Laredo arrest.

Q: I don't know too much about Zen, but how do you feel that complete sense consciousness or sense awareness would mix with Zen consciousness?

AG: I'm not a specialist in Zen; I know some Zen people like Gary Snyder and Watts and Roshi Suzuki, and I've done some sitting, formal Zen sitting, that involves abdominal breathing, so that's my preparation for any answer. If mind consciousness is stilled, that is if the matter babble behind the ear, yakety-yak ticker-tape conceptual language consciousness linear gossip inside the cranium, is shut up—which means a stillness in the vocal cords and vocal apparatus, and a stillness in the body—if by accident or design or practice you're able to turn off the phantasm consciousness that beclouds sense consciousness of the immediate present, then you have sharper sense consciousness, smell, taste, touch, optical, because you're not beclouding the doors of perception* with preconception, you're not inventing universes which overlie this universe.

To be a little more precise: if I'm looking at you but thinking "Gary Snyder's supposed to get here tomorrow night, what time is he supposed to get here?" I'm not seeing you or addressing you, so I'm not in sensory contact with you, simple as that. That's what I meant by phantasm consciousness overlying present moment sense consciousness.

Q: I was sort of wondering whether you are aiming toward a complete transcendence of the physical world.

AG: I don't know, I don't know. Depends on which yogi you go talk to. The Zen people don't aim at transcendence—they aim at no-mind in which the question of transcendence or immersion in the world is a piece of conceptual furniture dragged in (from being told to go to the bathroom in the toilet, you know) from conceptual body habit training from childhood grammar school.

In the ten years since he first attempted to live peaceably with dignity of purpose in Millbrook, New York (where his privacy and freedoms were initially violated by Duchess County law officers including G. Gordon Liddy), Dr. Leary has been arrested 14 times and undergone seven prosecutions. His current legal co-ordinators are Vasilios Choulos and Kent Russell, of the Melvin Belli law firm, in San Francisco.

*From William Blake's *The Marriage of Heaven and Hell* ("A Memorable Fancy"): *"If the doors of perception were cleansed every thing would appear to man as it is, infinite."*
Aldous Huxley used the same phrase for his personal account of mescaline: *The Doors of Perception and Heaven and Hell* (New York: Harper & Row, 1963).

The Zen people would say that mind is conditioned to manufacture displaced fantasy mostly, fantasy continuously displaced from this Place: where we are right now. And so the whole point of a Zen tea ceremony is precise, accurate, attentive gestures to the object in front of you, to neutral objects like the tea, the tea bowl, and to the pouring and mixing of the tea. So it's sort of like an exercise in the staying-aware of just exactly what you're doing instead of drifting off, even to transcend.

Q: Yeah, because if you completely transcended, you probably wouldn't write poetry, I guess.

AG: Yep, likely. Except when you say *transcend*—we haven't defined what we're talking about really——

Q: Well, I'm referring to states in which you leave this uh physical . . .

AG: . . . body. Yeah, I don't know, I've never done that. I've never left the body entirely, so I don't know. I'm not a yogi, either, like that—I mean I don't have that much *siddhi,* power; I don't have that much experience.

Q: If you don't indulge in the babble of the mind how do you verbalize your consciousness into poetry?

AG: Occasionally I just simply turn on and listen to the radio—it's just like listening to the radio—and then write it down. It goes on, except if you focus attention elsewhere. See, like if I'm chanting, for instance, conceptual language does stop. That's sort of the interesting thing about chanting—to see what it can do to a room. If I can stop my conceptual fantasy by forming myself or my identity into a column of breath that goes Om, vibrating in the body, and if other people do that or it sets up a sympathetic vibration in the sympathetic nervous systems of other people —you know like if you pluck one chord on a string and the other chords vibrate—so if other people tune in on that, sometimes it can reduce the room to a sort of frankly physical place where everybody is sitting in the immediate eternal present. Without having another thought, except being where they are. Or that's the ideal, that's my fantasy of what I'm doing, half the time. Actually someone told me that was the effect of the singing this afternoon on the quad. But I guess that varies with people. Does that seem like a believable fantasy?

Q: But it seems like when you're chanting you can't create something.

AG: No. You simply *are*, without creating any further. You're not creating any more universe than there already is right here.

Q: What's the advantage of that?

AG: Um, man, haven't you ever wanted to rest from all your godlike creations? Ain't you created enough? I mean what's the advantage of creating more? There's already so much here. And if you pay attention to what's already here, like accounting what's already here, being aware of what's already here, then you can go out and create some more stuff to fit in over there, if there's a place that's missing a piece of stuff like a piano or hard-on.

Q: Then creating is kind of like a relief of guilt.

AG: It's more a seeking out of an eternal state of consciousness, or trying to articulate an eternal state of consciousness, or seeking a response from other self in the terms that I was talking about before—that we are really all one self. Or at least that's how I see creating, that's how I see my poetry. You see it as a byproduct of guilt of some kind?

Q: Well, it seems to me that people who feel guilty are the most creative. People who fit in perfectly just become blocked, they don't have rough edges.

AG: I don't agree with you. There are different varieties of creation, but all those people making those breakable and atmosphere-befouling automobiles are also creating. They sure are creating, and creating real solid objects.

Q: What do you think about this town in terms of the technology you were talking about this morning?

AG: I haven't seen enough of the town. The campus is low, which is interesting. I was at UCLA last weekend, and gee, it's all these giant monolith buildings, whereas here everything's low. I don't know. I imagine that the agronomic-economics here is like bank capitalist creepy Moloch agricultural technology rather than anything more musical.

Q: I guess that's the foundation.

AG: Yeah, and I assume they haven't converted to anything more humanistic in their agronomy, or anything more ecologically attuned.

Q: I was wondering what you thought about the layout and the architecture of the place and the way the money is spent. The construction.

AG: It's nicer than most of the modern U.C. schools I've seen Partly because it's surrounded by farm fields, so that's sort of interesting.

Q: Yeah, but aside from comparing it to other places, if you had a chance to live here how would you feel?

AG: Well, what do you think about it?

Q: Well, I don't like it a lot of the time.

AG: Because of what particular details? From what particulars in the construction.

Q: From I guess the planning of it. . . .

AG: In what particular detail?

Q: A lot of it's very cold.

AG: Like where? How about this room, say?

Q: Well, classes and the administration building.

AG: Oh, I passed that by car. I didn't get a close-up look but I was surprised, I was told that was like the big tall building from which you could see the entire campus, so I was surprised to see it was only about four stories.

Q: Well, nothing else is very high around here.

AG: Well, it was a relief it wasn't a twenty-story monolith, it was only four stories. That was almost like a——

Q: Well, the trees planted on campus, I don't think it's natural, like it's all landscaped all the way long.

AG: Yeah, there is very little wildness around, that's true. But then this is a flat plain anyway.

Q: What do you think about the environment in human terms, from a sociopolitical view point?

AG: The only thing I feel about that, a little, is I wonder if it isn't a little like an artificial paradise in the sense that it's nicer here than Berkeley—it's calmer and more tranquil, but at the same time it's a little island of luxury and conspicuous consumption in the midst of a starving, torn-apart, freaked-out world. And I don't know to what extent the luxury here depends upon the exploitation of the Third World. Probably a good deal. I was at Kent and a lot of other places the last couple of months (this is the last reading I give for quite a while). So after two months of running around fifteen or twenty schools, I came to a view I hadn't seen before, similar to the hard-hat proposition: which is, basically, that the students in the United States are enjoying a very specialized way of life, compared to the rest of the world. They've really got it easy—you know, they have these great lounges, they can go around in their shorts and be as sexy as they want and get laid all they want, they get fed in cafeterias, and they have an unlimited supply of milk like big babies, and then they get these big jars of peanut butter like overgrown television pubescents, get all the books they want. . . Sort of like—at Kent State, for instance, it's sort of like an old folks' home for young people in that sense. Leading a very cloistered, sheltered, and spoon-fed life, you know, in which all the charming indulgences of American youth are indulged in, like having an unlimited milk supply and having little cars and gasoline they can run around in, bicycles and dates, and nice dormitories—a little cramped, you know, that's the only obvious sort of squeeze on consciousness there, that the dormitory rooms are being made smaller and smaller and the buildings larger.

Eternity

2

BLAKE/POETRY CLASS: KENT STATE
April 7, 1971

One day in 1948 at the age of twenty-two Allen found himself utterly alone in his Harlem apartment. His closest friends–Neal Cassady, Jack Kerouac, William Burroughs, Herbert Huncke, and others–were gone, love relationships had been broken, and he was graduating from Columbia with no prospects. In a moment of idleness, lying on the bed with his eyes drifting over a poem he'd often read before, Blake's "The Sun-flower," he suddenly understood the Sun-flower to be himself, the Self:

> Ah, Sun-flower! weary of time
> Who countest the steps of the sun;
> Seeking after that sweet golden clime,
> Where the traveller's journey is done.

Simultaneously he heard a deep ancient voice, which he identified as Blake's, as the Creator's, pronouncing the poem, bringing him into a deepening understanding of the poem and the universe. He then looked out the window and recognized that this existence, "existence" itself, was God, that this was "that sweet golden clime," that he was the son of a creator who loved him.

"Eternity" opens with Allen's response to being asked what brought about that precise experience or "opening" of consciousness, and in Chapter 3 he focuses on the means of communicating that consciousness.

15

AG: I didn't understand what caused the opening of consciousness, except solitude and inattention and giving up. In other words I'd given up on love——

Q: Like out of frustration?

AG: No, given up in the sense that St. John of the Cross[1] says that when finally after seeking and seeking you give up, you go into a night of despair, a dark night of the soul; when the soul then is passive, when it's not straining, striving, not seeking, when it is open unto the sky, then it sees. In other words when your attention is not focused on what you think you're supposed to be doing and seeking and praying for, but when the attention is completely open like a blossom, then the entire consciousness comes, in complete relaxation.

Q: That's the way moments of illumination would come to Wordsworth.

AG: Yeah. So it's actually in inattention, so to speak—when you're not tensed up and looking, because in the act of looking you're just using a small part of your rational consciousness, saying, "Well, let's see now; if I focus my eyes out the window and say that that window is Eternity and anything I see outside that window is a composition in Eternity," well, then, my mind will be filled with the language and I'll be thinking *about* a composition in Eternity instead of being actually in it, reflecting on being rather than being.

So the problem is how do you not think about being, or how do you get completely absorbed into your own presence, and the presence of Presence around you without mulling over and over, revolving around the corpse of a thought about it, or trying to go back to it in memory, or stepping in the same river over and over and over again. Well now each epiphany, each incarnation, each illumination, is going to be different, so that you can't reproduce next week the same one you had last week and it will probably come in different terms, just like everybody knows every trip is different on drugs.

Q: Isn't being enrolled in a university kind of eliminative of that type of consciousness?

AG: Any routine is, probably. On the other hand, being enrolled in a human body is also somewhat eliminative of that (unconditioned) type of consciousness. So the yoga is freeing yourself from habit-pattern conditioning, no matter what condition. A university tends to overaccentuate language babble in the head and language articulation, rather than complete open-mind sensory input—to the extent that in a sense you can't quite conveniently take an acid trip on campus (you can, but not quite conveniently), you also can't quite conveniently have a visionary experience on campus. Partly it's because there's no solitude, especially in these dormitories, it's like a real horror scene, everybody sitting on your bedsprings, many a body squeaking above you.

Q: I think it's partly because your mental machinery isn't working unless it's pushed to extremity, your powers aren't working . . .

AG: Yes, well, it's like the old thing "God works in mysterious ways his wonders to perform," God knows how people ever get to that point of balance where no matter what they're into—either despair, or an excess of joy, an excess of success —that finally there is nothing more to desire and all of a sudden—Bam!—everything opens up. In other words there is satiation instead of frustration. Or satisfaction can also precipitate awareness. Or, just by accident you're walkin' down the street, and—Bam!—where is the universe? You know, it isn't Chance and it isn't Times Square, it's Eternity Square, all of a sudden, and that's happened to a lot of people too.

Q: I was trying to think of a justification for a university because books do push you, and they're very frustrating.

AG: Well the books are all about nonbook experience. Though Western civilization has certainly come to this funny kind of contradictory point where finally its technology has produced a chemical which catalyzes a consciousness that finds the entire civilization leading up to that chemical pill absurd, because the consciousness was always there all along with the animals in the forest, or when you were huntin' the animals in the forest. And finally, the most sophisticated anthropologist comes to say, "Oh yes, of course, the Australian aborigines without written language have the most complex human consciousness" and live in Eternal Dream Time, naturally.

The function of Blake art or Blake's art, is to catalyze that experience in other people. In other words I'm interpreting the "aesthetic experience," as they used to say in the 1890s, as none other than the good old psychedelic flash. Or vice-versa—the language is interchangeable. What people now experience as a psychedelic universal cosmic consciousness, to the extent that it is describable as such, is probably what Yeats was talkin' about when he said in "Gratitude to the Unknown Instructors":

> What they undertook to do
> They brought to pass;
> All things hang like a drop of dew
> Upon a blade of grass.

Wordsworth has descriptions of this, Shelley has descriptions, Blake has descriptions, William James. . . . So really what I'm saying is that there are modalities of consciousness and there is a definite mode of open consciousness, of which the more you talk the farther it flies from you. The more you describe it language-wise the more you use up your attention and distract yourself from absorption in where you are. *Unless* you finally get to a point where since you're not chasing your shadow, since you're not chasing your own consciousness in order to cling to it, it comes on its own, it comes and goes on its own, 'cause you can't command it anyway, consciously, so you give up trying to and then it comes like a little doggie to your hand. But you have to be totally relaxed and not give a shit any more, whether you're high or not. In other words you have to sacrifice entering heaven in order for heaven to come down on you. 'Cause if you're still grasping and desiring even heaven, then you're still stuck grasping and desiring!

I spent about fifteen-twenty years trying to re-create the Blake experience in my head, and so wasted my time. It's just like somebody taking acid and wanting to have a God trip and straining to see God, and instead, naturally, seeing all sorts of diabolical machines coming up around him, seeing hells instead of heavens. So I did finally conclude that the bum trip on acid as well as the bum trip on normal consciousness came from attempting to grasp, desiring a preconceived end, a preconceived universe, rather than entering a universe not conceivable, not even born, not describable.

Q: I was wondering what relationship there is between chanting and this visionary experience you've talked about—like if chants are an attempt to invoke a particular experience or just any experience or if there's any relation like that at all.

AG: Well, things have gotten very complicated with me through longtime experiences and all different kinds of experiences: there's art and then there's visions and then there's dope and then there's India and then there's politics and there's Apocalypse itself. Like the whole scene is a vision at this point.

And some weird visions too. I remember once at Columbia I went to a bookstore and that was the site of another sort of epiphany. I saw the bookstore clerk and his face looked like that of a horse or sumpin', some wounded, weird animal. Before I had just thought he was like a not very sexy bookstore clerk, but all of a sudden I saw this enormous *Houyhnhnm* animal horse-face soul and looked around and everybody had these "Marks of weakness, marks of woe" on their faces—that's a line of Blake:

> I wander thro' each charter'd street,
> Near where the charter'd Thames does flow,
> And mark in every face I meet
> Marks of weakness, marks of woe.

So their karma or their experiences were written right out there on their faces—whether a joyful expression or a suspicious one, tight-assed or open. Everybody had their expressions and you could just read where they had been and who they were, all their karma right out front, which you actually can do when you're high.

And wandering around the other night I got into an almost similar state as a result of staying up late and going visiting in people's rooms and seeing people living on top of each other three and four at a time. Like I was actually trying to get laid, sort of, and I was going around to all the nicest-lookin' boys I could find and visiting their rooms, not making out, because I got distracted suddenly realizing there were thousands and thousands and thousands of beautiful-bodied boys here, all of them stuck in little cubicles, no longer heroic at all, no longer really individualized, no longer romantic as I always thought them, but they were just sort of like these robot bodies, reproduced and reproducible, millions of them, and long golden-haired girls, all the same, living like one on top of the other in tiny cubicles, like a 1984 thing, and then all of them wandering around and coming down to the open public space and wondering if the other one was a spy or an agent.[2] And it was like the weirdest vision: instead of a bunch of romantic, happy young muscular kids it was all this overpopulation robot CITYCitycity[3] building blocks with everybody in little cages. Like a young persons' old folks' home, an old-folks' home for young people, all suspended in this so-called luxury, you know, everything provided: jukebox, meat from a machine, lots of meat.

What I mean is that everything's gotten so complicated that just everyday life is a vision now, at least when you think of the earlier simple-minded terms of 1945 God-Country-Anti-Hitler-We-Won-the-War and whatever was going on then. 'Cause history came to an end I think about 1948 or so, and it opened up into some eternal planet place where whatever magic takes place is all going to be of our own creation cause we're the magicians.

So given that complication I found it useful after visiting India to try and simplify my mind a little bit—rather than intellectually casting around through the window to see if it was the Eternal Field, maybe try and eliminate all that thought about eternity and concentrate all of my energy and my effort in one single place, you know, simplify everything down to one single note, like Hūṃ. Something that would be physiologic, involving my body, not just my mind—that's what yoga is, yoking of the body to the search, the path that you're into.

So the mind strays and creates universes all the time, past present future, and I've been sitting here talking about Harlem 1948 all this time, so I've been taking your mind away from your bodies and away from this place where we are, and putting it back into an old movie that I had, and making you compare your consciousness with my supposed consciousness as verbally delineated and pictured as of 1948—which is not leading you or me anywhere at all.

The mantra refocuses mental and physiological activity right back into the present, in a world of frankly physical sound, pure sound, body sound, a continuous humming body sound that wakes up the body to some extent. It vibrates inside the body, it's a gesture of the body, the whole body. In other words, instead of being taut from this part (*chest*) of the body you actually have Hūṃ (*sighs deeply*) from the breast or even lower if you can get lower in making body sounds. So what you're doing is involving the whole mammal body in one effort; at the same time focusing your mental field on a single image continuously, like on a candle flame, if you're doing that kind of yoga. Perhaps a picture going along with the mantra or just eliminating all picture if you can and just reducing all sensation and all universe to one single sound which vibrates through the center of your body—that's basically the theory of something like Om.

It's said that sound is the first sense to come and the last sense to leave—you know that theory? If you ever go to a dentist and go out on laughing gas you will find that the last sense to depart and the first to come back is sound.[4] And maybe even in dying sound is the last strand of consciousness to disappear before the void. I think touch goes out fast and sight goes out late; smell goes out very early, taste probably, too. If you get hit on the head there's nothing left but some picture, sound movies, and you suddenly realize, oh, the whole thing has been a sound movie with a couple of extra features like touch and smell and taste. It's always been an illusory sound movie, and suddenly the screen goes blank and there's nothing left but "Good-bye!," like the Porky Pig "Th-th-th-that's all, folks!" Da da da da da duh!—what is that little honky tune that comes through?

Sound is the primary sense. So therefore if you want to focus on the primary sense, the first and last sense, it would be a sound vibration. The reason one practices focusing, or as they say centering, concentrating, is to collect all the scattered consciousness into one spot. Because when the consciousness spreads itself out it gets lost in the movie and thinks that the movie is real, and forgets that it's created the movie, and that the movie is totally an unreal spectacle created by the grasping of senses.

Q: Were you able to make sense out of your visionary experiences at the time you had them?

AG: No, I think the experiences made sense by hindsight and have come true since. In a sense they were glimpses of what I feel now, all the time. And the voice I heard, the voice of Blake, the ancient saturnal voice, is the voice I have now. I was imagining my own body consciousness, I think—that's what it means to me nowadays. In other words I was imagining my own potential awareness from a limited more virginal shy tender blossom of feeling, I was imagining the total power and feeling and universe possible to me. So in that sense it was prophetic, you know, just like childhood daydreams are prophetic of what you grow up to be. A front porch daydream I had when I was a kid was that I had a Magic Spell. And it occurred to me the other day that mantra is defined as magic spell.

Q: Would you sing us a song?

AG: I was just going to try some mantra chanting. The effects are different for everybody, like the effects of smoking grass are different for everybody the first few times. But there's always some kind of interesting curious effect if you throw your body into it. In other words the quality of the Om is dependent on the quality of the Om-er. You get just about as much out of an Om as you put into it. Except that one thing you can trust is that the Om itself, the sound, the mantra itself, is inviolably perfect, and magical, and cannot be desecrated under any circumstances— you can chant it shitting, you can chant it fucking, you can chant it dying, you can chant it climbing a mountain. No matter under what circumstances, if you're chanting Om the Om carries the awareness of an eternal consciousness, and a universal consciousness.

And that's what's interesting about it, because that's the very nature of it, because that's what it symbolizes. And that's also what it is physiologically because what you're doing is expiring and inspiring life-breath and forming it from the middle of the body to the edge of the lips, a single rounded sound which is rounded within itself. Theoretically (one theory) an opening of the Gate of Heaven in the back of the mouth, "O."; traversing the phenomenal world, the "u" part or the "ooo" part; and then theoretically closing the Gates of Hell with the "m," closing the lips. So you're opening the Gates of Heaven, traversing the World, and closing the Gates of Hell. Closing the Gates of Hell gets you high because if you close your lips as you are breathing the air out with the "m" it begins vibrating the lips and the bones that hold the teeth and the lower palate under the brain case and part of the cranium, and that gives a slight massage to the brain if it's done properly, 'cause you're working on your actual physiologic brain as well as your whatever spirit thing.

Now, applying that vowel and that voice to poetry. In setting Blake's *Songs of Innocence and of Experience* to music, I found a lot of mantric sounds in the poems, even in the simplest. Do you know "A Dream"?* An emmet is an ant, in case you don't know. (*Sings* "A Dream," *ends with repeated choruses of* "Hūṃ Hūṃ Hūṃ Home,/ Home Home Home Hūṃ.")

So you find in Blake or in any good poetry a series of vowels which if you pronounce them in proper sequence with the breathing indicated by the punctuation, as in Shelley, "Ode to the West Wind," or "Epipsychidion," or "Adonais," or as in Hart Crane the text "Atlantis" or in "Howl," the Moloch section, or in Shelley's "Mont Blanc," or in some of Wordsworth's "Tintern Abbey," or in Milton, you find a yogic breathing. Yogic's a bad word 'cause it's un-American—you find a "phys.-ed." breathing that, if reproduced by the reader, following the poet's commas and exclamation points and following long long long breaths, will get you high physiologically (which is why I say phys.-ed.), will actually deliver a buzz like grass, or higher. And so I think that's what happened to me in a way with Blake.

Q: Could you sing that love song you sang this morning?

AG: Yeah, but I'd rather sing more Blake, actually. Are there any specific Blake poems that anybody's interested in having articulated?

Q: Can you do "Tyger! Tyger!"?

AG: No, I haven't finished it yet. I'll put that last. I've done about thirty-five or forty-five of the *Songs*. I've worked on "The Tyger"—the rhythm is the same as heartbeat—but that's like revolution, or the total wrath to come, so I'm not quite capable of looking it in the eye yet.

---

*AG's music pp. 240–241.

3

Words and Consciousness

EPISTEMOLOGY CLASS: WISCONSIN STATE UNIVERSITY
Platteville, Wisconsin
April 13, 1971

Q: Would it be fair to say that language gets in the way of truth or in the way of obtaining truth?

AG: Very often—because of the way language is used. But there are one or two uses of language that are identical with truth, as in certain poetry practice, where language is used as mantra, purely as magic spell, not as rational description (which one would usually assume to be nearer to truth), where any attempt at rational description is abandoned from the very beginning and it is understood that the language is purely magic spell, and that its function is to be *only* magic spell, or mantra, or prayer, so to speak—that its function is only to be a physiological vehicle for feelings and understood as such.

In other words if you know you're going to use language to say "Oh!" then the "Oh!" is identical with the body movement of saying "Oh!" or with the feeling. Or the cry "Oh!," the exclamation, the exclamatory use of language, is identical with its function, so it's complete truth in that sense.

When I said magic spell or magical use of language that's all I meant—emotional affective exclamatory use where the language is not attempting to carry any weight of "reality" other than a purely subjective projection from the body. So that's a theory of mantra.

25

Basically what I am saying is that experience as well as reason shows that when we have to reduce our multiple-sensory consciousness of an event which we know about into words, we have to abstract so much that we eliminate most of the details of the event. Right? So a language description of an event is not identical with the event, is an abstraction of the event. And it is such an abstraction that it picks out only certain aspects of the event that we're preoccupied with at the moment. And so in no way can a language description of an event be said to be comprehensively representative, really, of the event. In fact we don't even know if an event exists and we only call the thing an event because we see it and hear it and smell it and these are all strictly very specialized human functions, human functions—seeing, smelling, hearing.

What might be a big color event to us wouldn't be nuthin' to a dog 'cause dogs see black and white. And a bee sees more myriad facets. So it's our particular senses that collaborate with whatever's going on outside to make an event to begin with. And then when we reduce everything from whatever went on outside, plus whatever we could pick up of it with our scanning patterns, with our senses, plus the further remove of what we reduce it to when we say "It was an explosion," or "It was a music concert," or "It was a big bust, a big university bust"—by the time we've reduced it to just a word description it's so far removed from anything that might have ever happened in eternity that we can't claim to be talking about anything coherently real.

However, if someone wanted to, they could redefine the whole use of language and say there's another use of it which is purely expressive, subjectively expressive, where the breath exhaled is a conscious articulation of feeling... therefore the spoken breath, "Ah-om" or "Oh" or "Ah" or "Uuuh," is identical with the event that it describes, because it is the event... As Blake says, "For a Tear is an Intellectual thing,/ And a Sigh is the Sword of an Angel King."* The tear and the sigh... well, the sigh at any rate you could speak of as language. The sigh articulates clearly a body state, a state of feeling, a state of consciousness; not merely articulates it but is identical with its own Idea.

---

*From Blake's "The Grey Monk." For some political comments on this poem, see "War and Peace: Vietnam and Kent State."

So, like the tear, it is also presumably an intellectual thing. Just like the orgasm is identical with itself, so a sigh is identical with itself. And the sound of the sigh—well it isn't the entire sigh because there's also the breath moving—the sound of the sigh is identical with what it means, unlike most other statements, or unlike most other sounds. Most sounds are not completely identical with what they refer to.

Another aspect of language is not generally taken up in discussing the use of language to communicate knowledge, is not generally considered when we try to dissect and analyze what language is, how it's functioning and what it's being used for: the tone of voice or affect with which it's pronounced (if the language is pronounced aloud), because that makes it different from when it's just eye-read. You can use the same words and say them with different tones, from "I love YOU?" to "I *love* you." Two people can say exactly the same thing with the same intention and one person really mean it and the other not mean it and you can tell the difference by whether the voice comes from the center of the body or whether the voice is just a little superficial weakened yak from the top of the larynx center.

So between David Dellinger saying "We must end the war" and Kissinger saying "We must end the war" there's like a difference of content, though they're both saying the same words. Voice tone is one aspect of sound I would point to particularly nowadays when we're confronted with the image of one single person talking multiplied myriad on television. People intuitively do hear it, but it is essential to consciously check the tone of voice, of body, as a way of finding out whether or not the voice is genuine, whether or not it means what it says. And the best way to do that is not to get confused by the intellectual presentation or the associational pattern presented for hypnotic purposes by the words themselves but to look underneath the words to the vehicle for the words, which is the voice, and see if the voice itself—on the level of voice affect—is an acceptable vehicle. We have a right in that sense to be aesthetic, or to put it another way, we have a right to be emotional—we have a right to our feelings, most of all, so we've got to check out the feelings in the voice, realize affect.

So there's tone, or affect, or feeling of the voice, and that's connected very much with the rhythm of the language—whether it's a natural rhythm of language or whether it's a forced artificial bureaucratic dry rhythm affected by multiple machinery, affected by its being passed through many typewriters, whether it's an authentic human personal voice talking, or whether it's a voice that has been filtered through so many machines that the human rhythm has been lost.

Most public speech is pseudo-event in the sense that it is not the product of a literal human being; it's literally non-human. It's passed through so many hands and so many machines that it no longer represents a human organism inspiring and expiring, inhaling and exhaling, rhythmically. The sentence structure no longer has any relation to any affect that could be traced along the lines of inhalation and exhalation—in other words, sad to say, the voice can finally be separated from the body. If the voice is completely separated from the body, it means that the rhythm will be fucked up, it means the affect will be fucked up, it means it no longer has any human content, actually. It probably means it doesn't mean anything, even, finally—by *mean*, anything that could be connected back to the physical universe or the human universe.

So the characteristics of mantra, then—or poetics (the seed of poetics is mantra)—are attention to rhythm, connection with the breath, with the actual breathing, and affect, and so connection with the body. Charles Olson talks about poetry as an extension of physiology, language as an extension of physiology.[5] Mainly from this point of view: that the words we pronounce do connect finally to our body, connect to our breathing, particularly, and breathing connects to feeling, feeling articulated in language. Poetry is a rhythmic vocal articulation of feeling and the content of poetry is feeling as well as whatever else you would call it if it were removed from feeling—I suppose conditioned reflex language chain associations.

The Hindu proposition is that there are faculties for body sound language that have atrophied in the transient and very recent temporary cultures that substitute mechanical reproduction of imagery for interpersonal communication of imagery. Sort of in McLuhan's terms, the very nature of reading and linear thinking and reproduced language—language images reproduced and read silently—has tended to abstract language communication and thin it out, actually, give it less body, less meaning. And so faculties of body sound and rhythmic deep-breathed language behavior have atrophied.

But that's only a temporary condition in the sense that out of say twenty thousand years of intellectual history recorded from the Magdalenian cave paintings to the present, it's only in the last hundred years or so that we've so completely abandoned direct voice communication and exercises of voice communication including chant which are characteristic of almost every tribal group scattered all over the globe over a much longer, viable period of time than our own very transient mechanical civilization.

Now we're examining epistemology under very specialized circumstances, using language to discuss the limits of language. We don't have the philosophical or the educational armamentarium of more sophisticated tribal societies who have a much more varied knowledge of body sounds. American Indians did community chanting and dancing too, as well as meditation, as part of their food-gathering rituals. In order to kill buffalo there would have to be meditation on the soul of the buffalo and imitation of the buffalo and a buffalo chant and an identification with the buffalo, and a sacramental knowledge of the buffalo that we don't have when we get a prepackaged piece of frozen meat in a piece of plastic. So it also required sitting, patience, internal observation, and rhythmic chanting, just to get buffalo, or to get a rabbit even—the patience required to sit under a tree and smell and wait and listen.

That patience required for food gathering conditioned mind consciousness to greater attention to immediate minute particular detail around the body, conditioned the tribal food gatherer going about his practical business to a more direct relationship (through his senses) with the outer world, just as our division of labor and mental absorption with written language conditions our consciousness to accept as real that which can be formulated in verbal sequence and put down on paper and read silently and Xeroxed. It means that to us only a *written* event is credible or real, whereas Indians or members of other cultures would take their event, their reality, and act on it, more directly.

Whether our system's an advantage or not I don't know. As it stands, it seems to be ruining the planet. The very nature of our power of abstraction dooms us to lose touch with detail. And therefore the very roots of the trees are shriveling, withering, and the oceans are being polluted simply because we have reduced everything to a language which can be passed through machines. Obviously machines aren't sophisticated enough to take account of all variables, aren't as sophisticated as men and women in that sense. We've lost our world by pursuing our kind of language specialization.

According to the Buddhist Diamond Sutra, "All conceptions as to the existence of the self as well as all conceptions as to the non-existence of the self, as well as all conceptions as to the existence of a Supreme Self, as well as all conceptions as to the non-existence of a Supreme Self, are equally arbitrary because they are only conceptions . . . " and are not the entity (or non-entity) that we are actually sitting in the middle of, which hath no category, name, or abstraction but is itself, and as such is "open"—that is, unlimited by language.

Since "life" cannot be categorized, magical behavior within it cannot be ruled out, since there are no rules. Therefore, for highest knowledge of the center of it all, or for one aspect of knowledge of it, one would have to use language that was identical with the behavior of the entity itself, rather than descriptive of the behavior of the entity. And that language behavior itself is prayer. So I would say the highest form of epistemological research would be prayer. By prayer I mean a kind of mantra. In other words, use of rhythmic language to rouse the senses, arouse perceptions, and arouse sense of inner space, to alter all of consciousness itself, rather than to rearrange the language digits within one realm of consciousness. It could be quiet or silent, it could be prayer without words, i.e., just pure attention, attention maybe to breathing, or attention to no-thing.

Recently I read a Sadhana of the Nyingmapa sect of Tibetan Tantric Buddhism, the same sect which teaches the Oh Ah Hūṃ Vajra Guru Padma Siddhi Hūṃ mantra now in America. The ritual involved a series of preparatory prayers to and visualizations of ideological deities, and formed an attitude of mind toward meditation, and toward the end of the Sadhana the instruction abruptly reads: "Rest in state of non-conceptual Mind as long as possible."

And that's like the heart of it, the rest of the magic was just an invocation of blessings preparing you to sit still . . . you know, having exhausted all sorts of conceptions of Buddha-forms sitting on top of your head showering your body with ambrosia and everything, finally you remain in nonconceptual mind.

There's a guru in New York teaching this, and I asked him,

"How do you do that?" 'Cause I'm used to doing a mantra, you know, like sitting, meditating with a mantra, so he said, "Oh, well, one way is to look *in between* thoughts, in the interstices between thoughts." So that that theory of knowledge is a very pragmatic, practical thing: these teachers actually examine the procession of thoughts in the head, dig. In other words, meditation doesn't take for granted the exclusive reality of "thoughts," as Western epistemology does in a sense. It doesn't take for granted the substantialness of the language-thought process which considers the nature of knowledge. Meditation means not merely examining the definition of words, it means examining the mind-stuff of which the words are made, or the mind-stuff of which the consciousness is made. And so one practical suggestion for getting into that is "Well, now, look at the gaps *in between* thoughts." Which means that you have to actually literally examine thought—not get lost in it. In other words you don't become part of thought and get swept away in it, like in a boat. You get out of the boat and examine the nature of thought itself, and that I suppose is true epistemology . . . and that's where Western epistemology does lead, ultimately, in certain writers. It would have to, unless it were to exist within this closed dream system, you know, and never really get outside itself, for I would imagine real knowledge begins with examining the nature or stuff of thought about knowledge, examining the ground in which thoughts take place.

In Western culture the equivalent of that kind of research would lie in the gnostic tradition. You'd have to start with Heraclitus and examine Porphyry and Iamblichus and Jakob Boehme and Pythagoras. There is, in fact, a heavy Western tradition in this area, though it's not studied extensively as part of formal philosophy because around A.D. 300, when Emperor Constantine took over the Church, it got stomped out by the so-to-speak CIA of that time as being anti-authoritarian.

Around the 1750s in England there was a great Greek and Latin scholar named Thomas Taylor,[6] who translated all the fragments of the church fathers that had survived burning by Constantine and the Council of Nicaea when they damned all the heretical doctrines, burned all written record of the fact that alternative modalities of universe might be seen or examined, and reinforced the central authoritarian one of Jehovah-Constantine-Emperor-Pope. Made a deal, that Constantine would be the head of the Church and also the head of the state, and also his boys would determine what theories of the nature of reality were acceptable to the Church and State. In other words there was an official reality imposed—within words, "Don't get outside of words, either!" That was part of it.

So Taylor got together all those fragments, and his manuscripts were examined by William Blake at great length and by all the revolutionaries of his day, even Thomas Paine. Coleridge drew a great deal from Taylor, as did Shelley. Bronson Alcott went to England to get a library of Taylor's work, which he brought back to Brook Farm—which affected the whole American tradition of Transcendentalism. When Brook Farm communists weren't reading the Upanishads and the Vedas, they were drawing upon gnostic Neoplatonic texts from Taylor. Which may have affected Herman Melville, who probably also saw those texts. And the specific books that Alcott brought back from England were loaned to Emerson and annotated by Alcott and Emerson.

So examination of mind is very much a part of our own American tradition. That's where William James comes in, when he begins to go into practical phenomenology and gets at the praxis of altered consciousness in *The Varieties of Religious Experience*. And that set up a situation for pragmatic experiments with transcendental insight at Harvard which led to the poetics of Gertrude Stein, whose poetry was a form of meditation or examination of language itself by means of repeating it over and over again in different combinations to see if it could be removed from conditioned associations, as if associations could be cleaned off the words so that they were just mantric sounds.

That also led to the situation in 1919 when Virgil Thomson (later a friend of Gertrude Stein) was a young musician around Harvard talking with S. Foster Damon (who was a great Blake scholar), and I think Damon gave Thomson *Four Saints in Three Acts* or some text by Gertrude Stein as a study of language and consciousness. And in that old context of William James (the anesthetic revelations chapter of *The Varieties of Religious Experience*), Virgil Thomson gave S. Foster Damon two peyote buttons in Harvard Yard.

So the Western gnostic tradition can best be studied in such sayings as Pythagoras's "Everything we see when awake is death, and when asleep, dream"; or, regarding the use of language for generalization, the old Heraclitus statement still holds:

"You can't step in the same river twice." Meaning that you can't make a generalization which will be good a minute later, not exactly the same generalization. You can't make a statement absolutely descriptive of an event even if the statement is identical with it. Even an Om is not eternal, in the sense that the Om changes with the Om-er, from minute to minute, so there's no hiding place even in mantra. There's no rest from continued creation or change.

Any questions?

Q: I have one on your statement about the chant and how in contemporary society, at least in America, it seems to have gone out of existence. Could you explain that? Why are people thinking differently, why do they think that's not of consequence any more?

AG: Well, a lot of different reasons. It's not exactly even true to say it's gone completely out of existence, because the Black tradition keeps the chant going, in the sense that the body chant is still there in jazz and in spirituals, up to the political use of it in "We shall Overcome"—there still are remnants of Afric chanting and dancing and drumming.

But while in Black culture something very deep-souled is the dominant mode, in white culture something very shallow and un-chanty, like Mantovani, Musak, or Pat Boone is dominant, except for some Promethean folk-rock. I would say the reason for that is maybe capitalism—that is, usury. People trying to make money out of mass production, monopolizing the replica machines, dominating the printing (image reproduction machinery) and television and radio. The fact that the radio and television air space is for sale, is not common property but is just integrated into the commercial Wheel, means that only such body sound as is commercial will be broadcast.

Television is a connecting neurological link between the separate cells of the body politic our culture. And our communications network is dominated by capitalistic usury—in other words you've got to make money on it. To the extent that the body chant is an assertion of a nonusurious common communal communistic sharing of soul among all members of the body politic, not merely members of the body politic, but members of the body of nature, including the animals and the trees and the grasses . . . to the extent that the highest communal chant is a chant of unison and oneness with all of nature, and that capitalism and our economic system require the excessive chopping up of nature into lumber, or the mining and exhausting of nature—to that extent I think it's partly our economic system that forbids us to chant. Partly the very nature of the machinery.

Q: It's interesting too that in the churches nowadays you won't find anything like Gregorian chants. I remember my experience when we had chants—not in a Catholic church but in a Protestant one—we'd do it, but it wasn't very popular.

AG: Embarrassing, probably. Because it's a whole area of feeling, of communal family ritual feeling, which is feared. And the reason it's feared is because it's a breakthrough onto a new consciousness which is not like the social consciousness inculcated by television or radio or newspapers or politics, it's another animal mammal consciousness that's unified with the world—you know, the consciousness that we share, the compassionate consciousness of the mind and the heart that we share with the bald eagles and the blue whales. And since we keep killing all the whales and the bald eagles it wouldn't be appropriate to voice that consciousness—I mean it would be revolutionary to voice that consciousness, to articulate that consciousness and welcome it to surface front-brain awareness.

And that's why African ritual jazz forms were in a sense always revolutionary and when they were passed on across the Atlantic through the Beatles and the Stones, through Rock, through electronics, back to the children of another generation who began shaking their hips and making that chant sound, it was part of the revolution, as the John Birch Society said in 1965, very prophetically. They said the Beatles were using hypnotic rhythms and body movements and strange vibrations to alter the consciousness of the kids and to hypnotize them and to get another consciousness through that was not like American "reasonable" morals. Rock was supposed to dissolve the rational consciousness of the Western world. They saw it immediately as a threat and a danger—remember those pamphlets in the sixties?

NOTES

2. ETERNITY

1. See St. John of the Cross (Juan de la Cruz), *The Mystical Doctrine of St. John of the Cross* (London: Sheed & Ward, 1948), especially "The Dark Night of the Soul," pp. 71–115.

2. See pp. 196–7; 209–210 ("War and Peace: Vietnam and Kent State") of this book.

3. An allusion to Jack Kerouac's science fiction "CITYCitycity," anthologized in Leroi Jones's *The Moderns* (New York: Corinth Books, 1963).

4. See "Laughing Gas," pp. 66–82 in A. G.'s *Kaddish and Other Poems* (San Francisco: City Lights, 1961), and "Aether," pp. 83–98 in his *Reality Sandwiches* (San Francisco: City Lights, 1963).

General note: Allen's most thorough exposition of the Blake epiphany itself appears in his *Paris Review* interview (*PR* 37), reproduced in *Writers at Work*, Third Series (New York: The Viking Press, 1967)—see pp. 301–311.

3. WORDS AND CONSCIOUSNESS

5. See Olson's "Projective Verse," in Robert Creeley, ed., *Selected Writings of Charles Olson* (New York: New Directions, 1966), pp. 15–26; or same in Donald M. Allen, ed., *The New American Poetry* (New York: Grove Press, 1960), pp. 386–397.

6. Princeton University Press has recently issued in its Bollingen series *Thomas Taylor the Platonist* edited by Kathleen Raine and George Mills Harper. Bollingen Series LXXXVIII, Princeton, N.J. 1969.

Political
Opium

(HISTORY OF DOMESTIC MANIPULATION OF
OPIATES AND ADDICTED CITIZENS AND U.S.
RELATIONSHIP TO WORLD TRAFFIC)

SEMINAR LECTURE AT THE INSTITUTE FOR
POLICY STUDIES
Washington, D.C., March 19, 1971

*Many policemen and narcotics agents are precisely
addicted to power, to exercising a certain nasty kind
of power over people who are helpless. . . and if they
lost that power, they would suffer excruciating
withdrawal symptoms.*
—William S. Burroughs (from *Writers at Work: The Paris Review
Interviews*)

*For most of twenty years Allen has shared his drug research
with the general public and with legislators, enforcers, and
victims of drug statutes, in an effort to avert increasing police
state omnipotence in that area. His research has not been con-
fined to his personal drug experiences, which he has described
in writing, in public, and before a congressional committee, but
has also involved collecting all printed data available, including a virtually comprehensive gathering of all relevant articles
in* The New York Times *throughout the 1960s.*

*By the end of 1970 Allen was winding up this research and
had drawn up a preliminary fourteen-page summary, "Documents on Police Bureaucracy's Conspiracy Against Human
Rights of Opiate Addicts & Constitutional Rights of Medical
Profession Causing Mass Breakdown of Urban Law & Order,"
which he circulated to fellow scholars, journalists, and congressmen. In March of 1971 Marcus Raskin offered him the
resources of the Institute for Policy Studies in Washington to
conclude his work and make it accessible to colleagues. In the
two weeks that we spent there Allen had a long talk with then-
CIA Director Richard Helms, and we both spoke with former
CIA and AID agents and journalists who had served in Indochina as well as former members of congressional investiga-
tive committees and Washington-based editors and columnists.*

*The material presented here was offered as a seminar lecture
at the Institute on the last day there. Before the tour was over,
occasion arose to draw from this material again. We were to
arrive in Platteville, Wisconsin, a week after its first university
bust. Eleven students had been arrested through the undercover
efforts of a cop/student employed by the town police. Several of
those busted were his fellow athletes; one was his girl friend.*

Addiction Politics, 1922-1970

STUDY OF HISTORY & CONSEQUENCES OF
CRIMINALIZATION OF OPIUM ADDICT POPULATION
INCLUDING POLITICAL DOCUMENTATION OF
NARCOTICS BUREAU'S "WAR AGAINST
PHYSICIANS" & POLICE OPPOSITION TO MEDICAL
TREATMENT OF OPIUM ADDICTION, THUS
ENCOURAGING A MAFIA-DOMINATED BLACK
MARKET CASH NEXUS JUNK BUSINESS THUS
CREATING EPIDEMIC ADDICTION, WITH A CURE
FOR THIS SOCIAL DISEASE PROPOSED

AG: To understand the present dope situation you've got to understand that the original Harrison Act of 1914 was a reaction to lots and lots of old lady and men addicts who were consuming opiates in patent medicines like Lydia Pinkham's. The Harrison Narcotics Act originally, around World War I, 1914, was intended to limit the supply, to regulate the supply of opiates, so that people could get their opiates in clinics or regulated stores or through doctors: it wasn't originally intended to shut off the supply of opium to addicts—that was a move that came later and was an *administrative interpretation* of the original Harrison Narcotics Act.

Among the early key documents is testimony from Lester Volk, from New York, the only M.D. in the House of Representatives at the time (1922). What had happened was that around 1920 the Internal Revenue Service, which was in charge of administering the Harrison Act, began expanding its bureaucracy in Parkinson's Law style, saying that the act gave them power to shut off supplies of opium to people who were already addicted, and also gave them power to regulate doctors' treatment of addicts, and to prohibit doctors from giving addicts maintenance opium.

In the twenties there were federally funded clinics, similar to the clinics now in England and similar to the present methadone clinics, where addicts could go and get junk, could go and get opiates, laudanum, or tincture of opium or regular opium; I think also heroin,* even, because heroin had been invented as a substitute for morphine a little bit earlier. The Internal Revenue Bureau cut off the funds for the clinics, and so by 1921,–'22,–'23, most of the addicts were thrown out on the streets. So the actual problem of "dope fiends" as criminals as we've known it over the last twenty or thirty years didn't begin with the original Harrison Act, but rather with an administrative interpretation of the Harrison Act around 1922.

The question is, what were the local politics that began this new policy? Volk's speech explains a great deal of it. You can get a good outline of the whole scene if you refer to Dr. Alfred Lindesmith's *The Addict and the Law*,[1] which is the classic work on the political history of the junk problem. Lindesmith turned me on to this particular Volk document. It's a speech in the House of Representatives, Friday, January 13, 1922. Volk said:

> There has developed a tendency in carrying out the objects of the Harrison Law to substitute for the provisions of the act arbitrary administrative opinions expressed in rules and regulations which amount to practically a repeal and nullification of the law itself.
>
> These rules and regulations have been promulgated by those in charge of the administration of the Harrison Law upon the representation and statements coming as the official pronouncements of the New York City Board of Health, presented by a particular small group or clique among whom stand out prominently the names of Royal S. Copeland, health commissioner of the city of New York, Drs. E. Elliot Harris, S. Dana Hubbard, Alfred C. Prentice, and a lawyer, Alfred C. Greenfield. Reliable records, reports, scientific information, and experience have been swept aside by these men and in their place has been set up a campaign of publicity intended in the end to benefit this small coterie who seek to control the avenues of narcotic treatment throughout the country.
>
> The agitation emanating from New York City from these men and the department of health is spreading over the entire country and knowingly or unknowingly has evaded and ignored sound medical findings. As a substitute for open discussion of known medical facts there has been set up a propaganda for the incarceration of all drug users, their treatment by routine methods, and

---

*Heroin was first synthesized for commercial use in 1898 by Bayer.

complete elimination of the family doctor. An undeniable effort is now being made whereby physicians are to be denied any discretion and power in the prescribing of narcotic drugs and to force all those addicted to the use of these drugs into hospitals exploiting questionable "cures."[2]

What he is proposing, which he documents later, is that the people he named all had private sanitariums which charged a great deal of money for cures and were trying to get rid of the competition from the public clinics. And that was the original seed of lobbying in New York State for the system which spread very rapidly throughout the country, because it also played into the hands of the bureau of Internal Revenue, which thereby increased its power and its aegis.

It would be interesting to discuss the actual qualifications and connections of this interlocking directorate (of lobbyists), but time and space would be better utilized in outlining the general subject and leaving these matters of detail to a future investigation. [Which never did take place.]

However, in passing it would be of interest to quote from an editorial in the *Illinois Medical Journal,* October 1921 issue which states:

"The present attempted interpretations, and so forth, are based somewhat beyond any doubt upon representations and statements and opinions and conclusions coming from people like Drs. E. Elliot Harris, S. Dana Hubbard, Alfred C. Prentice, the lawyer, Arthur C. Greenfield, etc., and also somewhat from statistics and statements and deductions coming from the New York City board of health.

"Their reliability and validity must therefore depend upon the qualifications of these people, as compared with the bulk of recorded workers and men of real experience. We believe that without any question at all their reports and statements and conclusions would be utterly overthrown and discredited by comparison with the bulk of reliable record and report and experience and scientific information."[3]

In other words, it was a group of very specialized bullshit artists who took over the propaganda and lobbying in '21-'22.

The report of the committee on legislation of the New York State Medical Society, beginning on page 209 of the June, 1921, issue of the *New York State Journal of Medicine,* voices mistrust of these narcotic committees and of the "10 men in the medical profession and a couple of lawyers" who have gotten mixed up in this addiction matter. . . .

These principles were completely aired at the several hearings on restrictive antinarcotic legislation before the New York State Legislature in 1920 and 1921, and met with just rebuke to the men propounding them. Yet they appear in this solemn screed issued by the United States Government and are followed by the remarkable additional statement:

"Doubtful cases (of addiction) or those not falling within any of the above instructions, upon request will be investigated and special instructions based upon the recommendations of the inspecting officer will be issued."

Let this statement sink in. Consider it. The Government in positive terms says in its regulations or rules of October 19, 1921, that a physician may treat a drug addict only for a certain length of time, no matter what physical conditions may arise, or may commit or advise commitment of that addict to a sanitarium regardless of whether there is a sanitarium to put him in or whether he may regard the treatment of that sanitarium judicious or injudicious.[4]

Well, you will notice that the arguments being rehearsed here are the same arguments that you could hear half a century later regarding Rockefeller's New York State plan of the sixties for dealing with addicts, which was to give all of them medical facilities instead of prison treatment. So there was the Rockefeller plan beginning '62 or '63 which was, on paper, to build facilities for medical housing of addicts, there being it was considered at the time, 50,000 to 150,000 addicts in New York state alone. Well, the plan was preposterous because it would have required billions of dollars to build hospital facilities for permanent or semipermanent incarceration of, like, a hundred thousand people.

So the state legislature in New York never did appropriate the money, but since laws based on those fantasies were passed, judges, as of the last few years, were remanding addicts to treatment or hospital facilities which didn't exist. Addicts in New York City were being sent to the Tombs and then sent to Rikers Island or a few other places which were not hospitals, and finally the Tombs became overcrowded, and then there was a series of scandals which were noted in the papers over the last half year where judges were getting exasperated and saying, "According to law I have to send somebody to a treatment facility and there's no such thing going now," or, "There's no room in the treatment facilities," "There's no room in the methadone program, no room in Phoenix House, so the people that I've sentenced to treatment facilities are just being held over in prisons." So that gave rise to a series of suits prepared in New York for some addicts saying that since the law requires they be given treatment and since there is no treatment available, it's illegal for them to be kept in jail: it's contradictory to the law for them to be kept in purely punitive jail circumstances.

So what's interesting about this is that the junk problem, the medical junk problem as we have it, as we know it now, was known fifty years ago, a half century ago, and there hasn't been any change at all in terms of the public arguments back and forth. Volk's thing, though, as a time capsule of the immediate pressures of his day, of the people, of the personnel involved in the politics of it in his day, is invaluable if you want to know where the condition originated, from the point of view that those who don't know history are doomed to repeat it over and over again.

Volk had an absolute, clear grasp of the facts as a medical man and was presenting to a totally unknowing Congress a series of facts which they neither heard nor could understand, actually, through the barrage of lobbying that they were exposed to:

> Apparently it takes but a twist of the wrist of the Revenue Department at the bidding of ignorant and egoistic, self-centered, and perhaps criminally involved professional men and administrators to put in force in these United States a set of regulations, drastic in their inception, unethical in their administration, and calamitous in their effect. . . .
>
> Be it David or Goliath, judge or degenerate, prostitute or preacher, opium plays no favorites. Race, color, creed, physical and mental ability alike are no bar to contraction of addiction. And once addicted there follows a symptomatology represented by practically unvarying manifestations recognized even by that small band who apparently are backing the latest regulations of the post-addiction school of misinformation conducted by the New York City Department of Health and others and later indorsed by the Department of Internal Revenue. . . .
>
> The next man to rise in his[5] place and declare that clinical observations of addicts and their symptomatology could only be explained in terms of disease was Dr. Ernest S. Bishop, of New York City, who will go down in medical history as one of the few

fearless men willing to stake a reputation and a livelihood on honest observation and truthful deduction. . . .

For this opposition Dr. Bishop was indicted, and still enjoys that distinction, through the failure of the United States Government to find out the truth about the narcotic drug problem and apply it. His persecution is a medical and political scandal and an obstruction to solution of the drug problem.[6]

Bishop was the consulting physician for the New York State prison system, and so presumably a politically powerful doctor and an expert in this particular area. Bishop wound up trying to treat addicts with maintenance therapy, like methadone therapy, and was indicted for it in 1920.

Volk also has a few comments regarding the sanitarium systems these guys had:

If he [a patient] has plenty of money these pseudomedical savants recommend that he go to Dr. Jones's or Dr. Smith's sanitarium where he can take a "cure" of more or less efficacy, which very likely is challenged by everybody who has been through it. And if this same gentleman happens to be without funds these learned administrators of our law provide nice, cool jails, where the suffering addict can get every attention that their humanity suggests, including incarceration in a padded cell and a liberal douching with a fire hose upon occasion.[7]

What's curious is, like, the "early primitive" or "naive" rhetoric, because Volk and Bishop and the others were unused to this shocking or outrageous—to them—intrusion on medical practice by the federal bureaucracy.

These private sanitarium treatments are expensive. Many or most of the decent addicts have not the means and many more have not the courage again to invoke some of their drastic regimens. *Both classes, shut off from attention by legitimate physicians, are driven to the street-corner peddler and the underworld for narcotic supply.* *[8]

So that's the key to the whole drug problem as it stands now, as put forth very clearly in 1922.

---

*Emphasis A.G.'s.

> The result is a tremendous increase in smuggling and illicit
> traffic in drugs, arrests and convictions for illicit possession, and
> the incarceration of many innocent individuals in city jails and
> institutions where it is common knowledge they are herded with
> degenerates and worse. To put it plainly, this is making criminals
> of innocent people and involves aggravation of underworld con-
> ditions which has its reflection in court records and the
> newspapers.[9]

They did have at the time some public clinics, to take care of
addicts, and here's an example of what happened:

> The Board of Health of Louisiana, alarmed at the growth of
> morphine addiction and the ruinous victimizing of patients
> through underground peddling of the drugs, opened a clinic in
> New Orleans, where addicts were under the continuous oversight
> and care of the best physicians, and where they received the drugs
> at cost price. The plan was very successful. Underground ped-
> dling practically disappeared, and the situation was very much
> better.
> About November, 1920, without reason or explanation, the
> Bureau of Internal Revenue at Washington ordered the institution
> closed. The first order being ignored, a second order was issued,
> which was reluctantly obeyed. The result was that the patients
> were again driven to the underworld and the situation became as
> bad as before.[10]

So that's the inception of the black market in America for
drugs. Regarding the continuous aggravation of doctors by narcotics fuzz, Volk observes:

> . . . it seems to me that the untutored narcotic agents of this great
> Government under the last administration might have been better
> employed than in taking sides in a medical controversy involving
> the broad subject of what will or will not constitute the proper
> medication in the treatment of addiction. Yet this was done, and I
> am sorry to say is now being done, by our Government and will
> continue to be done until the end of time unless some protesting
> voice is raised against undue interference by lawyers, policemen,
> and detectives in the practice of the science of medicine and the
> furtherance of its research and study.[11]

I'll leave off Dr. Volk, 'cause I think he's presented the entire
grounds of present-day arguments forty-nine years ago.

Naturally the doctors protested, and one Dr. Linder in Seattle kept treating junkies, so the Narcotics Bureau sent in an agent to pose as a junkie and then arrested him for giving drugs to some-one who was not a narcotic addict and didn't need the drugs. So Dr. Linder appealed to the Supreme Court, and the Court ruled, in the Linder decision of 1925, that the Harrison Act *was not intended to interfere with proper medical practice, with doctor-patient relationships.* So that actually, since then, we have had the British arrangement where doctors are really le-gally, constitutionally entitled to treat addicts.

And the Linder decision was theoretically reaffirmed by Fed-eral Court Judge Yankwich in 1936:

> I am satisfied, therefore, that the Linder case, and the cases which interpret it, lay down the rule definitely that the statute does not say what drugs a physician may prescribe to an addict. Nor does it say the quantity which a physician may or may not prescribe. Nor does it regulate the frequency of prescription. Any attempt to so interpret the statute, by an administrative interpretation, whether that administrative interpretation be oral, in writing, or by an officer or by a regulation of the department, would be not only contrary to the law, but would also make the law unconstitutional as being clearly a regulation of the practice of medicine.[12]

So since the Harrison Act of 1914 and the 1925 Linder deci-sion, the junkies have been a totally unconstitutionally and il-legally persecuted minority group in the United States who at this point require some sort of Junkie Liberation Front, simply to get their civil rights. Their major right being the right to go to a doctor for relief of symptoms incident to addiction. Junkies are not and never have been in a position to go to the press or to form a liberation group because administrative interpretation of the law has made them subject to immediate arrest if they're caught with any of their medicine. And so they can't come out from underground, they can't come out front and make political rep-resentation as, say, the gay group can or women can, because though once it was illegal to be gay, it's not formally illegal to be gay and say you're gay. Or once, you know, you could get busted for camping, perhaps, or caught *in flagrante.* One doesn't have to be as cautious these days. So the gay group is able to come out front and form its own liberation group; junkies are not, and so actually need help from the outside. They're the one group, probably, that is so submerged in institutionalized violence that they require a hand from the outside to end state violence against their persons.

There was in the fifties very little discussion of the matter, and the reason for that is given in "Report on Drug Addiction—II," in the *Bulletin of the New York Academy of Medicine* for July 1963. There was also an earlier report in the *Bulletin* in 1955, and they both were extremely important in their conclusions in regard to present-day fact, because they both said that *"profit is a major force in the spread of addiction."*[*13] Heroin itself is not a magically interesting thing: it's not that people turn on to it and naturally more and more people get addicted. The magic in the spread of addiction lies in the profit motive.

Just yesterday I had a conversation with a man named Gene Rossides, who is the Treasury Department's chief thinker on drug policy, who doesn't know any junkies personally and actually knows absolutely nothing about street functioning, about the street market. Any policy he makes is going to be so purely theoretical that it's automatically going to crush human beings. Most of you know junkies, I guess, so you may have a clearer idea of the scene. The point Rossides didn't know is as follows: I have a friend named Herbert Huncke who is a junkie and who has been one for many years. Now in order for him to maintain his habit he has to take junk three times a day, every day. A habit, formally speaking, results when you've taken an opiate three times a day for at least three months: it takes that long for a physiological habit to begin.

Chippying around is not a habit. A habit is a physiological condition, perhaps a change in the actual cellular structure, or a change in the metabolism. And there's very little known about the metabolic effect or biochemistry of junk addiction, for as Dr. Vincent P. Dole (of Dole and Nyswander who developed the methadone therapy) pointed out in conversation about two months ago, when he came into the field in 1963 there was not one single paper on the biochemistry of addiction.[14] Although the problem had been seen in medical terms as early as 1914–1922 (as in Volk's speech), there was not, from 1920 to 1960, in that whole forty-year period, one single research paper on the biochemistry of what the sickness and addiction pain

---

*Emphasis A.G.'s.

actually was. And that was because the doctors were driven out and the police took over control of the field.

To get a habit you've got to take junk three times a day for at least three months before it settles in physiologically. And that's a habit that's not too difficult to kick—I mean you're sick but you get over it. A second habit, a second time around, of another month or two of taking junk will reinforce the first habit, and that will *really* be a hard habit to kick. And that's when the real difficulty comes in for a junkie. Kicking the first habit: difficult but not impossible; kicking a second, third, and fourth sequence of junk: more and more impossible. The body simply gets conditioned and habituated to the drug; perhaps the glands are made to function in an abnormal manner to balance the intake of a foreign substance in the body. That's Burroughs's theory. You withdraw the junk, the glands are still operating abnormally; and so Dr. Dent in England experimented with Burroughs and other people in what he called an apomorphine cure which was to rebalance the metabolism by apomorphine which, like, altered functioning of the hypothalamus, which altered glandular functioning, which then altered metabolism and restored it to some semblance of normality.[15]

In other words—I'm circling around the point—what does a junkie have to do every day to keep straight? He's gotta get his junk three times a day. Now given present prices for someone like Huncke that would probably be . . . well, there are six-dollar bags, say, at the moment, and he probably uses up two bags per shot, being a junkie of forty years' standing. So say that's two six-dollar bags per morning, and another twelve dollars afternoon, and another twelve dollars evening. To do that, he has to go to the street corner on Tenth Street and Second Avenue in New York and make a meet with his pusher. That means he has to wait around in the coffee shop there, or in the drugstore, maybe an hour or two until his pusher shows up.

So if he leaves the house at 6 A.M. or 8 A.M. or 10, he may wait there two hours, meet his pusher. Or the pusher may not arrive so he'll score from somebody else who'll take his twelve dollars and give him milk sugar instead. So he'll go home, shoot up the milk sugar, and not have the loot, and not have the junk. So that means he'll have to go out and come to my house and say, "I'm out of money, I just got burned, would you like a taste of junk today?," and maybe, "Would Gordon like a taste of junk today?

49

and if you give me twelve bucks I'll score for you, you won't have to take the risk, just give me the money—you got lots of money, Ginsberg, and I don't have the money, I can use it, and I'm sick, you know, I really need it, come on!"

So who can resist, finally. Or, if I'm not there, he'll get in and steal my radio and pawn it and go down to the corner and *maybe* score; by this time it's noon and he's several hours late for his fix, so he's in a state of extreme nervous tension and hysteria; he may have scored enough for the entire day and bought thirty-six dollars' worth of junk to cover the entire day. He'll go home and perhaps instead of shooting up his twelve dollars' worth, his two bags for the morning, he'll shoot up two and a half or three bags just to calm himself down after the long crisis of trying to scrounge for money, not meeting his connection, being beaten and burned for his junk.

Then by the end of the day, though he had perhaps scored for enough money for a day's supply, he may have shot up, pig-gishly, more than he should have, and so therefore in the middle of the night might have to go out and, say, rob a car or find some other friends to score from.

Now this is all referring to "It is reaffirmed that profit is a major force in the spread of addiction."[16] Rather than go out and bur-glarize, Huncke would much prefer to go around to his fellow junkies and his friends, collect five-six bucks each, or enough for a half a bag each, make the run, take the risk, and then redistrib-ute the supply. So he'll be proselytizing for other people to share the day's score with him. And that is the precise reason that profit is a major force in the spread of addiction: even on the lowest level the sick junkie has to collaborate with other people to get enough money to buy whatever he needs for the day.

Is that understood by everybody here? It's the key on the street level. What I'm trying to say, for those who don't know, is that this is like relatively common knowledge. In other words am I bullshitting or does this fall within your experience?

Q: Assume you have a mixed audience in terms of personal experience.

AG: Well, I'm assuming it's a mixed audience of people who have been friends with junkies and people who are involved with junk policy but don't directly know the street-level scene.

Profit is obviously a major force in the spread of addiction on the larger scale, in terms of motivation for importing it from abroad and growing it and selling it and wholesaling it and smuggling it.

This *Bulletin of the New York Academy of Medicine* has some other very interesting statistics put together by a doctor named Lawrence Kolb:

> ... From the year of the Harrison Act to 1938 it is estimated that 25,000 physicians were arraigned and 3,000 served penitentiary sentences on narcotics charges. About 20,000 were said to have made a financial settlement. . . . For most . . . it should be reiterated that they were following the then accepted medical precepts.
>
> It is evident that the Supreme Court opinion in the (1925) *Linder* case, removing restrictions on treatment of addicts, had no noticeable restraining effect on the Treasury Department in its war on physicians. . . .[17]

So there was a literal war, the casualties of which were three thousand doctors sent to jail over a twenty-five year period. Twenty thousand paid fines, though they were considered by the Academy of Medicine to have been practicing "ethical" medicine.

The result, as the *Bulletin* emphasizes, is that a trauma of such depth was inflicted on the medical profession that by the fifties and sixties younger doctors—and older doctors—no longer exactly knew why they weren't in the medical business in relation to addicts, but they sure knew they weren't, and they weren't going to get anywhere near it, because it was too dangerous.

The few doctors in the fifties that I knew who were attempting to treat addicts like my friend Huncke (whom I took around to all sorts of doctors and tried to pay for, say, reduction cures or maintenance or early methadone experimentation), said that they were constantly harassed by agents who would go as far as planting grass in their offices. Agents would also come in posing as junkies or send in stool pigeons to try and entrap doctors. So no doctor could maintain any kind of ethical practice, in treating junkies, particularly if he was a specialist in the area, 'cause he'd be knocked out of the business immediately by the Narcotics Bureau people.

"The abandoned addicts, in order to satisfy their compulsive needs, were driven to the illicit traffic. . . . "[18]

So this is the same statement in 1963 that Volk made forty

years earlier, pointing out over and over again that the addicts were abandoned by the medical profession, and that's why there were dope "fiends" on the street, and that's why their habits and their behavior were illicit. An interesting statement here:

> So thoroughly has the smear job on addicts been done, so outrageously but erroneously have they been depicted, that the mere mention of their name has conjured up an image of dangerous criminals or fiends. . . . [19]

And that's something to consider, because I don't think it has been: the use of the terminology *fiend* applied to a minority group. I think the junkies are the only minority group who have been categorized as fiends. Other minority groups have been categorized, like "gooks," or "niggers," or "wops," or "faggots," but *fiends* is a category of such extremity that it's staggering when you consider the psyche of the nation and the psyche of the bureaucracy that literally created *fiends*. Created the fantasy of fiends, but also in a sense perhaps did create a few human fiends, who internalized the fiendish fantasy of the Treasury Department. It's also an interesting commentary on the psyche of the United States that throughout this period it was swayed by such imagery applied to human beings.

Q: *(from Karl Hess)* Allen, is there any indication of how much an AMA doctor plus the Peoples' Drug Store would charge to keep a habit?

AG: Oh, a habit could be kept going for like thirty-five cents a day. The actual cost is very cheap, like aspirin, or maybe a little more. If you did it in the form of opium, which is one of the most stable of all habits (about as stable as methadone), raw opium, or smoked opium, it would be very cheap. The price of opium among the hill tribes of northern Laos and Siam is—how much? Probably two bucks a pound. That price is raised by middlemen all along the way from Southeast Asia to the vendor in the street here, who may sell just a smidgen in a twelve-dollar bag. I think it takes ten pounds of opium to make one pound of heroin, actually.

Q: Why was there no outcry from the medical profession?.

AG: Well, there was. But it was difficult for them to get it all together when 25,000 doctors were being arraigned and three thousand were paying fines. Also, the AMA was oddly infiltrated by the Narcotics Bureau and just simply came under its sway. I don't have too much research history on that, though there's lots of documentation available.* Leave it simply at this: in 1937, when Anslinger and the Narcotics Bureau proposed marijuana legislation, the AMA did send someone to testify against it. There was some political opposition as well, and so the La Guardia Commission was founded and reported several years later that marijuana wasn't really that bad for you. This report was reviewed in the *Journal of the American Medical Association* by none other than Harry Anslinger. So official Treasury Department thinking had infiltrated the AMA to a great degree.

The Narcotics Bureau also had campaigns of "public education" which included sending out agents to give lectures to doctors' groups, forums, and on radios and in schools. Their lectures to the doctors consisted of the information that heroin degenerated the body tissue and killed people and drove them mad and was responsible for deaths and murders, so the doctors were afraid that they were dealing with a substance which caused people to go mad and murder. And so they got a little scared. The one group in the AMA which did make some sense was a joint AMA-ABA narcotics committee, which did some studies in the late fifties and in '61 issued a final report[20] attempting to change only the terminology of discussion of the problem, by asserting that addiction is a medical rather than a criminal problem.

So that was the great semantic accomplishment of 1961. The report very definitely tried to set the wind going in another direction. It was issued very gingerly, around the same time President Kennedy's commission on juvenile delinquency made a very similar kind of report. The whole discussion had become so unreal that by the sixties it was a great triumph when a judicial or medical group would say that addiction should even be considered medically. And, three years later, the National Council on Crime and Delinquency advised

*See Rufus King's *The Drug Hang-up* (note 1, end of this section).

53

> ... that necessary action be taken, either by statute or by the appropriate bureaus and departments, to have the interpretation of the Harrison Act, as set forth in *Linder v. United States*, carried out administratively and the regulations of the Bureau of Narcotics amended to conform thereto. ...
>
> The nature of the [present] administration of the Harrison Act deters physicians from performing their ethical duties.[21]

Yet even now it's still somewhat under discussion—though many people do say "Well, OK, this is a large mental health problem or a large physical health problem or a medical problem," about half of the discussion is still in terms of law and order and police.

Q: Initially you tied in the rise of this attitude against junkies to the material interests of certain doctors in New York.

AG: Yeah, a very small group of doctors who had specific sanitariums which charged high prices for rich people, and were trying to sort of drive the junkies to their sanitariums for cures.

Q: Then you're explaining the traditional official attitude toward junkies in terms of some kind of puritanism or hostility?

AG: Well, the whole scene has changed in the last few years —everything got so scandalous, including corruption among the police, that in '67 or '68 or so the Federal Narcotics Bureau was shifted from the Treasury Department to the Justice Department. The present attitude is based on sheer ignorance of the whole field and of the history and of the facts and *everything*, including prejudice against "hedonism" and the assumption that drug users are immoral and criminal by nature. Like Rossides told me just yesterday, "Well, even if junkies are given their junk they'll still commit crime because they're criminal types, aren't they?" It's incredible!

Q: I'm curious what you were trying to accomplish by talking to him.

AG: Communication of information.

Q: Did you get anything out of it?

AG: Yes, my own information to them and also I was interested in getting some information from them.

Now the politics of methadone. You've got to get a license from the cops to do methadone therapy—dig?—as required by the New York State Department of Health:

> ... a class VI narcotic registration issued by the United States Internal Revenue Service Special Tax Section, with the approval of the Bureau of Narcotics and Dangerous Drugs, United States Department of Justice ... [22]

In other words you can't administer methadone on a purely medical basis—its use is still controlled by the police. Dr. Dole of Dole and Nyswander at present (1971) wants to expand the methadone maintenance therapy to twenty-five thousand people instead of four thousand five hundred people as it's now handled, but that can't be done because maintenance programs are still considered research programs and thus require the authorization of the police. Dole says the strategy immediately ahead for doctors is to change the terminology so methadone programs need not be research but regular therapy without police licensing. This licensing is very dangerous, because it means that if everybody who's addicted comes out from underground, from the woodwork, registers with the police as well as with a doctor, the police can perhaps decide that "This black cat is a junkie and he's on our program now, and he's working with the Black Panthers, so we ought to cut him off his methadone." Thus the real danger of political control of people—a point that's been raised by many of the Black Panthers here in Washington, and elsewhere—is a very important one.

Now, according to the New York Civil Liberties Union, after habits are stabilized addicts don't need to steal, so immediately the whole crime problem is wiped out:

> ... A four-year trial of the methadone treatment has shown 94 percent success in ending the criminal activity of former heroin addicts. ... [23]

Now, the next obstacle is the belief that if you give the junkies their junk it won't work, junk addiction will spread, "The English system doesn't work," right? That's the terminology that one hears from *The New York Times,* particularly via Richard Severo: *The English system doesn't work.* This was a propaganda line begun many years ago by the Narcotics Bureau, which has always been sending high-level delegations to England to fuck up their system, as far back as the fifties when Anslinger went over and tried to get the British doctors to have heroin eliminated from the pharmacopaeia, as it is here. The British doctors rose up en masse and said, "We don't want any more American imperialism!"

Dr. Donald B. Louria, Rockefeller's narcotics adviser until recently, and Dr. Brill, the head of Pilgrim State, who are New York state and federal advisers, have always been going over to England and then coming back and badmouthing the English system here. They badmouthed it because in 1960–62 there were five hundred addicts registered, and in 1968 there were two thousand five hundred. I'm not a statistician, but that means what, a 500-percent increase? Five times as many addicts in eight years: horrifying! If you apply that to New York, like the whole population would be addicted in ten years if we gave out "free heroin."

When I asked Representative Edward Koch, who's like a representative of the largest group of junkies in America—he should know more about it than anybody else, therefore, it being his constituency (i.e., Greenwich Village and Lower East Side)—why he wasn't pushing for some kind of English system, he said it was because he'd read *The Times* and Severo said the English system didn't work and so he was stymied and baffled.

We do know there's increased interest in drugs and everybody's experimenting around, so there's naturally going to be some rise, though not too enormous. The British did have a few writing croakers, doctors like Lady P., who was a friend of Alex Trocchi and Burroughs, who were making opiates available in overly large quantities. So there were five or six doctors overwriting and unbalancing the scene there. When the Americans came in and pointed that out and made a big stink, the British got a little frightened, so they decided to change their system by taking it out of the hands of private doctors.

An addict was still allowed to go and get his drugs, but he would get them from a clinic where a group of doctors would supervise it. Well, there was one unfortunate thing, which was that the date for cut-off from private doctors coincided with the announcement of where the clinics were, but not with the actual opening and operation of all the clinics, so that half of the patients in Britain were assigned to clinics which did not yet exist. So immediately a tiny black market arose in England. Once the clinics did get into operation, all the junkies who had never registered (or "notified" or "been notified," as the British say) notified the Central Addiction Office. So in '67–'68 there was a sudden rise in the statistical or paper record of the number of addicts in England, a jump of fifteen hundred or two thousand, actually. That's all explained by the Home Ministry in a *Report to the United Nations* by Her Majesty's Government, '68 and '69, and by a speech by Lord Stoneham in the House of Lords:

> ... We direct attention to this and to other encouraging pointers to a diminution of the heroin problem. ... The notification scheme brought to light more than 1,000 possibly addicted persons previously unknown, most of whom have been seen by the treatment centers. The number who remain is anyone's guess, but it does not appear likely to be substantial. The weekly rate of notification has been steadily dropping for some time. ... Of course it is too early to say whether the spread of heroin addiction has been checked or is petering out.[24]

In other words, the British system actually does work, in the sense that the enormous rise in addiction is primarily statistical rather than actual. That's a very important point, because people who don't know the politics and balance of arguments of the situation are continually being confounded by Narcotics Bureau assertions on this point.

Q: Why then is there a heroin black market in England today whereas there hadn't been five years ago?

AG: There will always be a little market, not much; one reason is that the English have been increasingly switching over to methadone recently, and also experimenting with reducing— not giving people as much as they really want and ask for (underprescribing)—so there's a small black market rising in heroin now. Partly on the insistence of the Americans, and partly out of recent unprofessionalism, and fearfulness, the British have been shifting over (1) to clinics, which I think ultimately will prove to be a mistake, and (2) to methadone, which I don't think is advantageous over heroin, medically or socially—it just fits in more with the American line. So naturally there are quite a few old schmeckers, older addicts, who are not going to accept this bureaucratic regulation.

In other words, a black market generally arises when a normal medical supply is denied, as was pointed out by Volk before and by the New York Academy of Medicine and many other commentators many times later. If you don't need a black market, you won't have a black market. The point is, there is not sufficient demand from virgins—from people who have not taken junk, who are not addicted—to call forth from Indochina or Persia or Turkey the whole apparatus of a black market. It's only the absolute pressure of people in total life-and-death pain-need that can call forth that much activity. And the remedy would be to balance out the demand with the medical supply, a regulated supply, as the Harrison Act originally intended.

Crime in the Streets Caused by Addiction Politics

A LITTLE ANTHOLOGY OF STATISTICS RELATING
BREAKDOWN OF LAW & ORDER & EPIDEMIC OF
CRIME IN STREETS WITH CONSEQUENT
POLICE-STATE HYSTERIA TO THE ORIGINAL SIN
OF DENIAL OF CITIZENLY CONSTITUTIONAL
PRIVACY & FREEDOM IN MEDICAL RELATIONS
BETWEEN DOCTOR & PATIENT IN CASES OF
OPIATE ADDICTION

AG: I don't know how many of you are familiar with the statistics and figures I have from New York City, but I understand that they are paralleled by data from other megalopolises that have a junk problem. What it boils down to is that the bulk of the famous political "law 'n' order" problem is not caused by the radical-left "hippies," not the "niggers"; it is the junk population on a rampage to score money for junk.

To begin with, in New York City by 1967 it was reported that there were a hundred thousand addicts.[25] Official figures vary all the time—in '63 it was supposed to be about twenty thousand.[26] By this year it's reportedly two hundred thousand, thirty-five thousand of them schoolchildren, according to Representative Koch.[27] Assemblyman Podell in New York City, linking the estimates of Dr. Ramirez, who was Lindsay's narcotics coordinator, and Lawrence Pierce, who was Rockefeller's, said that the hundred thousand figure meant that the city's addicts would have to steal ten million dollars a day to support their habits.[28]

So I've collected over a period of four or five years official persons' estimates in New York City as to what the relation between crime in the streets and the junk problem is, and to what extent this relationship effects the overcrowding of courts. Everybody's aware that the courts are breaking down under the strain of excessive case loads, and nobody can hear anybody or talk to anybody any longer because nobody has time to listen to anybody's case, much less judge it rigorously on constitutional standards, so there's wholesale plea-copping and switching of stands.

The point is that the bulk of street crimes, burglaries, and muggings are junk-associated. The Corrections Commissioner of New York City, George McGrath, was quoted as saying that 40 percent of the men and 70 percent of the women incarcerated in municipal prisons are junk-associated cases.[29] That means that half or more of the prison population which has recently been rioting because of overcrowded conditions in the Tombs and the Queens prisons in New York, is made up of citizens who have been denied their constitutional-medical rights. Back in 1968, Justice Botein said that half the crimes committed in New York City every year were by addicts, and advised:

> "We will have to give the addicts narcotics legally rather than have them roam the streets." He emphasized that (court) calendars were clogged and that there were not enough judges to handle them.[30]

And two years later Michael Pollina, the president of the city Criminal Bar Association in New York, said that the population of the Tombs, which was in the midst of rioting, could be reduced immediately by 25 percent if addicts were released and sent to doctors.[31] (That is, 25 percent of the inmates of the Tombs were charged with narcotics violations alone, just possession or sale—that didn't include the people who were caught stealing.)

The time spent by policemen at their tasks is also dominated by junkies:

> ... Some average times spent by policemen on different jobs were: burglary, 41.7 minutes of the day; intoxicated persons, 25.9 minutes; fire alarms, 30 minutes; traffic violations, 21.7 minutes; rapes, 59.9 minutes; and narcotics, 230.2 minutes.[32]

Representative Claude Pepper (Democrat, Florida), as a result of his investigation of the judiciary and the overloading of courts, pointed out that about 48 percent of the cases disposed of by the Supreme Court of New York County were for trafficking, or other junk-related crimes.[33] And a note by Chief Justice Warren Burger is interesting:

> From time to time Congress adds more judges, but the total judicial organization never quite keeps up with the caseload. Two recent statutes alone added thousands of cases related to commitment of narcotics addicts and the mentally ill.[34]

So is this point understood by everyone here?

Q: I understand that, but there's also an increase in violent crimes, like murders and rapes, so how do you relate that? Of gratuitous violent crimes.

AG: I don't. What I am concerned with is the fact that the volume of crime and the volume of court activity and the overcrowding of the jails is at this point attributed by almost everybody in the police and the judiciary as being related to the junk problem. The violent thing I think comes from the war, the overcrowding, and, in a way, a good deal from the fallout of the drug thing, (like a lot of it I think is speed, oddly,—amphetamines), aside from the general cultural horror scene that we're going through.

Q: Aside from the big problems, the violence emanates from junk?

AG: Junkies, if possible, try to avoid violent scenes.

Q: But if it comes to a point where they need it badly—

AG: It's more likely they'd do a sneaky burglary like steal your car, get in when you're out, or steal your television set when you're not there. Maybe pull a gun or a knife, less often—well, that's often enough, but usually in a situation where they're going to be faced with resistance. The very nature of junkies is torpor, anyway—toward torpor.

There may be an increase in violent crimes, but there has also been an overwhelming increase in burglaries. Like, every apartment in my building on the Lower East Side has been ripped off, including mine, three times.

Q: Is there evidence to show that efforts in the past couple of years to cut off the flow of narcotics traffic lead to a rise in crime?

AG: I don't have any figures on that except the opposite: cheap methadone cuts crime activity.

Cutting off marijuana during Operation Intercept* was followed by a flooding of New York with junk. The price of junk fell by half. It was very interesting, a synchronism, as if organized crime had been directing the government policy which cut off the marijuana. As the city was flooded with junk, simultaneously *The New York Times* began flowering with stories of people overdosing because the junk had become so pure. For the first time in years over a thousand people died of overdoses within a year—it was incredible! The normal six-dollar bag went down to three and it turned out to be pure junk and all of these people who were used to watered-down junk were keeling over all of a sudden. A thousand people in one year.

---

*Former Nixon aide and convicted Watergate burglar G. Gordon Liddy was enthusiastically involved in Operation Intercept. He had displayed the same gusto years earlier in the initial invasions of Dr. Timothy Leary's privacy in Millbrook, New York. Other Watergate figures involved in Operation Intercept were John Caulfield, John Ehrlichman, and then-Attorney General John Mitchell.

Narcotics Agents Peddling Drugs

BRIEF BIBLIOGRAPHY OF NEWS REPORTS
SHEWING THAT NARCOTICS AGENTS, FEDERAL,
STATE & LOCAL, THE BULK OF EACH GROUP, ARE
THEMSELVES INVOLVED IN DOPE TRAFFICKING

AG: The full extent of peddling conducted by narcotics agents is unknown as yet to the general public or to the specialists in the legislature.* My assertion is the bulk of narcotics police, municipal and even federal, are involved in corrupt narcotics dealings.

On the federal level, when Ramsey Clark took over as Attorney General he busted or forced to resign or indicted thirty-two agents from the New York area at one time—December 13, 1968.[35] A later *Times* story, February 26, 1970, said that the Bureau dismissed forty-nine of its agents, rather than thirty-two.[36] I asked Ramsey Clark how many New York agents there were altogether, and he said there were eighty. So that's forty-nine out of eighty. He also said, "These were the only people I could get evidence against"— in other words, this wasn't the total extent of the corruption, and that "The situation went back a quarter of a century."[37]

There was another bust of federal agents in Miami on April 21, 1965, according to an article headlined "U.S. Narcotics Chief in Miami and 2 Detectives Held in Bribery."[38] And that's very important because Miami is one of the crucial smuggling entry points. The bust of the Miami chief was part of a larger network of busts which led to Ramsey Clark's giant busts. You have to be like a fine detective specialist and read the various news stories and then do a little background checking to see the magnitude of

---

*1972 Knapp Commission assertions of grand-scale police corruption reached the public ear and led to the formation of permanent state investigatory bodies.

the corruption network and the association between one bust and another.

Q: What does this mean then about both municipal and federal law-enforcement officials—does it mean that it's a hopeless task to wipe out pushers?

AG: Right, because so many of the narcotics police are pushing. Given Clark's statement that this situation goes back a quarter of a century, it means that the corruption is at least half as old as the problem.

Q: Then the whole law-enforcement emphasis, new federal money—in effect it's utterly wasted.

AG: Well, not merely wasted. It *aggravates* the problem, makes it worse and worse.

On the municipal level much more has come to light. I have clippings of every bust of police agents recorded in *The New York Times* from 1967 to 1970. You have to read between the lines a little, but there's enough information to suggest the whole picture. To begin with:

> December 13, 1967: "6 Narcotics Agents Seized as Sellers—3 City Detectives, Two Nassau Investigators and Federal Man Indicted Here."[39]

That means a small group of local and federal people working together were found out. As a result Frank Hogan, the D.A., said that the hundreds of people these detectives had busted would have to be screened because the testimony of these agents could not be trusted any more.[40]

Then David Burnham, who was very good in *The Times*, one of the very best on this particular subject, did a follow-up:

> The three detectives arrested on charges of selling narcotics were members of one of the Police Department's smallest, most sophisticated, and least known operations . . . Special Investigating Unit of Narcotics Bureau.[41]

Now, the New York Narcotics Bureau is the biggest narcotics bureau in the world—hundreds of agents. The Special Investigating Unit is the unit that deals with the higher-ups, the Mafia, total corruption within the government (special investigations), international trade, wholesaling.

And it turns out that the people who were busted included a Detective Imp, who was the crack member of the Special Investigating Unit, which trained the other squads. This was the key unit, the most crucial, the "brains" of the New York City Narcotics Bureau. The head of the entire bureau, Ira Bluth, said the next day, "I feel as if someone in my family had been arrested."[42]

At this point the city bureau was divided into five subunits because of allegations by a former captain of the bureau that it was "riddled with corruption."[43] It wasn't just a few agents; it was *riddled* with corruption.

To understand the next few busts, you have to realize that 90 percent of narcotics busts (according to Professor Alfred Lindesmith in his book *The Addict and the Law*) are accomplished through the use of stool pigeons, because nobody is going to turn themselves in, and nobody else is going to bother to give information unless there's some self-interest.

This means that the policeman has a stable of four or five informers whom he keeps supplied with money, official money appropriated and kept in the safe in the precinct or in the Narcotics Bureau office. Or the stool pigeon may be kept "coming home" all the time by giving him smack—though that's sort of illicit, and would not be considered proper in court if it were known in court; but possibly it wouldn't even be considered proper if it were known that the stool pigeon had been given money.

But anyway, most arrests are accomplished thus: marked money is given to the stool pigeon, he scores four or five times from a pusher, then his detective and he make the bust. So they bust the pusher and he's got say five ounces of heroin. A common practice is to take one ounce and bring it back to the station and give it to the court for evidence, maybe give an ounce to the stool pigeon as pay for his work, and then the stool pigeon and the policeman divide the other three ounces and peddle it and get money from it. That's standard operating procedure, according to Sidney Zion of *The New York Times*, who went around with the detectives for many years; and according to many junkies I've talked to who have been stool pigeons; and according to my friend Huncke who's been in the business for forty years.

Now, February 14, 1968: "City Audits Police Narcotics

Fund."[44] They were auditing stool pigeon money. February 17:
*"Shakeup in Police Shifts 3 Top Aides in Narcotics Unit
—Renaghan Replaces Bluth as Four Inquiries Go On—Force is
Stunned."*[45] In other words Bluth, the head of the Narcotics
Bureau, was then shifted because of hanky-panky with the stool
pigeons' money and other suspicions associated with peddling.
Actually, he was never indicted, and the next time he appears in
The New York Times he was accompanying President Johnson
on a surprise visit to New York.

March 7: As a result of the inquiry on narcotics funds, fourteen
detectives and a captain are scheduled to be transferred.[46]

March 9: Twelve more detectives transferred:

> . . . 34 men removed from the bureau during the present
> investigation . . .
>
> With an authorized strength of 350, the New York Narcotics
> Bureau is the largest narcotics enforcement agency in the world.
> Two and a half weeks ago, the three top men of the bureau were
> relieved.[47]

On April 25, 1970, in a survey on police corruption, David
Burnham gave an outline of the conditions of corruption in the
Bureau of Narcotics:

GRAFT PAID TO POLICE HERE SAID TO RUN INTO
MILLIONS—
Survey Links Payoffs to Gambling and Narcotics

> . . .because the potential profits are higher, individual narcotics
> detectives are constantly tempted . . . charges of selling . . . trying
> to bribe . . . extorting $1200 in cash, 105 "decks" of heroin and a
> variety of personal possessions. . . .
>
> But there is some evidence that a more regular kind of corrup-
> tion is not entirely unknown. One policeman . . . said one of his
> fellow detectives arranged payoffs to policemen from the largest
> heroin dealer.
>
> These payoffs, he said, ranged from $5,000 for changing
> testimony . . . to $50,000 for sale of a "wire"—the recorded con-
> versation made by a police wire-tap or bug.
>
> . . . they had the evidence and then waited for a bid from the
> criminals. The bid came and the money was collected. . . .
>
> Many narcotics detectives . . . to meet a quota of four felony
> arrests a month . . . resort to stealing drugs from one addict and
> giving to another to buy information.

(Now this quota system is important, because in other words police have to drum up business where there is none.)

> In addition, . . . pressure on owners of bars . . . because a narcotics arrest . . . means the owner can lose his license . . .

(Which is another subject entirely—in other words if a bar owner gets busted for narcotics, planted or real, or just accumulated because his clientele is a bunch of junkies or young hippies, it's like really a total suicide, so the payoff from bar owners is another source of revenue for the narcotics agent.)

> A detective with several years of experience in narcotics enforcement said he heard a top commander in the narcotics division chastising another official for not demanding and receiving regular payoffs from the bars in his jurisdiction.
> . . . This sort of corruption . . . is woven into the very fabric of the policeman's professional life.[48]

That's that, for that area. However, we haven't finished with the tale of Renaghan and Bluth, the chiefs of the Narcotics Bureau in New York. August 2nd, David Burnham again:

> . . . a suspended detective . . . [was] indicted for perjury and contempt in connection with his contacts with a reputed major New York bookmaker, Hugh Mulligan.[49]

Mulligan, according to *The Times,* was the big fixer around New York for the Syndicate. He could fix narcotics businesses and gambling arrests, and he could also arrange placement of detectives in special places through payoffs. So,

> According to Detective Keeley's testimony, he met with Mulligan "five, six, or seven" times to discuss "police investigations." Also indicted in the case was the former commander of the Narcotics Division, Thomas G. Renaghan, a retired assistant chief inspector.[50]

This is the first time Renaghan reappears in the scandal papers; last time he was the chief of the Narcotics Bureau and now he too is indicted. That means that two successive heads of the largest narcotics bureau in the world have been involved in hanky-panky, shifted around, or actually indicted for criminal activities. What was the criminal activity that Renaghan was involved with? November 24, 1970: "Corruption Jury Indicts Gambler—Mulligan Is Arrested After Refusing to Testify":

> ... "Mr. Mulligan, did you offer payment of a bribe to former Assistant Chief Inspector Thomas Renaghan during the summer of 1969, through Detective John J. Keeley, in order to obtain the assignment of a certain Detective Lawrence Sangirardi to the Special Investigations Unit of the Narcotics Bureau?"[51]

So once again the key Special Investigations Unit is in the shadow. Which means that all along, and presumably continuing, the key agency in the New York Narcotics Bureau, which is in charge of actually investigating the Mafia part of it, the large-scale, wholesale pushing (not the street addict like Huncke who's just trying to scrounge around the street and get a little score for the day), the one which is really investigating the thing as a business, the business as Business, is itself corrupt. Not only is it corrupt, but the last two heads of the agency were corrupt. So the municipal situation combined with the federal situation completely X's out the police role in containing the problem of addiction.

Now it must be borne in mind that all the last three decades of lobbying for the criminalization of the junkie has historically come precisely from the groups who have been peddling. Very little of this lobbying has come from legitimate medical people, very little from sociologists. All the congressional testimony for harsher and harsher penalties always comes from police agencies, federal, state, or municipal. The very terminology and language of legislation used by congressmen, senators, and state legislators in reference to junk has originated precisely in the bureaus many of whose personnel have been most involved in dealing and smuggling.

Traditionally a congressman or senator concerned with presenting a bill on the junk problem discusses it with Treasury Department people, and the Treasury Department comes up very quickly with a model legislation program. Back in '56, I think, I saw a picture of Anslinger and Senator Price Daniel, I believe, shaking hands over a new proposition that was introduced to the Senate: death penalty for junkies who were caught peddling. And both of them in the picture were grinning.

Anyway, the structure from the beginning till now, from 1925 on, can be understood basically as a byproduct of Parkinson's Law: that a bureaucracy finds more and more work for itself, and encroaches more and more on the rights of private citizens. Plus the heavy motive for peddling on the part of a bureaucracy that has written its own prohibition laws and spent public money in propagandizing them.

In that area there's an interesting statement in a book called *The Murderers*, written by Anslinger around 1944, in which he describes very proudly how the Narcotics Bureau itself went on a campaign to convince the public that marijuana was no good and was an "evil weed" that "led" people to the "madhouse." He describes the methods of the bureau in "public education," or lobbying, or brainwashing, as you might call it. That's how the imagery of the dope fiend versus the heroic efforts of the Treasury Department T-men or the local dope fuzz got spread into public consciousness. And unless legislators and theoreticians on the subject realize that the pressure and the lobbying has come primarily from this interested agency, nobody will understand what the whole argument is about. The basic point, as anyone would know, know simply by one's own heart and humanity, is that you cannot treat human beings like *fiends,* and you cannot erect a system of law and order by billing some people as fiends and others as heroic, *macho* fiend beater-uppers.

There's a book by Dr. Howard Becker, sociologist, called *The Outsiders,*[52] which gives a statistical survey of the number of articles appearing in the slick magazines from 1932 to 1938 regarding the "marijuana menace," compares the imagery and information in them and traces them back to the first articles in '32 in the slick magazines; and then traces those articles back to direct information from the Narcotics Bureau. In other words, Becker traces very precisely all the imagery and the activity emanating from the Treasury Department offices through the slick magazines such as *Saturday Evening Post, Life,* etc., for a period of six years, till the accomplishment of the legislation in '37—the Marijuana Tax Act. In other words, it isn't as if there were a cultural thing where different anti-grass scholars were working in different areas and all writing different articles; it's that *all* of it came from one spot, the Treasury Department. And Becker does a linguistic analysis and interviews the authors and things like that.[53] It's a very interesting piece of sociology.

Now, in order to formulate domestic policy, you should first determine the best substance for stabilizing a habit. Methadone is probably all right, except it's a synthetic; probably the best thing would be opium itself, because it's more natural—because it's "organic." There's an ancient tradition of very stable opium addicts in the Orient. You can have a regular, stable life on opium. The high lasts a long time and also, like methadone, you don't have to take it three times a day. And actually the reason methadone comes into favor now is that it's convenient for the bureaucrats, who are attempting to control the addicts. Not that it's convenient necessarily for the addicts, unless one considers that the bureaucrat's convenience is the addict's convenience, which is present bureaucratic thinking, naturally.

Q: Is maintenance your approach, then?

AG: Well, if one were to be concerned with the problem of maintenance, I'm just contributing the information that opium is just about as good as anything else. Though it's never been discussed as medical evidence.

Bureaucrats have always been imprecise as well as medically incoherent and inaccurate in dealing with this problem, and that's why it has always been so grossly mismanaged. It may be just ignorance at this point, actually, just absolute total stupid ignorance which dictates draconian policies, see, because if they think opiates degenerate your body tissues, then they can't really think in terms of maintenance. And if they can't think in terms of maintenance, then they have to think in terms of enforcement; and if they have to think in terms of enforcement, well, the argument's been lost long ago.

Half of the discussions I get into with officials, always, oddly, I'm surprised to find, have to do with the basic material facts. Can somebody on junk lead a relatively normal life or not? And the junk bureaucracy doesn't know, they don't know the answer, or even enough to ask the question, actually.

CIA Involvement with Opium Traffic at Its Source

AG: A year ago I began getting heavily into the notion of CIA involvement with opium traffic in Indochina as a result of conversations with David Obst, Al McCoy, and a few other scholars. Since then I've done a lot of research and gone to original committee members and consuls and gotten the original documents and transmitted them to various people who are working in that field. There are now five or six scholars working on this subject—Alfred McCoy, Peter Dale Scott, Banning Garrett, and others who have written for *Ramparts* and are specialists in the area, as I am not, because I've never been to Laos. So you'll forgive me for generalizations because I'm just dealing with documents and papers and not with anything that I know directly, except through extrapolation from my experience domestically.

One very important book is *The Quicksand War* by Lucien Bodard. Bodard was a correspondent for *Le Monde* and was present at a conversation which took place in the early forties between a "Major Savani, a scarred, tough Corsican, the chief of intelligence in Cochinchina,"[54] who took Bodard with him to see Bay Vien, head of the Binh Xuyen, the bandit group that controlled the underworld in Saigon. "Savani was going to offer the hunted Bay Vien the alliance of France."[55] The Binh Xuyen was a rebel gang allied with Ho Chi Minh and the Viet Minh of the day; however, there was some rivalry. The Binh Xuyen was a bandit group against the central government or whatever law and order there was, whereas, the Viet Minh were fighting a political struggle. They didn't quite trust each other, so the

French chief of intelligence tried to play the bandit chief against the Viet Minh and offered him control of opium in the Cholon section of Saigon. The book is interesting because Bodard was present at the original conversations, and describes the actual terms of the treaty. And also describes the later history (several pages further on):

> Bao Dai [who was then the French puppet ruler] did not quite dare appoint him [Bay Vien] chief of the general staff in 1949, because the French high command would not have stood for it. But it was then that he caused the Grande Monde to be given to Bay Vien. Now the conquest of Cholon was complete: and from now on he could not be touched. Instead of being a mere tolerated gangster he was one of the pillars of nationalist Vietnam. . . .
>
> Five years later he accomplished the highest point of his ambition. Thanks once more to Bao Dai he became the official head of all the police forces and of all the security agents in the state of Vietnam. The Binh Xuyen, once hunted down by the police, had turned into superpolicemen.[56]

That's important to understand as background for what later develops with CIA and others. In other words, the head of French intelligence gave Bay Vien the franchise in opium dealing and whoring and other things in Cholon, and this same Bay Vien from, I believe, 1949 until 1953 or '54, until our men came over, was the head of police in Saigon and the chief opium dealer. The Saigon chief of police has always been the chief dealer since then to this very day, including the man pictured in the newspapers with pistol in hand blowing a Viet Cong suspect's head off. He, apparently, according to my research and the research of others in the area, is precisely the head of opium operations in Saigon.

To begin with, one must understand that 80 to 90 percent of the world's illegal opium supply since the 1950s has come not from Turkey, but from Indochina. Now the Narcotics Bureau and the Treasury Department say that 80 percent of the American heroin supply comes from Turkey via Marseilles into Montreal or Mexico City and is then sent to America. That has been the traditional line of our narcotics agencies. But my own research and the research of many other people increasingly leads to the suspicion that the source of this 80 percent that comes into

America is this fertile triangle [*Allen refers to map*] in northern Laos, including Ban Houei Sai, the opium capital of the world.

According to the U.N., some, but not very much opium comes from Yunnan, China (although the Hearst press and the Narcotics Bureau have long insisted that China is a major producer); some from northern Burma, which provides 40 percent of the opium from this area; some from Thailand; and some from the hill region of Laos and formerly the hill region up here in Vietnam. Altogether one thousand or twelve hundred tons of opium a year.

In 1965 a U.N. study was done in this area by Dr. Joel Fort, who made an on-the-spot investigation for the World Health Organization. Fort talked to all the newsmen there, went up into Ban Houei Sai, and traveled all around. He wrote a twenty-eight-page report which has not been published yet. When I spoke to Dr. Fort, he said that most—80 percent, he was willing to say—of our domestic heroin comes from Indochina. Which is like a revelation because it reverses all the thinking of the professional bureaucracies.

Q: Does there have to be any doubt on that? Can't you tell from inference where it is grown?

AG: Oh, everybody, including the Narcotics Bureau, accepts that 80 percent of the *world's* illegal supply grows there in Indochina. The question is whether it's 80 percent of the *American* supply—that's the point of bureaucratic distinction, the point of argument, and it's a crucial point, because it means: do we have to investigate the CIA and the Kuomintang and the Laotian general staff and General Thieu's family at the moment?

Q: Is this source of supply determined by a chemical analysis of heroin?

AG: No, from an analysis of the supply routes. Chemical analysis of heroin is the basis of the Narcotics Bureau's contention; they say that they analyze it and can tell where it's from by machines. But Dr. Fort told me that if the heroin is pure you can't tell where it came from. That's a very important thing to consider.

A second source in my study is recent research into patterns of traffic into Canada done by the Canadian Commission of Inquiry into the Nonmedical Use of Drugs, otherwise known as the

LeDain Commission. They are finding that 80 percent of the Canadian supply comes from Indochina. There have also been statements by George Belk, who was assistant to Giordano, head of the U.S. Bureau of Narcotics in '67, that most of the American supply comes either through Canada or, when it gets too hot in Montreal, through Mexico City; then when it's too hot in Mexico City, back to Montreal—shifting back and forth. If the major source of Canadian supply, according to the LeDain Commission investigators, is Indochinese, then it's likely that it would also be the major source for the American opiate market.

We'll get into that further, later. I just wanted to open up the discussion, the possibility, that the traditional myth, "U.S. Government sources were quoted today as saying . . ." (that's usually the way *The Times* puts it), or "Narcotics officials here said that 80 percent of the heroin coming into America comes from Turkey via Marseilles," may not be a stable language statement, and it may not be borne out by research which will be done in the next year, and by research which has been done by Fort and others previously.

The story of US involvement with the Indochinese drug traffic begins in the fifties. The army of Chiang Kai-shek, the leftover Nationalist KMT 93rd Yunnan Division, driven out of China by the Communists, came into northern Burma in '46-'7-'8-'9, and, according to Professor McAlister, who is California Senator Tunney's adviser on Indochinese affairs, hung around the hills to collect the opium harvest of the year '45 or '46.

Two weeks ago I met Richard Helms here in Washington and got into a conversation with him about whether or not the Chinese KMT troops were still in the dope business and were still active in the fertile triangle and he said, "Oh, no, no, no, you're . . . wasting your time investigating that, researching that, that's out of the question."

But then I met Gene Rossides of the Treasury Department, who had just come back from Indochina, at a party and he said the Chinese Nationalist KMT army people were still very strong in the dope business there. So I made a date with Rossides to find out more about that, particularly what they thought the drug traffic route was. They're convinced most of it is Turkey–to–Marseilles–to–New York and I'm convinced it's Indochina–Beirut–Marseilles–New York.

In any case, Rossides was not willing to bet with me about that.

The bet I offered him was that he could have my dorje* if under 25 percent of the supply came from Indochina, but if over 25 percent came from Indochina he would have to meditate half an hour a day for the rest of his life. I think he was a little unsure, ultimately. It was a heavy thing to do if he was unsure.

Q: Did he accept any kind of bet, finally?

AG: He accepted on terms that he would meditate once a week for half an hour.

Now for some news clippings from the fifties. According to a Reuters report in 1954, there was a KMT army of perhaps ten thousand who hung around northern Burma for many, many years, attacking into Yunnan, China, raiding, smuggling—partly subsidized by the CIA, partly making their living on opium trading and trading the opium for guns.

The guns were brought from Taiwan in old World War II Liberator bombers and exchanged for opium. So Taiwan and Chiang Kai-shek's agents were involved in the opium trade of that time. Reuters reported:

> Empty cartons and packing cases bearing the names of Thai, Japanese, and American firms were evidence of the Kuomintang's trade outside Burma. The Chinese obtained the money to buy these goods by means of extensive opium smuggling.
>
> General Li Mi even imported a kerosene refrigerator. . . . They had built an airstrip in 1951 to bring in supplies and ferry men to and from Formosa.[57]

So this dispatch gives the supply route and the details: an airstrip in northern Burma, supplies going to and from Formosa, opium smuggling as a source of their loot.

On May 20, 1959, there was a very interesting article in *The New York Times:*

> Burmese ground troops have seized three plants set up by Chinese Nationalist guerrillas in Wanton to process opium . . . and morphine. The guerrillas have been driven from town, the War Minister announced tonight.

---

*Tibetan religious symbol representing lightning bolt, magical power.

Burmese troops also were said to have seized a jungle airstrip used by the Nationalists to fly in reinforcements and supplies.[58]

So as far back as '59 it was established, definitely, that there were plants for refining opium all the way up in northern Burma, operated by Chinese Nationalists, who at the time were being subsidized by the CIA. Regarding General Li Mi, who had been awarded the U.S. Legion of Merit and the U.S. Medal of Freedom, there's a little piece of odd scholarship being done by Peter Dale Scott. (Li Mi was the head of the Chinese Nationalist group.):

> Sea Supply Incorporated, another CIA front based in Miami, was identified in the 1950s as the vehicle for the CIA support on the ground for the opium-running KMT guerrillas of General Li Mi's Anti-Communist National Salvation Army in Burma and Yunnan.[59]

Q: The company was in Miami?

AG: Yeah, Miami. Sea Supply Incorporated. That's one of the reasons I was interested in the bust of the narcotics chief there. Also, Meyer Lansky moved money through Miami banks, and Santo Trafficante, one of his aides, took a trip to Saigon in '68, by the way. Sea Supply also helped Thai General Phao Sriyanond build his mammoth police force in the 1950s into a powerful military organization which competed with the army at that time.[60]

But to return to the KMT: a *Times* editorial from 1956 indicated that Burma held the United States responsible for the continued presence of KMT troops:

> Rangoon broke off a profitable aid relationship with the United States because it felt that this country was not vigorous enough in getting Nationalist Chinese out of northern Burma.[61]

An article in the *New York Herald Tribune* around the same time gives the number of Chinese there as

> Some 10,000 fleeing Nationalist soldiers [who] crossed over. Unwelcome guests, they took to murder and plunder. . . . In Tokyo a [Red] Chinese broadcast was heard accusing the United States of

supplying arms and sending agents to foment Chiang Kai-shek forces in Burma.[62]

So the Red Chinese began complaining. Simultaneously around '56–'57–'60 there are a lot of busts by MAAG Air Force (Military Assistance Advisory Group) of Americans in Taiwan who had been bringing opium from Indochina into Taiwan, and there was the Burmese seizure of the KMT morphine plant in 1959.

In 1960 American newsmen begin reporting Corsican Union activity in Luangprabang, the ancient royal capital of Laos. The Corsicans were running Spotted Butterfly squadrons of Piper Cubs, souped up with larger gas tanks, that transported the opium which had been brought by the KMT troops from the Meo tribes' area in northern Burma down to Ban Houei Sai in northern Laos, where it was then transported by the Corsicans to Vientiane or to Saigon or out to the ocean and dropped into the ocean where it was picked up by junks and either brought to Hong Kong or transshipped from Hong Kong to Marseilles. The people involved were

> ... Carlo the Corsican, a Eurasian called Moitie Gnakouey ... Petit Père, La Sèche Noire (the Black Cigaret) and Le Gorille Gris (the Gray Gorilla).
> ... The Meo are getting only the equivalent of $20 a kilo [in Ban Houei Sai]. ... The same kilo, when it reaches the Laotian capital of Vientiane, will be worth $60; at Saigon in South Viet Nam it will bring $1,000, and when it is safely put ashore in San Francisco the value may leap to $2,000 or more.
> ... The boys at the Snow Leopard [the Corsicans who hang around the Inn of the Snow Leopard in Phong Savan] get around the ban on exporting opium by maintaining a fleet of half a dozen single-engine Beavers and Pipers outfitted with auxiliary gas tanks. They fly into South Viet Nam and parachute the jam [*confiture*] to agents in isolated valleys who carry it to Saigon. From there it is often smuggled by ship to Hong Kong. ...[63]

Many people say that the Corsicans ran the opium trade for a long while around this period until '62–'63 when the United States' CIA people began building up General Vang Pao, Touby Lyfong, and General Ouane Rattikone as our men in Laos, and from then on the Laotian Royal Air Force took over the transport of the opium (and there's more on that which we'll get to later). In other words, the U.S. Department of Defense subsidized the Royal Laotian Air Force, who took over the transport of most of the opium from Ban Houei Sai to Vientiane and thence to Saigon from around this time, '63.

There is another little piece of information regarding the Corsicans which was brought to my attention by a fellow named Gary Busch, who was formerly International Affairs Representative of the UAW. He wrote me a letter after I requested some information:

> Following the close of World War II, the U.S. was still supplying arms and munitions to a small number of Nationalist Chinese generals operating along the Chinese border in Laos and other areas of Indochina. . . .
>
> Later, as the French began their Indochina campaigns, this traffic fell under the control of two families of the Union Corse. These two families of Corsicans regularized the process. They used this form of exchange to pay for the cost of transport and to aid the French in counter-insurgency warfare—mercenaries, sabotage, and espionage against the Viet Minh. When the U.S. took over the burden from the French, it took over these flights. Air America and similar non-chartered airlines began transporting the drugs. Indeed, one of the first group of pilots flying missions on this route is said to be Nguyen Cao Ky.[64]

And he also sent me a thing from *Private Eye*, London, issue 191, 1968, regarding the Corsicans in Marseilles:

> Since late 1947, the intelligence services of many nations have been actively engaged in the refining and distribution of narcotics derived from opium and hashish. . . . The story starts in Marseilles in the days preceding the Marshall Plan. The U.S. government found itself opposed by the CGT dockworkers whose Communist leaders refused to handle Marshall Plan supplies. In an effort to curb CGT power on the docks, the U.S. hired Mr. Pierre Ferri-Pisani, a noted Corsican gang leader, to beat up any dock-worker who opposed handling the assistance. His thugs were very successful and soon were in total control of the docks.
>
> For his efforts, Ferri-Pisani received $225,000 from Mr. Irving Brown, then head of the AFL-CIO mission in Europe.*[65]

*Carl Braden, ex-CIA head of this operation, confirmed this story in conversation with the author.—A.G.

78

I checked this out with Leo Perlis, who is still with the AFL-CIO, and who was with Irving Brown in Europe, and he said yes, of course, it was government policy to oppose Communism by financing anti-Communist unions. He wasn't sure about this particular deal with the Marseilles docks, but said it was not outside the pattern of activity of our OSS people or of the AFL-CIO. So actually the famous Marseilles trafficking and smuggling activities were originally a by-product of interference by our intelligence agencies in that area, as present trafficking out of Vietnam may also be a by-product.

What's to be understood is that the Corsicans who controlled the trade in Indochina were also controlling transport from '47 on in Marseilles. Now a quotation from the 1965 McClellan subcommittee hearings on organized crime and illicit narcotic traffic:

> Prior to the early 1950s, the bulk of U.S. imports of heroin flowed into the port of New York. Rigorous law enforcement brought changes in the routes. A great deal of heroin was directed to Canadian ports of entry, principally Montreal and Toronto, where the narcotics were delivered to confederates of the Corsicans, such as the Agueci brothers in Toronto. The French Corsican traffickers, greatly disturbed by the costly seizures of heroin shipments in the U.S. and Canada, established an operating point in Mexico City from which large quantities of heroin have been dispatched to the American underworld.[66]

And later on in the hearings report:

> During [World War II] . . . the Bureau of Narcotics' statistics on addiction showed very sharp decreases in numbers of addicts because the drugs were not available.
>
> At the end of the war, however, shipping lines opened everywhere, and the racketeers moved back into the field of trafficking as a major criminal enterprise. This was particularly true in Italy, the Commissioner [Henry Giordano, Bureau of Narcotics] said, where the Mafia took advantage of the postwar opportunities under the leadership of the late Charles "Lucky" Luciano, who had been deported from the United States. Mr. [George] Gaffney [Deputy Commissioner of the Bureau of Narcotics] testified that the Mafia "had this thing sewed up. They stepped into a vacuum there and took it over completely."[67]

If you'll remember, Lucky Luciano was released by our secret intelligence agencies to aid us as a bulwark against Communism and Fascism in Italy. He was released from federal penitentiary and sent over to Italy to help prepare the way for our own invading forces and also to help us fight the Communist menace in Sicily. General Li Mi and others also thought of themselves as bulwarks against Communism or "guardians of the northern gate," as one general is quoted in a piece by Peter Braestrup in *The Times* in 1966.

One last item from the McClellan subcommittee report:

> ... in the early 1950s the clandestine processing of heroin from morphine had shifted to the hands of the French Corsican traffickers, along with a substantial share of the import trade into the U.S. The advent of the Corsicans as major traffickers brought changes in the smuggling operations. For years the main port of entry had been New York, but now the French Corsicans smuggled their drugs through their French-speaking Canadian confederates[68]

Now this Corsican control of traffic from Marseilles into Montreal occurs at about the same time as Corsicans begin supervision of traffic in certain parts of Indochina.

Meanwhile, by 1963, there was an enormous amount of tension emanating from all the Nationalist Chinese fertile triangle activity. The Red Chinese got very upset because the 93rd Division was foraging into Yunnan, and it wound up with Chou En-lai actually coming down to Rangoon to argue with the Burmese, asking them to kick the marauders out. And it was also a drag for the Burmese, whose army was working with Chinese Communist troops in the border areas in order to preserve a trade relationship between the two countries.

But as early as February 10, 1961, *Time* magazine had reported that it was the end for the Nationalist Chinese in northern Burma, and that all of them, including crusty old General Li Mi, were being airlifted out.[69] Some of them actually were lifted out and went to Formosa, but actually most of them hung around northern Thailand, where they were still being supplied by the CIA.

The Burmese, on February 17, 1961, formally charged that the United States was dropping arms to the Chinese Nationalist

guerrillas, using World War II Liberator bombers. They actually
shot down a bomber, and that was followed by a riot against the
American Embassy on February 17–18–19, 1961, in Rangoon.
The government on Taiwan disclaimed these guerrillas, deny-
ing

> . . . any connection with the Chinese forces in Burma for the last
> seven years. Taipei and Washington cooperated in the large-scale
> evacuation of thousands of Chinese from Burma under United
> Nations sponsorship in 1953–4.
> But it is believed here that at least 10,000 Chinese remained in
> the Burmese jungles and refused repatriation.[70]

That's as far back as 1961. Earlier,

> The leader of the pro-Western opposition Democratic party [in
> Rangoon] urged the Government to declare war on Communist
> China if necessary to drive Red troops from Burmese border
> areas.[71]

See, the Reds had sent their troops to protect themselves from
the Nationalists, and the leader of the pro-Western opposition
Democratic party (perhaps another CIA payoff) was actually
urging the Burmese to declare war on Red China because of this:

> In Tokyo, a Chinese broadcast was heard that accused the
> United States of supplying arms and sending agents to foment
> Chiang Kai-shek forces in Burma.[72]

So the Chinese Communists were quite aware of this and
broadcasting to Tokyo, calling the play as far back as '56.
Then in '61 there was another phony airlift that was supposed
to rid Burma and Thailand of Nationalist Chinese armies. From
Taiwan it was announced (but no one reported observing it) that
anti-Red guerrillas had been airlifted out of Cheng Mai, Thailand, and had arrived in Taiwan. *The New York Times* reported
on March 19: "Officials here [Taiwan] are said to be planning to
request U.S. financial assistance for the costs of resettling the
repatriates."[73]
But as of the present moment, as far as we know, those armies
are still not gone, although it is still the official position that they

are. As I mentioned earlier, Helms told me two weeks ago that we were not subsidizing them, they were not important, they have not been involved in the opium traffic—as of the '71 invasion of Laos when Rossides and his group were investigating the opium traffic in Indochina (but they stayed in Saigon because there was all this military activity in Laos and they couldn't go any farther on to Ban Houei Sai or anywhere else, and so they just hung around and got official reports in their hotel rooms and came back because it was scary out there).

As I understand it, the basic CIA or government motivation is: we have to work with those in power in opium-growing areas because that's their business, and we can't interfere with it. And we'll wink at their business or even tacitly accept it or even make a little money on the side as individual CIA agents (probably Helms may not even know it). But the specific people we are working with as bulwarks against Communism everywhere are——

Q: Corsicans?

AG: Well, either Corsicans or royal elite as Toubi Lyfong, or military elite as General Ouane Rattikone, for instance.

Joel Halprin says this of Toubi, who's assistant to General Vang Pao, the head of the Meo army presently fighting at Long Cheng:

> He has traveled abroad   ely and is reputed to be quite
> wealthy as a result of op·µr· t· de. . . .
>   Concerning the opiur rade he said that currently the price of
> this commodity is stabⁿ⁴ ᵉ.[74]

Toubi was backed by the French as head of the Meos and then later was displaced by General Vang Pao. Vang Pao made peace with him, according to another ex-CIA agent I talked to these last two weeks, by giving him the opium concession in and around Long Cheng, the great CIA base which is presently under attack by the Pathet Lao.

Other Laotian army leaders like Phoumi Nosavan and Laotian Royal Air Force Chief General Ouane Rattikone and General Vang Pao, heavy receivers of military and CIA backing, have been deeply involved in trafficking. Phoumi expanded Laotian trade considerably by bringing Burmese opium into Laos, and in 1962 he appointed General Ouane chairman of his Laotian Opium Administration.[75]

Q: What are you suggesting the relationship between the CIA and the people who are in the opium trade is? That they support people who are also in the opium trade, or that they support people for the purpose of insuring that they are in the opium trade?

AG: No, no. Merely that they support people who are the *major opium traders.*[*]

I haven't gotten to any general theory yet. I'm just trying to establish what facts we know. I don't even think you need a theory by the time you know all the facts. 'Cause like, everybody is so corruptly involved, you know—let's get rid of the rascals!

Phong Savan [Laos] was named in 1962 by *Time* magazine as headquarters of the thriving opium trade bossed by a crew of Corsicans, so the Corsicans were heavily into it in '62 and accounts of their involvement were appearing in the media. And the Laotian trade was associated with Phoumi Nosavan, and that was just precisely the time when the CIA was very much involved with the Laotian elite, at which point it got to be a little bit scandalous:

RED CHINA REJECTS OPIUM ACCUSATION

Communist China heatedly denied today a United States charge that it was growing opium as a money crop.[76]

That was in April 1963. A year and a half later a Nationalist Chinese Weekly in Hong Kong, *Tien-Ti Hsin-Wen,* accused Red China of opium trade profiteering.[77] That charge was picked up by *Pravda* and subsequently by Pierre Huss in the Hearst papers and spread throughout the United States as part of our general official party line so that now a general impression (as reinforced through announcements by narcotics bureaucrats) of Red Chinese involvement pervades.

---

*A policy termed "hitchhiking," using networks of opium-trafficking corrupt allies as vehicles for combat against native "Communist" insurgencies.

At the same time, however, a *Times* article by Walter Sullivan reports U.N. disbelief:

> Interviews with a number of United Nations specialists disclosed general skepticism at reports originally circulated by the Nationalist Chinese that Peking was intentionally flooding the world market with opium.[78]

So what I'm pointing out as just a little side issue is that simultaneous with the crescendo of understanding and information coming out about the trade itself (a good deal of it in *Life* by Stanley Karnow), there's also a crescendo of interested propaganda trying to implicate the Red Chinese, all of it unfounded, and denounced by the U.N. The odd thing is that the Russians picked up on it and accused the Chinese of trading in opium, and then the Chinese got upset and denounced the Russians, and that becomes part of the Sino-Soviet argument after a while.

Actually, one story that I heard from an ex-CIA agent who was in the area at the time was that the Chinese Communists stopped growing opium in the late fifties when they paid off their hard currency debts to Russia. In any case, the U.N.'s World Health Organization definitely says the Communists are not heavily involved in the opium trade and never have been. Of the thousand tons of opium produced in Indochina, perhaps 5 percent comes from Yunnan, from hill tribes even in China growing it independently, and some of it is brought down by the Nationalist troops after their raids into Yunnan, brought down into Ban Houei Sai or Thai railheads. But apparently Chiang Kai-shek has always been associated historically with the opium trade, because after he betrayed and defeated the Communists in Shanghai in 1927 he legalized opium as a revenue measure, and gave the gangsters who had helped him a large hand in its administration.[79]

Now to move on. In the mid-sixties one of the first suggestions of involvement on the part of the South Vietnamese power elite appeared in *Mr. Pop*, a biography of Edgar "Pop" Buell:

> Many days later, Buell drove with Albert to Phong Savan and watched from the side of the airstrip as a modern twin-engined plane took on a huge load of opium. Beneath the wing, talking heatedly with the plane's Corsican pilot, was a slender woman

dressed in long white silk pants and *ao d'ai,* the side-slit, high-necked gown of Vietnam. Her body was exquisitely formed, and her darkly beautiful face wore a clear expression of authority. Even Buell could see that she was Vietnamese, not Lao.

"Zat," said Foué, "is ze grande madame of opium from Saigon."

Edgar never learned her name, but he recognized the unforgettable face and figure when the picture of the wife of an important South Vietnamese politician appeared months later in an American news-magazine.[80]

Donald Schanche, who wrote the book, said that the David McKay Company did not allow him to publish the fact that Buell told him that this was Madame Nhu herself, the opium queen of Saigon. The book was published in 1970, and the anecdote referred to an event nine or ten years earlier.

In '65, when the Kuomintang group was still active in northern Thailand, working with the U.S.O.M. (United States Operations Mission) to block Communist infiltration and invasion from the north, they apparently received tacit approval for their trafficking:

"As long as the Kuomintang people stay quiet and behave themselves, we leave them alone," a Thai border official said.

"Of course opium running is illegal, but it's the only source of money for the hill tribes."[81]

In May, 1965, in a *Times* article by Seymour Topping, we have the first formal roundup of the ancient history of the whole Indochina opium scene:

NEW CHIANG RAIDS IN CHINA REPORTED

Troops commanded by General Ma Chuan-Kuo operate from mountainous areas of Hsi Meng, 170 miles northwest of the junction of borders of Burma, Thailand, and Laos. . . .

General Ma's troops are supported by the Nationalist Government on Taiwan. Unmarked planes drop supplies and equipment to his forces. [These are American planes, CAT planes, CIA-sponsored airlines.] The operation in Burma is believed to be under the supervision of Gen. Chiang Ching-kuo, son of President Chiang Kai-shek. . . .

Nationalist forces in Burma are also financing themselves through participation in the lucrative opium trade in border areas.

The "fertile triangle" of Burma, Laos, and Thailand is a source of much of the opium that enters the illicit international traffic. . . .

These forces had retreated when the Communists occupied Yunnan in 1949. For a time, despite the protests of the Burmese, these troops were supported by the Central Intelligence Agency as well as the Taiwan Government.[82]

So here for the first time in the news are all the elements put together: smuggling, the attacks on Red China, the support by CIA and Taiwan, the opium traffic, and even Chiang Kai-shek's son supervising.

Harrison Salisbury in *The Times* on June 22, 1966, balled up the issue by saying

The hill country is the stronghold of maverick Chinese Nationalist troops that were airlifted into the region in an operation of the American Central Intelligence Agency about 1950.[83]

So he did locate that much. But he also implicated the Chinese Communists:

That is the no-man's land where the writ of no government seems to run. Hill tribes conveniently move from Burma to Thailand or Laos or China as pursuit or the nature of their banditry dictates. Opium provides a common denominator for outlaws of all four countries. And they are not alone.

. . . Chinese Communists, it is insisted, and tribesmen act as intermediaries crossing into Yunnan, collecting raw opium and delivering it from Chinese Communists to Chinese Nationalists. . . .[84]

It had already been very firmly established in the early 1960s that there was very little opium left in Yunnan, and very little coming from Red China. It was unfortunate that Seymour Topping's tipoff of May 16, 1965, was followed by Harrison Salisbury one month and one year later, following up the story but attributing it to Communist junk instead of our own. And I think that's what inhibited further research into Topping's perspective.

So in 1966 we are still hearing about the Red Menace, as in

Pierre J. Huss's "Peking's Most Evil Weapon" in the Hearst papers:

> Where is the bottomless source of such murderous drugs? A new survey reveals the shocking fact that in 1964, the Peking warlords collected $800 million for the treasury of Red China by spewing into the world more than 10,000 tons of the stuff.[85]

The total Indochinese opium supply was only about twelve hundred tons, not ten thousand tons, anyway. Hearst and Huss and presumably the Narcotics Bureau were advertising a gigantic, insane, unreal figure for Red China.

Peter Braestrup in *The Times*, September 5, 1966, gives some intelligent reporting on the KMT troops in northern Thailand:

> Specialists in Bangkok estimate that a sizable percentage of the perhaps 3,500 men now commanded by [KMT leader] General Tuan and two associates act as paid escorts for opium caravans moving south through the bandit-filled Burmese mountains to Laos and Thailand.[86]

At this point the United States was beginning to bomb and disrupt northern Laos, and the opium production in Laos was diminishing, and so the Laotians began importing their opium more and more, and began acting as the main conduit for opium coming from the relatively calmer areas of northern Burma, northern Thailand, a little bit from Yunnan.

> But the Thais and some Western diplomats privately tend to agree with Tuan's estimate that "if we were not here, the Communists would be."
>
> "We are the watchdog at the northern gate," General Tuan said.[87]

And that's the motif, finally: we are the watchdog at the northern gate. And you must remember that the Americans had really very heavily established a military presence in Thailand by this time, 1966; that they were in complete control and had thousands of military and paramilitary people there at Udorn Air Base.

An interesting pilots' rebellion in Laos was reported in October 1966. Brigadier General Thao Ma, a Laotian Air Force commander, bombed out General Ouane Rattikone and the Royal Laotian Staff:

> His supporters said that part of the reason for the disciplinary measures was that General Ma, among other orders that he disobeyed, had refused to provide air force transports for the flourishing opium trade.[88]

And so rebellion by pilots and a little war was reported in '66. (Then an odd notice in *The Times* by Edwin Dale, January 7, 1967:

> In the case of opium, a new stockpile objective was established exclusively to meet the needs of atomic war. The need was put at 143,000 pounds.[89]

Just for whatever that's worth, the U.S. government was stockpiling opium.)

In 1967 there was a large opium war, and it's really one of the most interesting portions of the story. The power of the KMT in northern Thailand had developed to the extent where any opium caravan passing through its territory was required to pay a duty to the KMT for "protection." In '67 a half-Chinese half-Shan tribesman named Chan Shee-fu, as reported in *Time* and *Newsweek* and other magazines, got together a 500-man army of his own to protect his mule train carrying several hundred thousand dollars' worth of opium through KMT territory into Laos. The KMT had radio sentries posted all along the route, and by the time Chan's convoy crossed the Mekong into Laos they found themselves in pitched battle with a crack KMT expeditionary force of 1,000 men. At which point the local Laotian military chief freaked out and sought the aid of his boss, Royal Laotian Air Chief General Ouane Rattikone. Ouane was outraged, understandably so because an opium cooker he allegedly owned had been burnt to the ground in the course of the fighting. So he sent in Royal Laotian bombers and troops against both sides, forcing them to retreat back across the Mekong with heavy losses. The spoils of course fell to Ouane and his men, and that included nearly all of Chan's opium.[90]

General Ouane's involvement in the opium trade was brought to public consciousness by *Time* magazine in its account of the battle:

Watching both antagonists from a hill were two companies of Royal Laotian infantry, ordered there by Laotian Commander in Chief Ouane Rattikone, who depends heavily on his cut in the opium trade to buy the loyalty of his soldiers.[91]

And the article also had this to say about the fertile triangle region:

The annual harvest produces 1,000 tons of raw opium—90% of the world's supply.[92]

So that much was in public record by 1967. The next major scandal was in '67–68. Senator Gruening, investigating corruption of Southeast Asian allies, released two different reports in 1968, one of which dealt with opium smuggling in Saigon. The Chief of Customs in Saigon—I believe he was hand-picked by Marshal Ky—was busted with his niece, who brought opium in from Vientiane on Royal Air Laos planes.[93]

Simultaneous with Gruening's corruption studies and headline-making, U.S. Customs Advisory Team reports were made from Saigon in 1967–68 by special Treasury Department agents investigating corruption. The original copies of these reports are not available to us today because Rossides said that they were executive bullshit, executive privilege. I saw, however, a newsman's summary of a report made by George Roberts, Chief, U.S. Customs Advisory Team, November 29, 1967, and that summary made specific mention of smuggling not just of gold but of opium as well by the uppermost members of the Saigon government, including the chief of customs.* A series of stories on Saigon smuggling were then written on the UPI and AP wires, passed on to public consciousness and then forgotten, immediately.

The next scandal uncovered by the Gruening Subcommittee on Foreign Aid Expenditures began when it received a letter from a man who had been involved in CIA Operation Haylift**

---

*For further details on Roberts' reports on high-level South Vietnamese opium smuggling see *The Politics of Heroin in Southeast Asia*, pp. 170–72.
**Also involved in Operation Haylift was William Colby, famous for the "strategic hamlet" policy and mass assassination program Operation Phoenix. Mr. Colby was appointed by Richard Nixon and approved by Congress to succeed Mr. Schlesinger (who succeeded Mr. Helms) as Director of the CIA.

in the early sixties. The main activity of Operation Haylift was airdropping guerrilla fighters into North Vietnam for sabotage. But it wasn't a very successful operation and was discontinued after about '64 because the supposed guerrillas would all show up drunk, or scared of going, or not interested. And besides which Marshal Ky, who was in charge of the air crews, was transporting opium, according to the letter.

A copy of the letter was given me by Leslie Whitten in Jack Anderson's office. Its author identifies himself as having been an inspector and adviser to maintenance personnel for Aviation Investors (headquarters 505 Landmark Building, Washington), which was running an airline in Vietnam called Vietnam Air Transport. The name of the airline has never been made public, and what would be necessary would be to track down who made up the corporation. I have the incorporation papers data around—they're now actually in the hands of Peter Dale Scott, the specialist in CIA airlines.

Anyway, according to the author of the letter, the company was fictitious, was set up by the CIA, and the airline itself was a blind for Operation Haylift. He certifies that the CIA engaged Ky to command the air crews and that Ky used this opportunity to fly opium from Laos to Saigon (and adds that the CIA removed Ky and replaced him with Chinese Air Force pilots from Taiwan—!).

There's a great deal of detail given about Ky in relation to this in the *Washington Post* by Warren Oonam, April 19, 1968, and in *The New York Times* (A.P.), really exquisitely detailed, same date. Leslie Whitten also did a good solid job on this story for the Hearst papers, April 18, 1968. Ky denied he smuggled opium.

A very interesting bust took place in 1968. A small item which sort of ties East-West opium traffic together and also begins getting into something slightly different:

> Five-year terms were asked today for 15 of the 17 Sicilians and Italian-Americans on trial here on charges of running narcotics and currency rackets in Sicily and the United States.
>
> Seven of the accused are at large and believed in the United States. Among them is Joseph Bonanno, known as Joe Bananas.
>
> The others are in jail in Italy. Among them is Giuseppe Genco Russo, 73 and almost blind, a Sicilian long reputed to be a leader of the Mafia. . . .

The prosecutor said a five-year investigation before and after the arrests produced conclusive evidence that the defendants were among the most active figures in international crime.

According to the prosecution, narcotics were smuggled in from the Orient, refined in Italy and France, and then transshipped to the United States.[94]

So any further research linking Indochinese opium production and transport with the American situation would need reference to Italy and to this particular case, which probably would open up a great deal of information.

That about winds it up except for recalling to your memories that a year ago Senator Tunney, on the basis of advice by Professor McAlister at Yale, made a public statement on March 24, 1970, before the Chamber of Commerce in Los Angeles that the United States was getting involved in a secret war in Laos (and at that time, the war in Laos was secret) which was basically an opium war, the motive of which was Vang Pao trying to regain control of the hill tribe regions and the opium production of northern Laos.

There was also, August 30, 1970, in *The Times*, a one-paragraph account on the financial page which made me aware of the immensity of the problem:

Southeast Asia accounts for one thousand tons, 83 per cent of the world's illegal production of opium, an Iranian government official told the United Nations Seminar on Narcotics Control. Turkey is the second major producing area, he said.[95]

It was that little item, plus an article in *Ramparts* by Peter Dale Scott saying that Air America transported opium,[96] that first got me interested in research, plus my conversations with David Obst and Alfred McCoy.

So last we have Carl Strock, January 30, 1971, in the *Far Eastern Economic Review*. But first I'll offer an anecdotal addendum: I had a conversation with Helms about the whole subject. He denied that the KMT was at all active any more, and said he didn't know anything about the opium trade and all that, so I tried to specify, and asked, "Can I make you a bet? That your CIA-controlled Long Cheng is a major opium market in Laos." He said, "Impossible, you can't win," so we made a bet. The terms of the bet I won't talk about, but afterwards, communicating with my fellow scholars, they pointed out to me Strock's article:

> Long Cheng—headquarters of Vang Pao, the second military region and headquarters of the CIA's paramilitary operations—is still off-limits. Over the years eight journalists, including myself, have slipped into Long Cheng and have seen American crews loading T-28 bombers while armed CIA agents chatted with uniformed Thai soldiers and piles of raw opium stood for sale in the market (a kilo for $52).[97]

So that's the end of my exposition. Thank you for your interest. I'll leave copies of all my material here in the library. I also have a lot of other information, oral, that I got from AID, IVS, and CIA people here, from Helms on down—they're all very talkative, apparently, and they don't know what they're doing, any of them. None of them. Like it's a little tiny private club of people that are just totally unaware of the extent of their own activities. And probably it's a mistake to attack Helms himself because he's probably not particularly responsible.

Q: Could it be that drugs are just so powerful a force in the world that the activities of any major power or of anybody, if they're big enough and cover enough territory, will involve drugs sooner or later?

AG: Yeah. Well, in Indochina I think that's probably true for foreign "imperialist exploiters" like France and the U.S.A. The "Red" Chinese, NLF, North Vietnam, and Pathet Lao all seem to have clean hands. I have to make a three o'clock plane so I better cut.

NOTES

1. ADDICTION POLITICS 1922–1970

1. Alfred Lindesmith, *The Addict and the Law* (Bloomington, Indiana: Indiana University Press, 1965). Another excellent study has recently been published: Rufus King's *America's Drug Hang-up: 50 Years of Folly* (New York: W. W. Norton & Company, 1972).

2. "Extension of Remarks of Hon. Lester D. Volk of New York in the House of Representatives, Friday, January 13, 1922," *Congressional Record*, Vol. 62, Part 13, p. 13341.

3. *Ibid.*

4. *Ibid.*

5. Volk is referring to Dr. George E. Pettey, whom he describes in the *Congressional Record*, Vol. 62, Part 13, Appendix and Index, pp. 13343–4: "The late George E. Pettey, of Tennessee, was the American pioneer in this theory of addiction treatment, and his book, *Narcotic Drug Disease and Allied Ailments*, stands today as a milestone on the road to progress in American medicine. Pettey challenged the assertion that any routine treatment would free all narcotic addicts of physical reaction, and supported his thesis with a wealth of clinical observations extending over a quarter of a century. As a reward for this pioneering he remains to-day less known to the great body of American physicians than some who have forced the public and the profession to listen to the more noisy and less scientific reiterations of medical and lay owls possessed of a throaty voice and a fine intonation, who have persistently sat upon a dead limb of the tree of knowledge and impressed the public by advertisement and propaganda."

6. Volk, *op. cit.*, pp. 13343–4.

7. *Ibid.*, p. 13344.

8. *Ibid.*, p. 13345.

9. *Ibid.*

10. *Ibid.*

11. *Ibid.*, p. 13344.

12. *U.S. v. Anthony*, 15 F. Supp. 533 (1936).

13. "Report on Drug Addiction—II," *Bulletin of the New York Academy of Medicine*, July 1963, Vol. 39, p. 466. The earlier report by the Academy's Committee on Public Health, which was of the same purport, appeared in August 1955, Vol. 31, No. 8, pp. 592–607.

14. Dr. Vincent P. Dole in conversation with Allen Ginsberg, February 1971.

15. For Burroughs' discussion of Dr. Dent's apomorphine cure, see pp. xxxvii–xlviii of *Naked Lunch* (New York: Grove Press, 1959).

16. "Report on Drug Addiction—II," p. 466.

17. *Ibid.*, pp. 432–433.

18. *Ibid.*, p. 433.

19. *Ibid.*

20 The report was entitled *Drug Addiction: Crime or Disease? Interim and Final Reports of*

a Joint Committee of the American Bar Association and the American Medical Association on Narcotic Drugs (Bloomington, Indiana: Indiana University Press, 1961), with an introduction by Alfred R. Lindesmith. For a description of the pressure and harassment applied to Indiana University and its Press by the Federal Bureau of Narcotics prior to publication see pp. 246–251 of Lindesmith's The Addict and the Law. (The chapter is entitled "Obstacles to Reform.")

21. Advisory Council of Judges, National Council on Crime and Delinquency, Narcotics Law Violations (1964).

22. Hollis S. Ingraham, Regulations Regarding Administration of Narcotics Drugs to Addicts, New York State Department of Health mailing October 21, 1970, p. 4.

23. "The Narcotics Control Act: A Two-Year-Old Failure," Civil Liberties in New York, September 1970, Vol. XVII, No. 7, p. 4. Also, Herman Joseph and Vincent P. Dole, M.D., declared in "Methadone Patients on Probation and Parole," on the fourth page of a pamphlet reprinted from an article in Federal Probation, June 1970:

> Analysis of the records of 912 patients admitted to the program [the methadone maintenance program of the Research Council of New York City] over a 4½-year period showed a 90-percent drop in criminal convictions.

24. The Parliamentary Debates (Hansard): House of Lords Official Report, Fifth Series —Volume CCC, Fourth Volume of Session 1968–9 (London: Her Majesty's Stationery Office), cols. 12799, 1283, and 1284.

2. CRIME IN THE STREETS CAUSED BY ADDICTION POLITICS

25. Peter Kihss, "100,000 Addicts Reported in City," The New York Times, December 14, 1967, p. 52.

26. Ibid.

27. At the end of 1972, most estimates put the number of junkies in New York City at around 300,000.

28. Kihss, op. cit.

29. Donald Flynn, "Handle Addicts Apart, Crime Parley Told," New York Daily News, February 8, 1970.

30. Emanuel Perlmutter, "Addicts Program Held in Jeopardy," The New York Times, May 6, 1968, p. 21.

31. Francis X. Clines, "Tombs Officials Agree with Inmates," The New York Times, August 20, 1970, p. 29.

32. David Burnham, "Noncrime Jobs Dominate Police Time," The New York Times, August 3, 1970, p. 25.

33. Felix Belair, Jr., "Aid to Eradicate Opium Suggested," The New York Times, August 2, 1970, p. 56.

34. "Excerpts from Burger's Talk," The New York Times, August 11, 1970, p. 24.

3. NARCOTICS AGENTS PEDDLING DRUGS

35. "32 U.S. Narcotics Agents Resign in Corruption Investigation Here," The New York Times, December 14, 1968, p. 1.

36. Joseph Lelyveld, "Murder of a Key Drug Informer Under Investigation Here," *The New York Times*, February 26, 1970, p. 25.

37. Ramsey Clark in conversation with Allen Ginsberg, May 1970.

38. *The New York Times*, April 21, 1965, p. 1.

39. C. Gerald Fraser, *The New York Times*, December 13, 1967, p. 1.

40. Sidney E. Zion, "Hogan to Screen Narcotics Cases of 3 Detectives—He Orders a 'Fresh Look' at Pending Trials Involving Men Under Indictment," *The New York Times*, December 14, 1967, p. 1.

41. *The New York Times*, December 14, 1967, p. 1.

42. "Tough Foe of Narcotics: Ira Bluth, A Cool Crusader," *The New York Times*, December 14, 1967, p. 52.

43. David Burnham, "Police Dividing Narcotics Bureau into 5 Subunits," *The New York Times*, February 9, 1968, p. 95.

44. Richard E. Mooney, *The New York Times*, p. 33.

45. David Burnham, *The New York Times*, p. 1.

46. David Burnham, "4 More Police Officers Shifted in Inquiry of Narcotics Funds," *The New York Times*, March 7, 1968, p. 27.

47. "12 More Detectives in Narcotics Study Sent to New Posts," *The New York Times*, March 9, 1968, p. 26.

48. David Burnham, "Graft Paid to Police Here Said to Run into Millions," *The New York Times*, April 25, 1970, p. 1.

49. David Burnham, "Police Rewriting Manual of Rules and Procedures," *The New York Times*, August 2, 1970, p. 36.

50. *Ibid.*

51. Arnold H. Lubasch, "Corruption Jury Indicts Gambler," *The New York Times*, November 24, 1970, p. 1.

52. Howard Becker, *The Outsiders* (London: Collier-Macmillan Ltd., 1963).

53. *Ibid.* pp. 135–146.

4. CIA INVOLVEMENT WITH OPIUM TRAFFIC AT ITS SOURCE

54. Lucien Bodard, *The Quicksand War: Prelude to Vietnam* (Boston: Atlantic Monthly Press, Little, Brown and Company, 1967), p. 113.

55. *Ibid.*, p. 114.

56. *Ibid.*, p. 123.

57. "Chiang Army Puts Its Mark on Burma," *The New York Times*, May 31, 1954.

58. "Burmese Seize Plants," *The New York Times*, May 20, 1959, p. 3.

59. Letter from Peter Dale Scott to Allen Ginsberg, February 1971. For more information on

Sea Supply see p. 42 of Scott's "Heroin Traffic: Some Amazing Coincidences," in *Earth*, March 1972.

60. *Ibid.*

61. "A Mission in Peiping," *The New York Times*, October 31, 1956, p. 32.

62. Walter Briggs, "Red China's Intrusion in Burma is a Puzzle," *New York Herald Tribune*, August 3, 1956, p. 4.

63. "Laos: The Boys at the Snow Leopard," *Time*, February 29, 1960, p. 35.

64. Gary K. Busch in letter to Allen Ginsberg, December 17, 1970.

65. "Opium War," *Private Eye*, issue 191, p. 19.

66. Committee on Government Operations, United States Senate, *Organized Crime and Illicit Traffic in Narcotics* (Washington: U.S. Government Printing Office, 1965), p. 59.

67. *Ibid.*, p. 66.

68. *Ibid.*

69. "Lost Legion," *Time*, February 10, 1961, p. 22.

70. William J. Jorden, "Burmese Charge Taiwan Drops U.S. Arms to Chinese Guerrillas," *The New York Times*, February 18, 1961, p. 1.

71. "Burmese Assails China," *New York Times*, August 29, 1956, p. 27.

72. *Ibid.*

73. "Anti-Red Guerrillas Arriving in Taiwan," *The New York Times*, March 19, 1961, p. 88.

74. Joel M. Halprin, "Laos Profiles," *Laos Project Paper No. 18* (Waltham, Massachusetts: Brandeis University, June 1, 1961), p. 141.

75. For an account of the relationship between Phoumi and Ouane see pp. 258–262 of Alfred W. McCoy's monumental *The Politics of Heroin in Southeast Asia* (with Cathleen B. Read and Leonard P. Adams II) (New York: Harper & Row, 1972).

76. "Red China Rejects Opium Accusation," *The New York Times*, April 10, 1963, p. 3.

77. R. H. Shackford, "Opium and Red Propaganda," *The New York World-Telegram*, September 26, 1964.

78. Walter Sullivan, "Illegal Traffic in Opium Found a Rising Peril by U.N. Experts," *The New York Times*, September 17, 1964, p. 45.

79. See Leonard P. Adams II's Appendix to McCoy's *The Politics of Heroin in Southeast Asia* (pp. 380–383) for more details.

80. Schanche, *op. cit.*, p. 40.

81. Seth S. King, "Thai Village Winks at Opium Traffic," *The New York Times*, August 1, 1965, p. 8.

82. Seymour Topping, "New Chiang Raids in China Reported," *The New York Times*, May 18, 1965, p. 1.

83. Harrison Salisbury, "Peking Interest in Border Area Stirs Deep Concern in Rangoon," *The New York Times,* June 22, 1966, p. 6.

84. *Ibid.*

85. Pierre J. Huss, "Peking's Most Evil Weapon," January 23, 1966, Hearst Headline Service.

86. Peter Braestrup, "'Exiles' from China Wait in Thailand," *The New York Times,* September 8, 1968, p. 5.

87. *Ibid.*

88. "Rebellion by Pilots in Laos Reported," *The New York Times,* October 21, 1966, p. 1.

89. Edwin L. Dale, Jr., "Most Stockpiles Meet Goals for Nuclear War," *The New York Times,* January 7, 1967, p. 6.

90. According to Alfred McCoy, Chan's opium had been ordered by Ouane Rattikone himself. For more of the battle and the entire situation see *The Politics of Heroin in Southeast Asia,* pp. 315–328.

91. "Laos: Flower Power Struggle," *Time,* September 8, 1967, p. 22.

92. *Ibid.*

93. "Smuggling Ring Tie to Saigon Chiefs Reported," *Los Angeles Times,* February 29, 1968.

94. "Italy Seeks Prison for 17 in Mafia Case," *The New York Times,* June 12, 1968, p. 95.

95. "Asia Leads Opium Output," *The New York Times,* August 30, 1970.

96. Peter Dale Scott, "Air America: Flying the U.S. into Laos," *Ramparts,* February 1970, p. 39.

97. Carl Strock, "No News from Laos," *Far Eastern Economic Review,* January 30, 1970, p. 18.

(Note: See Appendix for additional notes on sources and cases.)

III

Recent Twentieth-Century Poetry

To find the Western path
Right thro' the Gates of Wrath
I urge my way
—William Blake

"Advice to Youth," *a meeting with a Kent State writing class, took place in a student union lounge with a frequently changing group of students as class bells rang. As Allen and fellow poet Robert Duncan sat with the students on the lounge's synthetic carpeting, the discussion of writing gradually evolved into one of self-discovery. The lecture begins with each poet answering a question about why he started to write poetry.*

"Early Poetic Community," *delivered to a Kent State honors class in a World War II quonset hut while bulldozers razed the land outside, maintained a much lighter mood highlighted by Robert's and Allen's magically different versions of one of their earliest meetings.*

In "Kerouac," *Allen's remarks to a fiction class about some of Jack Kerouac's early works, truncated by an early call to dinner, and complemented at the end of the book (p. 142) by an evaluation of Kerouac's lifework and relationship to the American nation.*

"The Death of Ezra Pound," *an excerpt from a live radio talk show, was recorded a year and a half after the other chapters in this section, and is included as a follow-up to the immediately preceding "Poetic Breath, and Pound's Usura," which begins with a discussion of the relationship between verse form and breath and Charles Olson's "Projective Verse" theories.*

Advice to Youth
(with Robert Duncan)

1

WRITING CLASS—LOUNGE TALK: KENT STATE
April 5, 1971

AG: I began writing poetry 'cause I was a dope and my father wrote poetry and my brother wrote poetry and I started writing rhymes, like them, until I went to Columbia and fell in love with Jack Kerouac, and then got into a sort of emotional rapport, a much deeper sense of confession, wanting to confess my feelings to him. But he didn't want to hear them so I had to find another way of expressing them, a way which would entrance him, and make him see into my soul.

That engagement with Kerouac began with a long conversation in which I described leaving a room that I'd lived in for half a year (where I'd originally fallen in love with him and some other friends, simultaneously), and when I left the room to move to a hotel, turning around as I left the seventh floor and went down the steps, and looking back at my door and looking back at the hall and saying, "Good-bye door, good-bye hall, good-bye step number one, good-bye step number two, good-bye step number three," down seven flights. And so I told him that story, and he said, "Oh, that's what I do!" So I suddenly realized that my own soul and his were akin, and that if I actually confessed the secret tendernesses of my soul he would understand nakedly who I was. And it was like I was already inside his body, we were identical in our most intimate feelings, so I came into an area of intimate feelings that I wanted to begin articulating outwardly to communicate with him, and join and be one with him. And that sincere talk replaced the earlier imitative rhyming that I was doing for my family.

Q: Is there a point where the direct sharing of your intimate feelings, in writing, can tend to hide or obscure the intimate feelings, or is it all straightforward, direct?

AG: Over the years, a more straightforward, direct attempt to share them.

Q: And the writing never obscures or is a defense against them in some way?

AG: No, or at least nothing that survives. My attention might be distracted one day or another and I might, say, try to write an imitation of Auden or sumpin' for some goofy reason, but——

Q: But the stuff that survives is this straight——

AG: By survive I mean anything I wind up typing up a year after I've scribbled it. And, you know, reading aloud and publishing is generally an attempt at sharing intimate feeling or perception directly. And this process deepened later on when as a result of reading poetry, other people's poetry, like Blake's, another dimension of awareness dawned on my senses. Besides the tender intimacies of friendship and yearnings, another psychedelic sense or modality of consciousness opened up within me, catalyzed by some short texts by Blake.[1] Then I began seeing poetry as not merely a sharing of human secrets, but a sharing of even the non-human, the cosmic, universal, archetypal knowledge of something beyond my own life, you know, beyond my own embarrassments, beyond my own loves.

RD: As Allen suggested, sharing also includes the discovery that you are the thing that you've been in love with or you've been excited by or that you adore. What comes to my mind now is something I was roundly reproved for—this would be college, my freshman year. I went to a poetry group and I was in love with stars and I realized I was a star. The poem was not only compassion for stars but stars had compassion for you, and Miss Miles said it was too big a subject. For me it was something like Allen's description, because being in love with Jack Kerouac he discovered he was Jack Kerouac: that's something love knows. Thank God for our universe Jack Kerouac said no and consequently Allen ... Actually, we all turned into Jack Kerouac, 'cause Allen wooed the entire scene, and had to then make all of us accept him, and nakedly. The original, literal nakedness had to be there, but it was nakedness like you all mean in love, essentially.

Maybe Allen's starting verse and rhyming was not just 'cause his father wrote in very respectable magazines. So did Paul Blackburn's mother—when readers opened *Harper's* or the *Atlantic Monthly* they read Louis Ginsberg, and they read Frances Frost, who was Blackburn's mother. And to have the kind of poets that Blackburn and Allen are come out of that world is incredible.

But I didn't. My father was an architect, not a poet. I wrote poems when I was little but ceased when I realized I was writing two kinds of poems: I discovered myself writing poems that were for Mother's Day that Mother would like, but they were terribly untrue; and I discovered I was also beginning to write about how "I am a tender pearl hidden in the middle/ Of a terrible, hideous, awful oyster/ And I look hideous to all the world around me." Then I quit, 'cause that was so nauseating. But I was getting vast appreciation: that's what my parents wanted to read, and now at last my poetry was expressing what they thought poetry ought to express. And that was sickening.

I discovered writing poetry again in high school when I'd fallen in love with a teacher. She would receive my adolescent agonies which were ugly to me, painful and *shameful* because all society around me considered them very shameful. They didn't even have the form of "Was I in love with Jack Kerouac?" They were just "Who am I, what am I," yearning, but not even yearning that could have that lovely feeling you get from that word alone—it was muddied at all the corners. I don't know how that English teacher ever believed I was a poet. I saw her ten years later and she said "You don't realize you were the only poet I ever had in a class in twenty-six years," so she knew what she meant. But her confidence, I thought, was everywhere; as a matter of fact, I thought she must be producing poets every minute. I didn't know that everybody wasn't in love with her, and it just takes being in love.

What really got me there, though, was the practice of imitating poems in class. When we read Chaucer, we read the Prologue and then we wrote prologues ourselves to an imaginary pilgrim- age poem. And then when we came to Robert Browning we wrote dramatic monologues, and there I discovered another thing that I had always loved, and that was "being" throughout the period of mankind. And Robert Browning suddenly showed you that you could go into words and be all sorts of people. And that was so exciting that then I knew I wasn't going to be an architect; I was going to be a poet.

In the late thirties it was a zero score to decide, to know you were going to be a poet. You could look around—you were never going to earn a living. And I didn't graduate from anything except high school; as a matter of fact, if anybody could have let me know you didn't have to graduate from high school . . . I was just still obeying everything, it took me till my sophomore year to figure out you didn't have to go to college.

AG: You didn't graduate from Berkeley?

RD: Oh, no, I never graduated at all. I didn't even have my degree. That's why I'm so informed!

Q: One thing that bothers me about contemporary poetry, if I can go back to Eliot, is like he said poetry is impersonal. He didn't mean that it's cold or didactic, but the primary concern of the poet is the creation of a thing of beauty or an artistic work. And very often in contemporary verse I get the feeling that some poets have subordinated that goal to almost preaching or making a statement, a matter-of-fact statement. I was just wondering, when you work, do you work with the idea that you're going to create a piece of art or that you're going to communicate?

AG: Just as I began by trying to voice my kinship and my secret perceptions to a dear friend, just as I began trying to get out the raw material of my heart, or to get out my actual feelings, heart-throbs, I'm not concerned with creating a work of art, because that's only a three-letter word, anyway, plus the four-letter word *work*. And I don't want to predefine it—I mean how would you go about creating a work of art, would you go by a set of rules or what?

Q: I'm not saying it's a rigid form. . . .

AG: Well, so, even to entertain the conception in advance of creating a work of art would block your mind from getting at the actual heart-throb or direct expression of the material you started out trying to articulate or voice. So what I do is try to forget entirely about the whole world of art, and just get directly to the most economical—that is, the fastest, not most economical—the fastest and most direct expression of what it is I got in heart-mind. Trusting that if my heart-mind is shapely, the objects or words, the word sequences, the sentences, the lines, the song, will also be shapely. And if I can directly deal out my feelings what will be dealt out could be put in a museum. "Art," see? In fact that's really what art is, I think—the stuff that later seems to be solid enough to put it in the museum of your mind.

RD: One of the difficulties with Eliot is that he's writing from a vast historical ignorance when he writes about perfection in a work of art. Although he lived in the thirties and forties, when great works were being written on art, he did not recognize that only a small segment of mankind for a very limited period of history had this idea of a "work of art," and of perfection. The Greeks had the idea of making something, and that's what the word *poetry* comes from—making something, like God makes Creation.

But poetry is not only this idea of making. If we go to the Jewish world, to the Semitic world, the one out of which the main line of Christianity comes, and the whole line of the Old Testament with its prophets (to which Allen belongs—but he also relates to Christopher Smart, which shows the continuity of this idea of a Christian tradition, and he relates to great Muslim poems, visionary recitals, as they're called), there it is absolutely forbidden to "make" a poem. They read the commandment in the Old Testament, "Thou shalt not make a graven image," to mean that one should not "create," should not "make" a work of art. The poem is, in this sense, an image. But one should pour forth what is felt to come from God and that one thing, the arrival of the voice, is the doctrine of inspiration. Inspiration means that something comes from great spirit into a man. I think you'll see that it would be something more than profound *hybris* to re-shape and perfect out of *our* human condition an inspiration which comes from great, divine spirit? No, you've got to speak out with it.

Now where does the craft come in, and the ability with words? The poet has to meet it, he can't just be shaken by this divine inspiration that comes, so he prepares at every corner: he's gotta have a massive access to rhyme, to music, to everything, so when he's filled with it, it comes into form.

When we go back to your idea of perfection, we find two things hidden within: the voice is perfect and it has arrived—the inspiration is perfect, the moment is perfect, and it's a reciprocity. One of the things we learn in our art, the true art of poetry, is it is like a ripening in you. You have to know when you're ready, you have to know when it is the time. In the beginning you ball everything up; you're so yearning to be filled with this voice you go bellowing with it at times, so it's lovely when it arrives. It *is* perfect, and it *is* beautiful, the thing Eliot's talking about. Eliot's talking about something very real in poetry. But it's not of the nature you're talking about. You'd never do it by trying to re-shape something you did to make it look like something you know nothing of. But those moments when the readiness, the inspiration, the whole poet nature and its ability combine—that happened to me first with "The Venice Poem." I started writing when I was eighteen; I was twenty-eight or twenty-nine when I wrote "The Venice Poem."[2] Think how long you have to go.

AG: I was twenty-eight when I wrote "Howl."

RD: I was twenty-eight when I wrote "Medieval Scenes" and that's the first time I knew what I had to do in a poem. You feel obedience when you've arrived there. Eliot is deficient on a formal level; that's why he talks about form. Pound actually rewrote "The Wasteland" and that's why it has the form it has. Eliot does not understand total form. "The Wasteland" has marvelous things in it, but one thing it does *not* have is a feeling of form. He flunks on the gestalt level. Whereas *The Cantos* are ever-present form. Eliot has to imitate form. He imitates Beethoven, propositions that come out of Beethoven. Beethoven wasn't imitating a form; he was *in* form. This is Eliot's weakness.

AG: Eliot's constantly adapting somebody else's forms.

RD: He goes to Poe and sounds like Poe, but when Poe was writing even he had form. Although Poe had a very grotesque thing: he kept thinking that his convention was his form. But we all feel the form struggling underneath.

Q: I think you're getting around to just what I wanted to say about enchantment. Let me tell you what happens here every day: you walk into a class, the teacher puts on one of your poems, or one of Eliot's poems or one of Keats's and asks, "What's the metaphysical implication of this word?," "What's the symbolic implication of this word?," and if you raise your hand and say, "This is very mysterious, this has mystery to it, isn't that good too?," they say, "No, no, you have to explain, give the justifications for this word, it's very rational." And in Keats's letters he said the problem with Coleridge was that he'll say something mysterious and then he'll spend the next twenty lines explaining all the mystery out of the thing. And I feel that quality of mystery is really very good in a poem.

RD: Then you should have stayed out of a poetry workshop. If you went to a magicians' workshop, you'd expect to learn how to take the rabbit out of the hat, not to be in the enchantment in which the rabbit appears from—where?—Well, man, what do you think enchantment is? Inspiration. You can't learn that, nobody can teach it to you, you either feel it or you don't.

AG: I think you can teach inspiration.

RD: Teach inspiration?

AG: Taking it literally, inspiration being a matter of breath, you can teach breathing.

RD: Oh, breathing, right. And you can teach vowels.

AG: And if you can teach breathing then you can teach a certain body looseness and mind-freshening——

Q: That's possible for a whole bunch of people?

AG: Yeah. First of all, back straight, spine straight, the general thing is as if you were being hung from the center of your skull, as puppets, so therefore spine straight that way. Secondly, when your spine is straightened out, you can let your belly hang out. If it means loosening your belt that's all right, so that you can actually let your belly hang out a little bit. It's the same kind of breathing girls know of from natural childbirth, abdominal breathing. So you inflate—push out—your stomach wall, push out the muscular wall of your stomach all the way, and then fill it with air. And then go "Uuuuuuh," the same sigh that you give after you come, "Uuuuuh"—you all know that, don't you? So now if you vocalize with that "Huuumm," closing the labia, closing the lips after, but not closing the teeth, "Huuumm," you won't feel it unless you try it—and it's fun if you try it—"Huuumm, Huuumm, Huuumm, Huuumm," [students join] a little more to the skull, actually, Huuumm, that will give you the inspiration buzz, Huuumm, Huuumm.

RD: If you were learning music you would not expect to sit around talking about compositions you were making in the beginning; you'd have to learn different things like scales and modes and get the language, wouldn't you? Where do poets learn? Not in workshops like this; they learn from poets they've admired, trying to be like them.

Another thing is, the world around you is language, so you're drawing from it, and if you return to it, it fills you with poetry, too. But Ben Jonson says: you find a model, and you write like it, and you try to enter its spirit. Keats entered the spirit of Shakespeare; if you read his letters you will find that he carried Shakespeare with him all the time.

So one of the discoveries is to discover a kindred poet, and to learn to write like him. That's your master; you don't study in a classroom with him. It's entirely voluntary. Blake recognized in Milton his master and that he was his antitype. To be a true son means that you are the antitype of your father and then you know that you belong to a generative order. And your spirit awakens to it. But at first it awakens only along the lines of admiration or the feeling of a power, or the feeling of wanting to *be* like that, and you go into it spiritually, and that means to write like it, to learn to write like it.

AG: Just like Dylan, with Woody Guthrie.

RD: And so you think and write day and night like what you admire. Yes, almost any model. This is the role of models, and sometimes you will find they crumble beneath you; they don't suit your spirit, you were wrong. There are many people who take a model in poetry and when the model in poetry doesn't unfold something in themselves never, never look for another one at all. And what poets do, endlessly, actually, is come into a huge love match with masses of poets.

I grew up in a middle-class professional art-centered family, and there could be nothing deader for you to be in. Every territory that was going to be meaningful for me was lied about there, and I would be a suicidal soul if it weren't for the fact that in writing that my family read and professed to admire I found kindred spirits. I found that Shakespeare was closer to me than Mother or Father, and that he told the truth when they lied.

AG: I want to put a footnote in: transfer from Kerouac to Rimbaud.

RD: Yes, right.

AG: I kept thinking I was in love with Kerouac and I also was in love with somebody else, another cat who looked exactly like Rimbaud, who actually looks like about half the people in this room, at this point. So I immediately transferred the same erotic *schwärmerei*, the same erotic pleasure, to Rimbaud, and then I fell in love with Rimbaud's writing because it was the manifestation of his seed, so to speak—I felt I could get inside his body through his writing. 'Cause I saw a photo of Rimbaud——

Q: The only time you'd write, then, is if your real-life love were blocked in some way, or failed in some way?

AG: No, 'cause there were a few people I began making it with, and I wrote even more. It was the *response* from Kerouac that made me awaken and want to write more. It was the recognition.

Q: Well, why the words then? Why write, why not just make it? I can't understand the necessity to write.

AG: The articulation of the inner sentiments was what created the recognition between us which led to—led to the banquet, finally.

Q: It's seduction poetry, then, in a sense.

AG: No, no.

RD: No, no. This word *share* was very important there. As our whole human spirit seeks to embody itself everywhere, in sexual intercourse we try to embody ourselves in the other body. And we strive to embody ourselves in language if it's allied to us at all.

AG: Yes, sexuality is just one aspect of that attempt to——

RD: Your true love is everywhere. I can't imagine the failure of certain models. Ezra Pound has never failed me as a model; I mean he still is my master. And a master is someone that in every sense is your superior. Superior in the way it is in yoga: you are obedient to a master.

Q: Isn't there a point of satisfaction, satiation?

RD: No, Goethe is right, Goethe is right about the nature of the soul.

Q: It's insatiable?

RD: Do you have a doctrine in which the soul is satisfied? That you can call upon in human——

Q: I don't have any doctrines.

RD: Well, do you have none at all, or are you aware of a doctrine that preaches the satisfaction of the soul?

Q: It would seem to me if the soul can't be satisfied that's a severe limitation.

RD: But don't *seem*—talk about what you feel, about what you know about the human spirit. Don't talk about what it seems to you—we're not a philosophy class! Talk about what you know. I guess both Allen and I have got to get across to you then the message that poetry has to do with the world of spirit.

AG: One thing I would say: the bliss of spiritual recognition is a satisfaction, but it's an endless activity also. Sexuality is one approach to that bliss. In other words it wasn't that literature was substituting for sexuality, that poetry was substituting for sexuality, or for frustrated sexuality, 'cause as time goes on, now that Kerouac's dead, I realize that the sexuality was just another little poem—not just another little poem, but that the poem itself was the subject.

Q: In other words frustration doesn't figure into the process you're talking about.

AG: No, no. Recognition: nonfrustration figures with it. It's realization—that's what figures in everything, not frustration of union——

Q: Do you put that much trust in words? Like don't you ever look at anything you've written and say, "That's not it."

AG: I look at something I wrote and say, "Ah, my attention was wandering," or, "I was thinking about writing like T. S. Eliot "

RD: Of course, you know that's different from mistrusting words, because words are themselves filled with meaning. We don't put meanings into words. Almost any word that we can mention has some six thousand years of human meanings poured into it; we have only to wake up to the meanings that are there. Yeah, yeah *(calling on a student with hand raised)*. I've got my damned crossed eyes as they say here. Yes, you.

Q: *(to RD)* You mentioned the fact that you grew up in a middle-class society——

RD: Architect's household, yeah——

Q: And given the fact that you're only one year younger than my own father, do you think that poetry came to you because you didn't have to struggle for survival?

RD: Oh, my family disinherited me, thank goodness, so I never got scared of the struggle for survival. And it took me about three years to realize, because I was so poorly informed, that I had a major skill—typing—and I never dreamed anybody earned their living at it. I didn't know how anybody earned their living at all. I had a feeling of security. I think. . . . But I've known poets . . . Corso, who is a great poetic spirit of our time, grew up in prison, so don't ask me whether or not I became a poet because I had that guarantee. How many years of his childhood were spent in prison?

AG: About six of his first twenty years.

RD: Yeah, right. Six of his first twenty years were in prison—so there a poet can happen. Poets happen in the damnedest places, sir. I find it more astounding than what happened in an architect's household. You know, poets happen anywhere, you can't prevent it. You can wear all the spiritual and mental condoms you want, but you'd think that if Louie Ginsberg was going to give birth to Allen Ginsberg and we tried to account for it all——

AG: Very unlikely.

Q: Even still—you mentioned the fact that Corso grew up in prison: at least he had the security of food and a blanket over his body, you know. I came from a community where survival sometimes was flour and water—if you could go down to the lake to get the water and build the fire to boil it because you had to boil it to drink it.

RD: I see what you mean. Only certain stages of society make it possible for art to arise, it's true. They will arise within that society in adversity, but what you're saying is that you've got to have not only the security, but certainly you've got to be able to have even just a little time in your youth to be reading books. To write a big novel like Tolstoy did, you damn well have to have the actual time that goes into it.

AG: Actually, the Australian aborigines, who live on the lowest possible level of subsistence, live in what they call Eternal Dream Time.

RD: Which is poetry time——

AG: —and make art objects, artifacts, ritual artifacts which connect them with Eternal Dream Time, and with the gods of Eternal Dream Time, and have the most complicated aural (auditory) memory epic literature of any social group. They're so complex and sophisticated they don't need writing.

RD: The Germanic and Celtic tribes were living a tribal food-gathering life and were not really great at killing their meat, so they really had to depend on wild plants for sustenance. They had their bards; they had to keep alive poetry, because poetry keeps the identity of the tribe alive—that's another thing it essentially does. It has the dreams for the tribe that they can hear and remember. Their main test was that the poet had to be submerged in ice-cold water in the middle of the winter and in the morning recite a poem that he'd made up. This is like yoga—naked and submerged in ice-cold water, he would deliver it rhymed and complete his epic.

AG: How long?

RD: For the whole night long: lying in a great stone bed of poetry which was ice water (well, what other kind of water?) with a nice crust of ice around. But this was almost at the survival margin, they would really inflict terrible pain.... We've got to have poetry, and for a tribe to survive they had to have a poet at least once in a while, and so they had this business of "That one must be the one." Often they had generations—they must have had generations—in which the one who was carrying poetry was no great poet. We've got impressions that are probably right that in back of the fathers, in back of Jacob and Isaac and Abraham are lots of Jacobs and Isaacs and Abrahams, and that the Jews—the Semitic and Bedouin tribes in the desert—went for a long time waiting for the full reoccurrence of this personality, and finally would say "Ah, he's here again!" I think in this country you can feel there's a great wanting to have a reoccurrence of Lincoln, for instance. We tend to make such people famous, but when you keep a tribal identity you wait for this person to reoccur. In the same way there was a great waiting for a poet to reoccur.

Poets also resisted writing so that they're the last group to learn writing, and only a dictator in Greece had the sacred texts of Homer written down. They *were* like the Australian aborigines; Plato reflects in his dialogues the damage he felt had been done to philosophy because it was written down. It was sentimental damage, because Plato is the first really great written book.

Q: How about that story—I'm not sure I get the point about the poet in the water. Weren't they stimulating the poetry then with a heck of a lot of pain?

RD: They're not stimulating the poetry; they're testing it. It's going through endurance. Sure, art is painful. Gee, there's a great moment when Schönberg speaks of the pain of the knowledge of art.

Q: This is directed at Mr. Ginsberg. Like in yoga, his whole body would become numb, and so essentially he wouldn't be conscious of his body after a while, and he could directly relate with his soul or his subconscious mind and therefore he could——

AG: Actually, I've never been in cold water all night, so I don't know the existential . . . but I would guess like any extreme physical situation like drowning (you know the visions of a drowning man), like the American Indian victim who was cut apart—remember that thing, did you [RD] read that thing?

RD: Oh, the thing Grossinger* has.

---

*Richard Grossinger, poet, author of *Solar Journal*, editor of *Io*, participating with Robert and Allen in Kent State Arts Festival Week.

AG: The Indian who was cut apart and reduced to a limbless tongue, finally, and given a song to sing at dawn after a night of torture. Actually I think the intent there is to call forth a consciousness that's totally nonindividualized, you know, that is really a complete cosmic consciousness, or a tribal consciousness, or just a mammal consciousness that has no name and no identity, that's looking on the planet listening for the first and last time. So there would be probably a glimpse of the brightness of the stars equal to the iciness and a glimpse of like a cold universe maybe that we were warm in for a few minutes—a glimpse of the relative nature of the universe that might be useful to the tribe when it went out hunting or gathering that afternoon. They might have had to go out and gather food in the cold.

Or like young kids now drop speed and spend a week awake to finally get to what they think they're going to get to. I mean that's a familiar thing.

RD: But it's the relation of suffering to poetry I'm thinking of. Sappho, for instance, where love-agony is essential to a great deal of love poetry. And it's the ordeal, not the deprivation. God, we don't feel that Sappho's got more passionate being than——

AG: *(to the students)* We haven't said, but I think both Robert and I are reacting to what you're proposing—that poetry is a substitute for love. We're saying love is a substitute for poetry—poetry at its highest, meaning the Creation.

RD: It can be written in deprivation. What the poet discovers is that what other people call deprivation is not emptiness but fullness, of agony. One thing that poetry's onto is that fullness of agony, fullness of death, fullness of sickness, fullness of love, all of it goes into depths of experience, and it does not try to select goodies or whatever, you know; it wants to be intensely experienced. The appalling thing about the state of our country is how much it doesn't want to know itself or feel itself.

[INTERMISSION PERIOD]

RD: Allen, could you open with a song?

AG: Yeah, I'll begin with singing. "The School Boy," by William Blake, which I set to music and which I never sang to Robert. Does anybody know Blake? I mean is Blake read here, his texts—is he taught here?

RD: Yes he is.

AG: Well some places he's not now. *(Playing harmonium, sings Blake's "The School Boy.")* Appropriate for Kent State: " . . . How shall we gather what griefs destroy?" "O father and mother . . ." I was partly thinking of the university situation, the school situation in America, when I was setting that to music, trying to find the right tune, the tones for those words, 'cause it's like Blake's rebuke to the elders of mechanical education, the elders of a satanic industrial education closing in on the spirits of the young of this generation and forcing a prison on all of us, a prison of war, but also a prison of war education and war mechanics.

RD: Long before you ever get drafted into the army, every child male and female is drafted into school. That school could not possibly be a school of the free spirit: free spirit has to be voluntary. Children go to playgrounds of their own volition, and we rightly would have minds that were alive if it weren't that our first experience of being drafted and coerced is the experience that our entire civilization lays on us and destroys in us, our spirit, just at the point when our spirit is supposed to be alive and in its own volition.

Years spent in the army are nothing compared to the utter destruction of children's souls from kindergarten until they're safely past the first and great period of their sexuality and its mystery. The joke of all this Blake has seen. He saw children who were locked away in factories, 'cause they locked 'em away in factories before they locked 'em away in education factories, and there was no volition there either, or with those who were imprisoned by their parents and put under that coercion. Yet the free spirit rose, over and over again. "The spirit is free!" Yes, Corso's an example.

Q: I'd like to know what ways there are to develop in your own direction.

AG: What ways to expand your soul and get out of the prison? A number of ways: practice of any art, poetry, or music, always, traditionally, was a way of getting out of the prison of conditioning of the society. Practice of any Vision Quest, as with American Indians, fasting, going into lonely places, seeking nature-spirit—physically removing yourself from the civilization and going up on a mountain, or into a desert, mountain climbing.

Dropping acid or mushrooms or peyote or psylocibin in the company of wise men and of mother nature. Doing yogas of different kinds, whether chanting or meditating or crosslegged sitting or lying in corpse position in the company of people who are practiced in that particular kind of practical body phys.-ed . . . working with intense attention at any kind of carpentering or physical craft task that requires complete absorption and care of the materials that you're working with . . . total absorption with tomatoes in gardening. . . .

Q: I can see how you can get it through those things, but I don't see how you can get it through drugs: drugs kinda make you into whatever's around.

AG: I had an argument with a man named Richard Helms, who's the head of the CIA, about a month ago as to the effects of LSD. He said LSD disintegrates your personality so it ain't good for you—he didn't say "ain't"—he said it's not good for you because it disintegrates your personality, how many times can people have that done to them without um? . . . He didn't finish his sentence, actually. So I said there's another terminology applicable, which is the terminology of a Dr. Jiri Rubichek, who did studies with LSD in the late fifties, in Czechoslovakia, in Prague, and wrote a book called *Artificial Psychosis.* He concluded that LSD inhibits conditioned reflexes—if you can follow the implications of that. *(Voice from audience: "He was right!")* In other words, LSD inhibits synaptic or neural automatic reactions (like, when I look at your face I see instead of a nameless being somebody I already know or think I know, and I plaster an idea over your face). It inhibits conditioned reflexes—in other words, it's an anti-brainwashing pill.

So to the extent that most of our sensations, feelings, thoughts, imaginations, visualizations, continuously are repeats, replays of old, conditioned, habitual sensory movies, to that extent the psychedelic drug experience can wipe that out and leave you staring there with an open brain for the first time perhaps in many years, for eight hours. So you get a perspective and can look back on the structure of the conditioning you've been through before. You can compare your present unconditioned open-eyed nameless consciousness with the over-named, over-used, over-categorized consciousness of the previous years. So it's like a useful bath in non-conditioning. Then you can go from there, having had that experience, that perspective, just as anyone who has had a religious experience of intermittent duration, like of an hour, half hour, goes back and attempts to reconstruct his life on the basis of a realization of its originally conditioned nature.

In other words, then you can practice an art anew, or practice yoga anew, or work at your carpentry anew. Perhaps build a table that's useful for the room you're in instead of a table that's like the one you saw in the front window of a department store.

Q: I guess you're equating learning with experience.

AG: I'm equating learning with return to direct perception—OK?

Q: Yeah.

RD: And actual skills. This is learning that really has to do with doing things.

Q: Facing whatever's going on.

AG: Yes, being present where you are. Perceiving with the senses given what's immediately in front of you as in, theoretically, Zen presence.

Q: Then you're saying that man should not be a social animal in that he should not be controlled by environment references.

AG: That man should be controlled by his deepest consciousness rather than his most shallow, sure. I'm also saying that all cultures provide such exercises in vision quest except maybe American culture at the moment. But most cultures have always provided a way out of the reference group—like the American Plains Indians told the young man at puberty to go up on a mountain and fast and wait till he was given a name by nature, until he heard a bird chanting on a tree or a fish came up and dropped a bubble on the surface of a brook where he was sitting. And then go back down into the town and say "My name is 'Bubble-Out-of-Fish's Mouth'" and the elder of the community will say "Yeah, you finally did get alone up there and wiped out the village and saw something with your own eyes and so therefore from now on your name *is* gonna be 'Bubble-Out-of-Fish's Mouth.'"

Q: Don't you feel that with the cultural revolution that is going on, hopefully going on, that eventually we can go back to the primary things that control us rather than continuing to be pressured by outside stimuli no matter how intensely involved we are in some type of art or some type of work?

AG: Actually, our conversation is getting so complicated I don't even understand it any more.

Q: Well, what I thought you said was that you should not be influenced by outside stimuli.

AG: Well, no, I was giving you an absolute answer to an absolute question—take it in context. The absolute question was like, "You mean to say we should not be totally influenced by whatever everybody tells us we're supposed to be?" In other words, "We shouldn't take our identity from what everybody tells us our identity is over television?" Well, obviously we shouldn't.

Q: Yes, but I don't see how you cannot in some instances. I mean you have to——

AG: Yes, but he was asking what ways are there to escape or to have vision or to get out of the cage, and I was giving six or seven yogas, six or seven *sadhanas*, six or seven paths, six or seven arts to do that: six or seven obvious activities.

Q: Actually I asked about learning and Allen kind of carried it over to getting out of the cage and finding a complete experience.

AG: And Robert brought it back to craft, to learning also, to practical application.

RD: Well this is the thing: when you stated the thing about the table, the essential of building that table is that you get from it what you're doing. This means that you step out of somebody else valuing it, because, as you said, *you* care for the materials you're working with. One thing we've lost is the care of the world—visible loss of care of it—and this is the product of this very educational system we're sitting in, the loss of care.

I'll tell you one thing, 'cause I taught under the conditions where you're given grades— A, B, C, D, E, and F. When you're teaching under those conditions and a student is trying to say something to you (in the first place they're made a student by it, so that's a loss of care), actually trying to say something, you don't really listen because you're employed, and you've got to divide that class up into A's, B's, C's, D's, E's, and F's, and you're frantic trying to figure out whether you're listening to A, B, C, D, E, or F.

You gotta return to that room so it's filled with presences, not students, not audience. As poets we fill you with your audience, possibly, so how do we talk . . . or socially I'm worried if I'm taking up some time that ought to be Allen's, or how come I'm sounding off here, what do you think of my sounding off, haven't I just about destroyed communication when I'm trying to talk to you, 'cause actually I'm sounding off just like a bird does; he gets on a limb and goes "Tweet, tweet, tweet, tweet," and actually if you weren't so uptight you could all "Tweet, tweet, tweet, tweet" back, and you would be pouring out what you think, we should be bombed out of our skulls so you were all singing *(laughter from those present).* No, really. I mean we keep wondering since I love to talk, how come I destroy all your talking? And you all listen, earnestly, or politely, or you think, "Oh, God, when will it be through, and I can get out—." But that isn't what boids do. They fly away, it's true, but most of them——

Q: You won't give us a chance to say anything.

RD: No, that's right! Does a bird wait for a chance? You got in there—go with it! You know I want to have the experiment sometime where everybody opens up—you can hear more than one person at a time.

Q: You spoke of freedom. What about tradition, tradition as a groundwork for meaning.

RD: Well, but there's volition in tradition, isn't there? I've already used this a couple of times as an example: Blake recognized that he was in the tradition of Milton. That wasn't laid on him; nobody came along and said, "Blake, you is in the tradition of Milton." He could have been in the tradition of a million other cats. True tradition is entirely voluntary; it's entirely in your own hands.

Q: OK, so you're saying what—to get out of the cage, and——

RD: You're out of the cage.

Q: OK, to get out of the cage and to free yourself from your conditioned reactions, and then return and look at the cage from the outside, maybe through the eyes of freedom or something?

AG: And get the other people out!

RD: Let's go back, we started with Allen's song: have compassion for all those children who're in compulsory education. *You're* not in compulsory education any longer. If something makes you go to school, you've already succumbed to it at this point. But they're compelled to go to school by *police* from the age of six through the age of sixteen or fifteen!

AG: There are many people who are at present compelled to go to school just to get out of the draft!

RD: There are truant officers that make them do it, and so you must have compassion for those who are truly coerced just as we've got to have compassion for the ones in the army.

Q: You mentioned that the other processes of getting out of the cage, of the educational racket or whatever you want to say it is, are being intensely interested in something that is your own personal thing, without really caring how other people react to it. I don't see how you can do this without having experience in this field, and if you don't have experience in this field, you're going to have to learn from others. And the only way you have of learning is going through the process.

RD: Yeah, but the process is not with other people's opinion of the process. On my mind now is Matisse's painting: he's gotta do that *fauve* scene. He can't worry about Paris thinking it's a mess, nor can he worry that overnight they think it's the greatest thing going and it's going to be a fashion in painting. Neither of those two things can he worry about, because he's actually there. This is why art is so liberating.

But you know we're at a gassy scene today in almost every art including poetry . . . now when we scribble on paper the so-called draft of the poem is worth money. So gee, they intrude everywhere; they wanna transfer everything into value, and we're talking about a non-value world; we're talking about an experimental world, because in the poem you are having care for the words and the thing that's happening there in your spirit, and you've gotta have care for the truth of the whole thing. And that's hard enough, you flunk it lots of the time.

AG: Let's sing—a minute—'cause there's something everybody can sing. I got another one you [RD] haven't heard yet: "Spring,"* which has an English language mantra at the end, simple enough so that you can sing it, and not have to just listen. *(Sings with harmonium. Many join, some clap rhythm. AG varies refrain: "Merrily, merrily, we welcome in the year" [the Great Year, the Apocalypse, End of Earth]. Followed by applause, then one "Boo!")*

AG: Boo! Hūṃ! Hūṃ! Hūṃ! [followed by exchange of short spontaneous mantras listed below]

Q: How!

AG: How!

Q: How!

AG: Mop!

Q: Barf!

AG: Crash!

Q: Gaylord!

AG: Bang!

RD: Trickle trickle trickle trickle trickle trickle trickle

AG: Help!

Q: Aaaah!

AG: Wow!

Q: *(louder)* Aaah!

AG: Shazam! Abracadabra!

Q: Ooooaaah!

AG: Om Ah Hūṃ! Om Ah Hūṃ Vajra Guru Padma Siddhi Hūṃ!

RD: *(giggling)* Don't say any bad things, Allen!

Q: Where do you start initially, then? Without any guidance at all, or do you have to have some kind of——

---

*For music see pp. 248–249.

AG: Start with a sigh—uuuuuuuhhhh. No, start with guidance, start with love, start with your loved one. Start seeking your loved one.

RD: It's like conscience; you got it in you, you follow it, that inner feeling. That's the guide you follow along.

AG: In other words, start with what you desire, heart, instead of what you think you are supposed to do.

Q: What about the person who doesn't know what he desires?

AG: Well, that's the worst misery, OK, that's the worst misery.

Q: A kid is very responsive: when they want something, they scream. God, they know better than anybody else.

RD: Yeah, they cry in misery when they're without. They know when they're without. A group of ten-year-olds has no trouble about "I talk too loud for them to talk" . . . Wow! They can hold their own in all scenes. It's taken the efforts of masses of people to get you to the place where you listen politely when somebody's talking and don't, you know, flow forth. We're talking about a vision about poetry that poets have always had. It's been left to us, that we would be the poets, but we know that there are lots of other civilizations where poetry is en masse with poets, sort of like it was when Allen was singing but the lead would pass around the circle. Instead we worry is the poet T. S. Eliot or is it Robert Duncan or is it Mickey Mouse or is it Allen Ginsberg.

AG: In the peyote ritual everybody is in a circle, and the fire chief takes care of the moon altar, and then everybody in turn in the evening gets the water drum and plays the drum and sings his song and the drum is passed around for the whole evening, so that everyone participates in the vocalization of the prayer.

RD: Haven't you all played that game where you tell part of a story and the next person tells the next part of the story? The Japanese, for instance, write great big poems this way, each person gets a line of the poem, and they get it going, and the music gets going like this—Allen was beginning "Welcome in," and you actually could have gone in all sorts of directions with this "Welcome in." Certainly they keep that alive in childhood circles, the making up of new elements in something.

Q: Finding answers is like returning to the awareness of a child, to that clearness of perception.

RD: Yeah, didn't Christ talk about "Become like a little child," right. "Except ye be like a child"—"The kingdom of heaven belongs to the child"—that's where Blake realized the child is the one we gotta look at, the child cries out in need, as was said here, you know. The child knows he needs and the rest of us have been taught that we don't need what we first cried for.

AG: The problem here though is how does everybody here confront the Kent State massacres and future fear of same as you try and break out and propose your own energy? So that's really the question that's being asked in a way: how do you confront the armed guards of the cage.

RD: The Mexican government broke the spirit of the students, and they still think they triumphed, 'cause they didn't kill just a small group, they killed over three hundred, and that broke a movement. But you can't break the spirit, or break an idea. And I'm not talking just about the goodness of ideas—you can't break Nazism by exterminating the Nazis; it grows all over again. In the world of spirit and ideas, evil as well as good grows all over again.

AG: *(to woman with hand raised)* Speakee!

Q: An adult may feel depressed, a child may know physically what he wants and needs (he may want to play rather than do something else), but how do you lead him in the direction of good instead of evil and still satisfy all his wants and needs so that he does not become like a Nazi?

AG: It's not good and evil, it's just something practical: if you're really interested in making a table or building a fence on a farm and you actually get into it, likely enough the child there will come along and want to hold the wires and want to take part in the play.

RD: He also wants it to come out so it fits; he may not know how and may go through quite a lot of what we call real work in order to learn how to join, and it takes years to learn. I'm in the same situation. You proposed the child can't do it; I still can't *do* it—I mean I've still got the same problems with poetry I had in the beginning because you've got to pay attention to language like you pay attention to and are careful of wood, and this is beyond good and evil. We don't talk about the good or evil of doing this work: this means you really are caring for something.

Let me clear up one thing. I see part of what you're asking about. You don't have an art in the beginning. You only find it working with the thing you're taking care of. I mean you don't have an art inside just to deliver like that.

There's a lot of difference between Henry Ford's Ford and the one which comes off the construction line in which no one is really involved in the making of the machine, and even the man on the drawing board is not involved. And then we get swamped by styles—"Has it got a jazzy line or something?" And we no longer have any feeling of a human being in back of this fender.

We're sitting on a rug right here—if you look deep into this rug do you have any sense of a human being making it? It actually has no human being in back of it. It has somebody who had a job, who's exactly like Blake's industrial child. The industries were coercing people, and they had a livelihood only in terms of the industry—that balustrade there, this rug, these panelings . . . that "brick" wall resembles no living brick wall built by a man. 'Cause it wasn't; it was built by a contractor who was in here to make a real hunk of money out of this place.

Q: I'd like to know why an inanimate object like the rug must have human traits.

RD: No, I'm not talking about "must"; I'm saying that they're not there, and I'm only talking to those who want such traits. Yes, of course a great deal of effort has gone into seeing that we live in a world without human traits, and that's what's called dehumanized.

Q: But look at a tree—did man make that tree?

AG: I have a poem* to read.

> Long stone streets inanimate, repetitive machine Crash cookie-cutting

---

*"Manhattan 'Thirties Flash" (1968), *Fall of America,* City Lights, San Francisco, 1972.

dynamo rows of soulless replica Similitudes brooding tank-
    like in Army Depots
Exactly the same exactly the same exactly the same with no
    purpose but grimness
& overwhelming force of robot obsession, our slaves are not alive
& we become their sameness as they surround us—the long stone
    streets inanimate,
crowds of executive secretaries alighting from subway 8:30 AM
bloodflow in cells thru elevator arteries & stairway glands to
    typewriter consciousness,
Con Ed skyscraper clock-head gleaming gold-lit at sun dusk.

In other words as we get surrounded by repetitive, exactly-
the-same robot-similitudes, they begin influencing our nervous
sytems, and we begin to take on their coloration and affect,
feeling-tone.

RD: We are different people from the ones that lived in
Romanesque churches and towns and built their own houses.

Q: Is that reality out there or in here?

RD: There's no out there and in here.

AG: It conditions us; the rug conditions our——

Q: See, that's why I run into hassles, because I say that rug
conditions you if you believe that rug conditions you.

AG: Well, no, let us say the rug conditions you until you become
aware of it as being a robot rug—then you've escaped from its
subliminal conditioning. I mean to a great extent we're
surrounded——

RD: We're not talking about this rug; we're talking about the fact
that we do not have a rug here——

AG: To give us joy!

RD: A great work of art like the Muslim carpet where a whole
lifetime is spent to make a carpet—they don't even get this size,
'cause it takes much more than a lifetime. Now those rugs are
meaning, and this is not only non-meaning, it is anti-meaning.

Q: Some fat sheik walks over that one anyhow, right? Some fat
sheik that doesn't even look at the meaning in the rug still walks
over it.

AG: Oh no—don't be a racist—they really look at them too; they get high on hashish in the middle of Persia and look at the rug! Why do you think they were making all that stuff about flying carpets?

RD: Flying carpets and the works, right? They fly, they go on trips, and they knew the carpet took them on their trip.

Q: But the expense of this—would you——

RD: All right. Let me give you it straight off. A Picasso today is worth over a hundred thousand dollars. It's pretty expensive, isn't it, to have? Does it cost Mr. Picasso a hundred thousand dollars to produce? I mean he isn't producing money when he paints; he paints straight into it. I'm talking about rugs that were not made because they were going to be costly; they were made because they were acts of devotion so that the whole life was devoted to a rug, and you can see it when you see the rug. The makers of some of those rugs were in their nineties when they finished. Do you think they were thinking about what they were going to be paid for the rugs?

I see the scorn of some fat sheik, but in that world of fat Muslim sheiks, those very fat Muslim sheiks thought of those rugmakers like Roman Catholics think of their priests and nuns. They didn't work to produce a commodity that was for sale, and no Muslim would think of being a fat ... he might be a fat sheik lots of places, but not when he was before his rug, because that rug was a holy object, and Soul had gone into it.

The Blacks, thank God, are reviving Soul. You know, we're the ones, those of us who are whities, are the ones who need Soul. We *had* Soul in the seventeenth century; it's evident, and poets have tried to keep it alive, and it *is* coming up again: I mean to have Blake sung again is the beginning of Soul, once more.

Q: Like to worship something that has a lack of soul is to be in hell.

RD: Worship? We don't worship this carpet. Do you?

AG: Some people do, in the sense that they put their devotion into it.

RD: But, oh, wait a minute. To work on this carpet is hell. And now I see what you're saying and what I really want to get across

Think of the ones who produce your automobiles: these are people living in hell because they work all day . . . have you ever asked why they demand such high pay? I found whenever I had a job that had nothing in it of human meaning I wanted to be paid back and I never could get enough pay because when I worked for eight hours and it didn't contain human meaning, I had to give myself a great time every night I finished because I had to pay back for HELL! which I was in for eight hours.

But there are many people who live in this hell—you can tell by how much they ask for what they're doing. An automobile . . . only Henry Ford and the very beginners were in the dream of what an automobile is, and the rest of those guys in the assembly line, they are in hell, and the machine itself is hell, and we drive it like hell, and we drive it to kill, and we actually succeed in killing people with that automobile like we kill them with our armies, and it is a hell-machine because it originates in hell. The original Ford wasn't a hell-machine, it wasn't designed to go a hundred miles an hour; you want to go a hundred and fifty miles an hour or one thousand miles an hour in a jet because you gotta make up for the fact that it's entirely a product of hell.

Q: OK, but we've got this reality to deal with. How do we deal with it?

RD: Well, one thing is . . . are any of you going into a rug factory? The ones who have this reality to deal with are the ones who are making it right now and who've got to wake up and get out of making or profiting from the spread of meaningless things.

Q: And this rug was probably made by a machine, and then sold to a middle man, and then——

RD: Yeah, right. There we're in the second thing. To go back to *The Arabian Nights* with the flying carpet: the merchant was the man with the wonderful secret magic goods in his shop (there still are some who feel that way). But the man who's selling this stuff is living in hell, 'cause he ain't got no wonderful magic secret goods, and he ain't in any contact with the thing they really used to bring all across Asia to bring some wonder from the human world. The goods are no longer really goods.

By the way, there are some shops, aren't there, where you still have the other kind of merchant: you go in and all of a sudden everything's wonderful and they know about their goods and they know where they came from. The true inspired merchant keeps himself alive just like poets. Merchandising is one of the most ancient, inspired human things; it is the one line that goes between civilizations. And this carpet is really a vast area of hell.

Q: What can we do to find meaning for everyone? Like our society has become so choked just with human beings—how is there a way to show all of these human beings how to get this individual consciousness?

RD: One thing: you leave it up to their own individual volition.

2

Early Poetic Community

(with Robert Duncan)

HONORS COLLEGE: KENT STATE
April 7, 1971

RD: In following our discussions I think you've already got an impression of how important to me is a kind of continuity moving through poetry and a relationship both of a fellowship of poets and, through time, of an inheritance of spirit. Since I've been here I've talked about the big inheritance of spirit in which you discover your own fathers—like Blake discovers he really is the next incarnation of Milton and the antitype of Milton. As later, for instance, Yeats is going to discover himself, as he discovers that he is immediately related to Blake and then to Milton and then to Spenser.

Today, though, I want to talk not about that area of magical discovery in solitude, but one that happens when you belong to a company of poets.

When Don Allen's anthology[3] appeared in 1960, it caused shock waves of outrage and horror throughout the American poetic establishment. He didn't edit it like anthologies are usually edited. He felt there was a poetry everywhere, and he consulted various people, various poets, and had informants, and it looked to the horrified establishment like there was another establishment forming. Well, what there was, was a community. Some of those poets I hadn't read at all and didn't know the existence of—like I was on the west coast; I didn't know the existence of the New York school. But you can draw a map and

131

find out that my poetry is intimately related to the poetry of Ashberry and O'Hara and Koch, and this is a true, actual community.

But what was revealed to us was that whereas we'd thought we were isolated before, and then we thought, well, there's a little group of us, we suddenly discovered that actually this thing that had happened in poetry had many different guises—the Beat Movement was one of them. The intelligence of Don Allen's anthology is that it included them all. Allen [G.] came bearing the message that there was Kerouac's poetry—I'm sure you all know Kerouac's prose, but we still try to get across the message that Kerouac was a poet. Actually, Kerouac paid no attention to his poetry, which was all right, he was in prose and he was junior James Joyce or something, and so he let go these marvelous *Mexico City Blues*. That wasn't part of what he projected in message, but for Allen, and Corso, and . . . there must be another one in there—Corso, Kerouac, you and who else?

AG: I think that Peter [Orlovsky] was writing a little bit.

RD: At that time. But for instance also properly in the anthology, but in a different section were people very closely associated with Allen [G.] personally in the west coast scene, because Snyder and Whalen were about a different business. See, that's the accuracy of that anthology.

Now, that's just one section. The section on New York poets is so beautifully, actually *it*, that you can't find one missing or one unfitting poet in there. I don't mean that the anthology formed us—it showed when it finally appeared how formed we were. And we were formed naturally—we belonged to environments. It's the *only* anthology I know of, and *the first* one, there's never been another one since that's been composed that way that was—an environment of poets the way they are. Usually we're exhibited in anthologies in no way that anybody who wanted to get the feel of things would accept.

Now, I was refusing to be in the anthology because I *hate* anthologies, and not until I saw a table of contents did I consent to be in it. Today I'm in anthologies because I gave up, finally, three years ago. New Directions was distressed, indeed, that I wanted to refuse anthologies, and that I had a formula, if an anthology is not edited by a poet that I think interesting—I don't mean that I agree with him . . . if Edith Sitwell or Yeats or Pound had ever wanted me in an anthology, yes, regardless of whether I agreed about it, and when Auden wanted me in an anthology, yes, regardless of my own distaste for Auden's role in poetry. He *is* a poet, and it's fascinating what's in that anthology,[4] until he came to my generation. But then he must have been right, because there I was with H.D. and Williams and people I really loved, and so did Auden, it turns out. So this must be an *entente* of some strange kind.

OK, I was in the Allen anthology. "No," I said, "Don, I don't belong in that group, in the San Francisco Renaissance." I never really came home and discovered that I had a place where my soul really belonged till after I met Charles Olson. Charles was both a contemporary and at the same time filled a paternal role. In Kabbalism—it's all in those fathers we talked about the other day, Abraham, Isaac, Jacob forming a four with Adam, called a chariot. And I had three: Pound, Williams, and D. H. Lawrence. And there was a missing wheel on the chariot. And I had that feeling and all of a sudden there with great resounding—and my own contemporary—was Olson with "Projective Verse." Well, that sounds like when I read "Projective Verse" and when I read Charles Olson's poetry it came like a light and I immediately saw what it was. Here was the man who is going to change me—not change, I didn't change—he's going to open up everything I am. And I'll tell you, it was a joyous experience. I had been writing poetry for more than ten years by 1950, since '37 or so, and Charles was just beginning to write it, and was just there. He had written poetry as early as '47 or so. I met the man in '46, when he had a grant to do work on the migration of people to our west coast, and in our first meetings we talked about that and about my own concept that the disorder of our civilization is the fundamental coercive disorder whereby we all live in cities and make farmers raise food for us. Now, did I recognize Olson at once? Boy, this story is going to send book collectors out of their minds. I'm sitting there, Olson had paid three visits to me, and I was thinking, "Oh, this historian recognizes I'm a poet," and, "Poet, poet, you're a real poet, I've wanted to know a real poet," this man was saying, hiding away like some cunning monster the fact that he's actually the secret thing I've gotta have in order to even realize I'm a poet. Well, let's see, I'm thinking, how does an historian know anything about poetry? I mean isn't it wonderful, OK, great. So he sends me *Y & X*. I don't know if you know what

Y & X was, but it was like his first thing in poetry; it was brought out by the Black Sun Press by Caresse Crosby, who is Mother Fairy Godmother of everything from James Joyce to Charles Olson, and who put a magic finger on "this is the thing" a million times. Not on any of mine—I could cry, I never got that magic appointment. So I must have burned to see this Black Sun Press, gorgeous thing, and I said "What is this?" and I tried to read this *Y & X* and I said "Oh, for Christ's sake, I can't make anything out of this," and I threw it in the wastepaper basket, where a book today worth twenty million dollars is floating away down the river to somewhere.

It was James Broughton who first brought "Projective Verse" to me. It had appeared in a magazine[5] as an essay in 1950, and at the same time in San Francisco we really preached the doctrine of reading a poem aloud. We weren't even interested in publishing, and we had already by 1950 an audience going. And when I read "Projective Verse" first I said "Yeah, yeah, right, man, that's exactly what it is—it means that we're right and you got the message from me, and you should read the poem aloud."

And not too long after that I'm reading this man and thinking I hope he never presumes to think he can write poetry again, but at least he's written an essay that says that it's great to read aloud. That was a zero reading; I hope that now one has to have classes that seriously read that document and that nobody slips by under the boards reading it that stupidly.

Well, by 1951 *Origin** arrived, and its first issue had such a blockbuster of Olson that I had to come off it. He was a poet, a poet like I had not seen in all my life. And I had been nursing possibilities of a poet in people I knew. It destroyed one of my closest poet friendships, which was with Jack Spicer, who was as genuine a poet as Olson, but Olson was to become *my* poet. I was very much Jack Spicer's poet, and his heart was broken when it was clear suddenly that someone would take his place, and so he was never able to tolerate the existence of Olson. I have pored over "Projective Verse." I mean I carry it like people carried *Pilgrim's Progress*. Like Keats carried Shakespeare. I can look at it right now and say, "God, did I ever sufficiently *feel* before, *move?*"

---

*Poetry magazine founded by poet Cid Corman featuring Olson, Creeley, *et al.*

Not every poet has exactly this experience. When Allen was talking about Kerouac the other day, I thought, "Gee, no wonder we're in a common area that can be defined. We know that the poem is an occasion of spirit. Yet my relationship with the New York school has been very difficult—O'Hara was absolutely intolerant of my existence. My correspondence with O'Hara was only one long letter to him when I read a marvelous love poem of his and said, "What a pouring-out of soul this is!" But for O'Hara it was wrong to have to read his poem as a pouring out of soul, I guess, really.

Now one thing I'd settled in my mind by 1950 was that I wasn't interested in the American language as proposed by Williams. Williams, you see, kept feeling that he really wasn't American. We find out that his grandmother spoke Spanish, so he had to stake a claim in the American language. Well, I couldn't possibly talk any language that wasn't American, because I happen to be, I think, twelfth-generation American. There is nothing in my family tree that is not pre-1800. So I couldn't *search* for an American language; the minute I open my mouth it must be American—it couldn't be anything else. I'm a phenomenon of it. Well then what did *American* mean? And Olson came charging in with, "Yes, there is a mystery in American letters as there is in British letters." There is an American spirit. I don't agree with Charles's picture of where that spirit is; Charles could be a narrow-minded bastard who misses out on three-fourths of the show. Great on Melville, but Black Mountain students were *not* supposed to read Emerson. And I was an Emerson person. There was an Index at Black Mountain. Henry James was another writer absolutely on the Index.

Nonetheless, Olson did bring an intense sense of company, and I don't have to worry about the fact that he was not going to acknowledge parts of that company, because every place he touched on the nature of that company in full confidence I could go and know it was there. Those Shakespeare plays that meant that much to him I know hold a secret. I mean even if I don't find it I know they hold a secret, and this is also the nature of your feeling of faith moving through. I will go over and over and over again to the texts, even though they still baffle me, because I have full confidence they belong to poetry. And the message may not be fully there yet—as I hinted the other day in relation to

Pound. Pound fairly points out that John Adams is one of those people. Now usually he's divided off as if you were studying history or politics. No, Pound meant John Adams is the matter of our poetry, and if you go to his letters, and if you go to John Adams's writings, you will find the matter of poetry.

All right, we've gone on for a long time and I only wanted to give you a picture. Here's a very short Maximus poem, delightfully, really, really, short, because it's a song, a written song. "Song 6" from "The Songs of Maximus."

> you sing, you
> who also
> wants

Gee, that's neat, reading this book. If you were to read this book, it says "You sing, you"—why the commandment? It's a great poem of division of labor in a democracy. Isn't that the only message in democracy? Oh, gee, how you'd all like to sit around and have me be the poet. Or I would like to sit around—and of course the same way you're not going to want me to be the poet, like I didn't want Olson to be the poet: what business have you coming up here being the poet? And my God, you are my poet. And that one really told the other part of that secret. You, you, you sing. "Who also/ wants."

AG: At Columbia College I never mastered poetics as analyzed by New Critical prose, and so tried to write sincere, though elegant, quatrains. However, falling in love over and over, I kept writing my poetry about or directly to the people I was in love with, so by about 1948 I had already been several years deep into a long physical love affair with a friend, Neal Cassady, who hitchhiked cross-country with me, from Denver, 1948, where we were hanging around with an old schoolteacher friend of his, Justin Brierly, down to a marijuana farm in east Texas where Burroughs was experimenting growing plants. Near Huntsville, Texas—New Waverly, where Burroughs was living with his wife and with another later-to-become prose writer, Herbert Huncke, whose long confessional novel* will soon be published by Harvey Brown, if Brown ever gets it on.

---

*The Evening Sun Turned Crimson, Frontier Press, Stewart Street, W. Newbury, Mass., 1974.

Arrived in Texas, spent a month wooing Cassady, trying to get into bed with him, making out, barely, and then coming into a financial problem—none of us had any money. So I was going to sail off to Africa and make a lot of money on ships, and he was going to meet me in New York, and then we were going to go off and be lovers together. All of which worked out, except that when I got to New York he had left New York—he'd driven Burroughs with the harvest of grass to New York City, sold the grass, and Neal hitchhiked back to California and got married —to a girl. So I was left out.

So I wrote a poem. Actually I went into a solitary phase, living in an apartment in New York City by myself, corresponding with Cassady, and then got a letter finally saying, "Well, we had better not really consider ourselves lovers, because I'm distracted with the wife and she's going to have children and I just won't have *time* now, much as I love you." So my heart was broken. As a result, my mind strayed into transcendental meditation, and I had various experiences of transcendental bliss. My heart having been broken, my earth heart having been broken, or my sexual heart having been broken, I thought, I found another heaven. So I wrote a poem to Cassady which was called "A Western Ballad," which I set to music a year ago. So as an example of the mode of poetry I was writing in 1948 I'll present that and then recite another poem and then get on to the relation between this form and other contacts, other friends, William Carlos Williams, and a change of form. *(Sings three stanzas.)*[6]

A WESTERN BALLAD

When I died, love, when I died
my heart was broken in your care;
I never suffered love so fair
as now I suffer and abide
when I died, love, when I died.

When I died, love, when I died
I wearied in an endless maze
that men have walked for centuries,
as endless as the gate was wide
when I died, love, when I died.

When I died, love, when I died
there was a war in the upper air;
all that happens, happens there;
there was an angel at my side
when I died, love, when I died.

So that registered both renunciation of what I held dearest in
terms of human body and breaking-open of consciousness. Thus
I gained what I held dearest in intuition, which was a sort of
eternal bliss contact with sumpin' beyond my body, or something that appeared beyond my body. Poetry, really.

So then began trying to write in that form more complicatedly.
Working in the Associated Press all night as a copyboy, "Stanzas:
Written at Night in Radio City," 1948 also:

If money made the mind more sane,
Or money mellowed in the bowel
The hunger beyond hunger's pain,
Or money checked the mortal growl
And made the groaner grin again,
Or did the laughing lamb embolden
To loll where has the lion lain,
I'd go make money and be golden.

Nor sex will solve the sickened soul,
Which has its holy goal an hour,
Holds to heart the golden pole,
But cannot save the silver shower,
Nor heal the sorry parts to whole.
Love is creeping under cover,
Where it hides its sleepy dole,
Else I were like any lover.

Many souls get lost at sea,
Others slave upon a stone:
Engines are not eyes to me,
Inside buildings I see bone.
Some from city to city flee,
Famous labors make them lie;
I cheat on that machinery,
Down in Arden I will die.

Art is short, nor style is sure:
Though words our virgin thoughts betray,
Time ravishes that thought most pure,

Which those who know, know anyway;
For if our daughter should endure,
When once we can no more complain,
Men take our beauty for a whore,
And like a whore, to entertain.

If fame were not a fickle charm,
There were far more famous men:
May boys amaze the world to arm,
Yet their charms are changed again,
And fearful heroes turn to harm;
But the shambles is a sham.
A few angels on a farm
Fare more fancy with their lamb. . . .

So I was writing, actually, a little after Marvell, a little after
Wyatt. Sent six or seven poems in that mode to William Carlos
Williams, who read them and sent them back, saying, "In this
mode, perfection is basic, and these are not perfect." I was trying
to actually perfect a rhymed, punning, silvery versification.

Same time I was reading Williams and keeping prose journals,
so simultaneous with that kind of rhymed verse I was writing in
prose form, in prose paragraphs, writing more directly out of my
own concrete experience. I mean I'd never been on a farm, so
how did I know about "A few angels on a farm/far[ing] more
fancy with their lamb," anyway? But while waiting in Denver for
Neal to get home from his job, I'd looked out a window and taken
down a prose note:

Two bricklayers are setting the walls
of a cellar in a new dug out patch
of dirt behind an old house of wood
with brown gables grown over with ivy
on a shady street in Denver. It is noon
and one of them wanders off. The young
subordinate bricklayer sits idly for
a few minutes after eating a sandwich
and throwing away the paper bag. He
has on dungarees and is bare above
the waist; he has yellow hair and wears
a smudged but still bright red cap
on his head. He sits idly on top
of the wall on a ladder that is leaned

up between his spread thighs, his head
bent down, gazing uninterestedly at
the paper bag on the grass. He draws
his hand across his breast, and then
slowly rubs his knuckles across the
side of his chin, and rocks to and fro
on the wall. A small cat walks to him
along the top of the wall. He picks
it up, takes off his cap, and puts it
over the kitten's body for a moment.
Meanwhile it is darkening as if to rain
and the wind on top of the trees in the
street comes through almost harshly.

So that was a little notation on whatever completely photo-
graphic, instamatic sensory detail could be seen through a window, or heard in the wind. That notation is 1946. But I didn't take
it as poetry, I took it as just writing in my journals, and so I didn't
until several years later arrange it into lines like that.

I read some of Williams's poetry later and thought I could
rearrange the lines according to how they might be spoken, and
where I might take a breath, or where a breath might run counter
to the movement of the line, or where the end of a line might
make a little syncopation with the way the breath was moving
along to the end of the sentence.

Also, using dream material, notating simple facts from dreams,
or descriptions of dreams: "In Society," which is 1947, so that
would be about a year before "When I died, Love . . ." or "If
money made the mind more sane . . ."

I walked into the cocktail party
room and found three or four queers
talking together in queertalk.
I tried to be friendly but heard
myself talking to one in hiptalk.
"I'm glad to see you," he said, and
looked away. "Hmn," I mused. The room
was small and had a double-decker
bed in it, and cooking apparatus:
icebox, cabinet, toasters, stove;
the hosts seemed to live with room
enough only for cooking and sleeping.

My remark on this score was understood but not appreciated. I was
offered refreshments, which I accepted.
I ate a sandwich of pure meat; an
enormous sandwich of human flesh,
I noticed, while I was chewing on it,
it also included a dirty asshole.

More company came, including a
fluffy female who looked like
a princess. She glared at me and
said immediately: "I don't like you,"
turned her head away, and refused
to be introduced. I said, "What!"
in outrage. "Why you shit-faced fool!"
This got everybody's attention.
"Why you narcissistic bitch! How
can you decide when you don't even
know me," I continued in a violent
and messianic voice, inspired at
last, dominating the whole room.

So those are literal renderings of actual material which, though
less pretty than the rhymed poems I was writing, actually had
more humor, more life in them, more detail, more minute particulars, less ideas, more things—"icebox, cabinet, toasters,
stove"—*presenting* material, rather than recombining symbols
that I had appropriated from Yeats or Blake or Marvell. Like "I
wearied in an endless maze/That men have walked for centuries" was just simply a paraphrase of Blake. *(Sings "The Voice
of the Ancient Bard.")*

Youth of delight, come hither,
And see the opening morn,
Image of truth new born.
Doubt is fled, & clouds of reason,
Dark disputes & artful teazing.
Folly is an endless maze,
Tangled roots perplex her ways.
How many have fallen there!
They stumble all night over bones of the dead,
And feel they know not what but care,
And wish to lead others, when they should be led.

In other words I stole his "endless maze": "Folly is an endless maze." So I was just recombining literary imagery, and that is the difficult habit-tendency if you repeat somebody else's rhythms, if you repeat somebody else's forms, or if you imitate archaic forms.

So I found I wasn't speaking in my own voice. In order to not merely speak in my own voice but actually make use of my own life, my own occasions, I had to stop writing poetry and had to just simply start writing writing or scratching out notes.

Conversations with Williams reinforced the insight, 'cause I went to see him, and he had written down on a piece of paper, on his prescription pad, I think, "I'll kick yuh eye." And he said now you're writing metrical poetry, but how would you measure that funny phrase "I'll kick yuh eye," 'cause it's got a little syncopation in it, "yuh eye," which would be very difficult to describe in a regular meter. What I picked up from him was that he was writing without any rules at all, really, except listening to rhythm that he heard around him. He was taking rhythms directly from his own voice, or he was building little rhythmic structures in his poetry directly from the changes that he heard in his own voice or in the Polish workman up and down his block, "I'll kick yuh eye." So he would get to little funny poems like "To Greet a Letter-Carrier."*

In other words Williams was arriving at little refrains, little rhythmic squiggles, that were unheard in previous lyric composition, because he was taking them from what he called, or what Pound spoke of in relation to Williams, the "raw material" around him. The raw material being the raw sensory material, actually, the input right into his own ear from the streets.

So what I did next, within a month, was to send Williams a whole bunch of little snippets I cut out of prose journals and rearranged in little lines to look like his poetry, and asked him what he thought of these as poems. (They're all poems that are in a little early book called *Empty Mirror*.) They were very short; one was "A Poem on America":

America is like Russia.
Acis and Galatea sit by the lake. [That's an image out of
    Dostoyevsky's *The Possessed*.]

---

* See "Poetic Breath and Pound's Usura," p. 165.

We have the proletariat too.

Acis and Galatea sit by the lake.
Versilov wore a hair shirt
and dreamed of classical pictures.

The alleys, the dye works,
Mill Street in the smoke,
melancholy of the bars,
the sadness of long highways,
negroes climbing around
the rusted iron by the river,
the bathing pool hidden
behind the silk factory
fed by its drainage pipes;
all the pictures we carry in our mind

images of the Thirties,
depression and class consciousness
transfigured above politics
filled with fire
with the appearance of God.

So Williams got turned on I guess by the local imagery, "the bathing pool hidden/ behind the silk factory/ fed by its drainage pipes," 'cause later he wanted me to take him and show him that specific spot in Paterson for his own research, for his own exploration of his place that he wanted to write his epic about.

So when I sent him those little poems, he wrote back to me, "Ah, this is it." Except that he cut out a few lines of some of the poems, and said like, they're vague, there's nothing in there. Leave the poem unfinished if necessary—just whatever is "active" in the line is interesting. Whatever presents an active piece of information. If you're just babbling on about the information and commenting on it, then forget it—just chop it out, cut it off, it doesn't even have to be a finished sentence; don't even finish your sentence if you're just gonna bullshit. Well, he didn't say that, but "don't finish your sentence if it is not active," was the purport.

And so in 1948 I went to hear him read at the Museum of Modern Art. I still didn't quite understand his poetry, I didn't know how to read it. Like Robert threw out Olson's first text that he received, it was not readable, 'cause the eye was used to reading a different kind of page, a different kind of line; the voice was not yet familiar, so I didn't know how to read with Williams's voice. I was expecting something else. I kept reading, waiting, where is the rhythm here, or OK, so it don't rhyme, but there must be some other . . . maybe it's like cummings, if you rearrange it it really makes iambic pentameter, or quatrains. I didn't realize the absolute rhythmic departure, that he was working out of his own ear, instead of an antique ear, like they taught in grammar school.

But Williams read a poem at the Museum of Modern Art which immediately clarified the whole process. It was a poem called "The Clouds." The subject is clouds of imagination, vagueness of imagination, what happens to your discourse if your mind is up in the clouds, to put it vulgarly, if you're not paying attention to detail, if you're not "present" where you are, if you're not making use of "minute particulars" as Blake said, or if you're indulging in ideas without things, 'cause Williams's formula was "No ideas but in things."

But the poem ended—I've forgotten how he built up to it—so the mind wanders and is distracted. Like he made a gesture, ". . . lunging upon/ a pismire, a conflagration, a . . ." and he ended the poem like that, on the stage of the Museum of Modern Art. And I had never heard a poem that ended in the middle of a sentence, though I'd heard people talk that way all the time, and I suddenly realized, oh, *he's just writing the way he talks.* He's really talking in his poetry, he's trying to say something, for real; he's not just making a lot of pretty words like I was, like "If money made the mind more sane." He wasn't just throwing out a line, you know, to complete the form, but the form was absolutely identical with what he was saying. It was so absolutely simple, simple-minded, almost—so *obvious!* I couldn't understand why I hadn't been able to read him before. And the reason I hadn't been able to read him before, understand what I was reading, though my eye had gone over the lines on the page any number of times, was I had never figured out that he just meant what he said.

And finally to arrive at a poetry that really means what it says, a poetry with a meaning which is identical with its form, with a rhythm identical with the arrangement of the words on the page, and the words on the page arranged identically with what you want to say and how you want to say it, was like a revelation of absolute common sense in my entire universe of complete bullshit! Aesthetically a totally hallucinated universe where like every possible poetic form made absolute common sense. And also made absolutely pretty rhythm, too—"Atta boy! Atta boy!"

Also, at the same time, independent of the contact I had with Williams, which was about '48, I'd already been in contact with Neal, as I said, and with Jack Kerouac. Kerouac till this time, '48, '49, was still writing *bildungsroman*, that is, giant family novels with regular prose. Till about 1950, he was still writing symphonic prose sentences out of Thomas Wolfe, out of Joyce, out of Milton, a little bit; a prose that had great beautiful voweled periods. He was still thinking of breaths as long prose sentences, hearing his sentences, but still thinking in regular syntax with semicolons, dependent clauses, semicolons. Proust!

He didn't begin to interrupt himself, he didn't begin to allow the movement of his mind to interrupt freshman comp syntax until about 1950 or so, '51, so I think probably it was Williams from whom I got the first touch of a natural prose poetry style. But I got it most insistently from Kerouac thereafter, because his precept, finally, after about '52, '53, was not to go back and revise what had been set down on the page, his idea being a very "naive" one, that is, naively arrived at for him, because he had not read Gertrude Stein for that idea, and he didn't have the literary experience that I had with Williams, and he wasn't in contact with a very similar practice arising in both New York City with Frank O'Hara and Kenneth Koch and through Olson and yourself [Duncan] in San Francisco. Sort of . . . all by himself. A good deal before I did, he arrived at an understanding that the gesture he made in language was his mortal gesture, and therefore unchangeable. And I still didn't quite believe it until I checked it with Robert Duncan a couple years later, '53 or '54—I went to see Robert, who was in San Francisco teaching a class in poetics at San Francisco. I walked into the room where Robert was teaching—Michael McClure was sitting there looking really beautiful, also—and brought *Empty Mirror* to Robert, and Robert later brought it back to a little room in North Beach where I was staying, and I had pinned on a wall a set of instructions from Kerouac on essentials of prose composition, I think "Essentials of Modern Prose," which are reprinted in the Don Allen anthology, which outlined like "Speak now, or ever hold your peace, write whatever comes to mind, adding vowels, adding alluvials, adding to the end of the sentence, and then rather than revising, if you have a new thought, go on to articulate it in the next sentence."[7]

So Robert looked at the page I had tacked to the wall and said "Oh, who wrote that?" And Robert I think was the first person who recognized the high literary quality of Kerouac's instructions. I was sort of astounded that he had the same insight, 'cause I still hadn't quite got it straight—that you had to attend to what you were saying, because you couldn't say it twice.

RD: Listen, can I give one little parenthesis to describe that scene? I'm just blowing my mind the way he tells the scene.

I'd read, you see, these poems in *Empty Mirror* and it had the William Carlos Williams preface with it. And in the preface Williams says first, Can you really write poetry in Hell? Well, I read *Empty Mirror*. And Allen had come to the door and left this manuscript.

AG: You were sitting having a conversation with Spicer, I think.

RD: And so I'm reading this manuscript and first I said did he leave this manuscript because he knew I was queer? And then I said I wanted to return the manuscript, so he gives me his hotel room number, and I'm to go there about nine o'clock.

OK, I arrive, I knock at the door, I open the door, and here sitting in his shorts is Allen, and I think "Oh God!" While Allen is blissfully seeing this—You see, in his angelic dream, I'm standing like your maiden aunt, and I've got my legs crossed already, I'm not going to be given this hotel room meet-in-shorts scene; I probably looked at what was on the wall in order to show "I'm not going to be looking at your shorts!" So it's that that shows the power of poetry—once I look at what's on the wall and *(voice drowned by laughter)* . . . OK, Allen, it's your turn.

AG: I had my mind at this point like completely on high poesy——

RD: I had mine on Allen's shorts——

AG: And so, I said, "Well, what do you think—how could you possibly just write without revising?" And Robert said "Well, look, I've taken a step across the room; how can I go back and revise my step? I've already done it. How can I go back in time and revise the step?" Which again made such complete sense —obviously if you've written a sentence it's there in eternity.

How can you change it? You could take another step, but can you go back and cross out the old step, without confusing history, or without confusing eternity, like? Or without getting your head certainly confused. Without confusing your own consciousness, and without confusing the record—what Kerouac said was that it was sort of like lying if you revised, in the sense that you make believe you didn't say that. Like you revealed what was on your mind, but he felt that most revision would be motivated by embarrassment—in other words you'd be embarrassed by the truth of what you were saying, therefore revise.

What that kind of writing proposes is an absolute, almost Zen-like, complete absorption, *attention* to your own consciousness, to the act of writing, to a focus of mind, so that attention does not waver while writing, and doesn't feed back on itself and become self-conscious—but that you are attentive to the object you're describing, whether it be the consciousness that is in the room at the moment or your own head, just as long as you don't get feeding back, "I am writing because I am writing I am watching myself writing while I am writing," which would be the great wavering of attention, which most young poets begin with, actually, you know, their first spontaneous thing is, "Gee, I'm writing. What does it feel like? Isn't it weird that I am writing while I am writing and here I am writing, and the ink is blue." Which is everybody's first poem, I guess. It's the archetype poem. But there's a lot of people that really get hung up on that first exercise.

I had come to San Francisco from New York, and simultaneously there were poets in New York also who, oddly, had picked up on Williams—the poets that Robert mentioned, Frank O'Hara, John Ashberry, and Kenneth Koch, among others. They had picked up on Williams from, again, the point of view of a common-sense statement. O'Hara had picked up on Williams because he saw Williams as goodhearted. O'Hara did have passion, and of all those poets was romantic in the sense of poetically romantic—in other words O'Hara did speak of love. And I remember him receiving that letter from you and his comment on it, which was, what he was going through was a feeling of complete freedom, that anything written—just as with Kerouac, or with yourself, I think—that any gesture he made was the poetic gesture because he was the poet, so therefore anything he did was poetry.

I'll just read a little poem of O'Hara's so we know what we're talkin' about.

POEM

Khrushchev is coming on the right day!
$\qquad\qquad\qquad\qquad\qquad$ the cool graced light
is pushed off the enormous glass piers by hard wind
and everything is tossing, hurrying on up
$\qquad\qquad\qquad\qquad\qquad\qquad$ this country
has everything but *politesse* a Puerto Rican cab driver says
and five different girls I see
$\qquad\qquad\qquad\qquad\qquad$ look like Piedie Gimbel
with her blonde hair tossing too,
$\qquad\qquad\qquad\qquad\qquad$ as she looked when I pushed
her little daughter on the swing on the lawn it was also windy
last night we went to a movie and came out,
$\qquad\qquad\qquad\qquad\qquad\qquad$ Ionesco is greater
than Beckett, Vincent said, that's what I think, blueberry blintzes
and Khrushchev was probably being carped at
$\qquad\qquad\qquad\qquad\qquad\qquad$ in Washington, no
$\qquad\qquad\qquad\qquad\qquad\qquad$ *politesse*
Vincent tells me about his mother's trip to Sweden
$\qquad\qquad\qquad\qquad\qquad\qquad$ Hans tells us
about his father's life in Sweden, it sounds like Grace Hartigan's
painting *Sweden*
$\qquad\qquad\qquad\qquad$ so I go home to bed and names drift through
$\qquad\qquad\qquad\qquad\qquad\qquad$ my head
Purgatorio Merchado, Gerhard Schwartz and Gaspar Gonzales, all
$\qquad$ unknown figures of the early morning as I go to work
where does the evil of the year go
$\qquad\qquad\qquad\qquad\qquad$ when September takes New
$\qquad\qquad\qquad\qquad\qquad\qquad$ York
and turns it into ozone stalagmites
$\qquad\qquad\qquad\qquad\qquad$ deposits of light
$\qquad\qquad\qquad\qquad\qquad$ so I get back up
make coffee, and read François Villon, his life, so dark New York
$\qquad$ seems blinding and my tie is blowing up the street
I wish it would blow off
$\qquad\qquad\qquad\qquad\qquad$ though it is cold and somewhat warms
$\qquad\qquad\qquad\qquad\qquad\qquad$ my neck

as the train bears Khrushchev on to Pennsylvania Station
   and the light seems to be eternal
   and joy seems to be inexorable
   I am foolish enough always to find it in wind

So his poetry was all his gossip, local gossip, social gossip, with sudden "ozone stalagmites," inspired images of New York, mixed with blueberry blintzes, also inspired. So that he felt any gesture he made was poetry, and poetry in that sense was totally democratic. So that there were no kings and queens of poetry. So when you wrote him, he saw you as the Queen of Poetry, giving him the scepter, and he said "Well, I don't want a scepter from that old queen!" He wanted to be independent, or, in the New York context, he felt it was like a San Francisco plot, so he got paranoid, a little.

The other poet in New York, working then, mentioned was John Ashberry. Do you know "The Instruction Manual,"[8] which for Ashberry's poetry is, say, the most easy to get into? He's sitting at the window daydreaming, and presents a complete universe, in totally authentic midtown New Yorkese discourse . . . just completely imagined, I bet, phrase by phrase, without needing any change, just adding, adding one detail onto another, beginning from the platform of pure imagination—a complete daydream transcribed. Oddly, then, we find in New York, a slightly different point of view, probably relying less than myself on mystics; less than the Berkeley Renaissance and San Francisco Renaissance scholars; relying less on Pythagoras and hermetic studies—nonetheless, an exploration of present consciousness in the New York writers. Later Ashberry texts, like "The Skaters,"[9] are very long exfoliations of association and improvisation; a little bit like "The Rape of the Lock," actually, as far as the gaiety of improvisation—like skating along the surface of consciousness.

The common theme, I think, or the common effort, between the two coasts, simultaneous, as I see it, or what to me is common, what to me is communal there, is a new consciousness being born in America, or an old new consciousness being returned to. The first steps of exploration of the contents of present consciousness during the moment of composition, a yoga of exploration of consciousness, a meditation on the nature of consciousness, beginning with the delineation of the contents and the operation of consciousness in the poets of the west coast and the poets of the east coast.

And also a language yoga—articulating that consciousness by means of normal talk, the syntax of our actual speech, our actual thoughts in our actual speech. That probably was aesthetically the key to the community that came to total clear consciousness with accompanying explosions of mystical visions and epiphanies around 1948, I'd say. I'd put 1948 as the date of this emergence into a flash, because '48 was when I had my Blake epiphany experiences——

RD: '48: my "Venice Poem."[10]

AG: '48 Robert's "Venice Poem." '48 also the Berkeley Renaissance community, which would be Jack Spicer, and oddly enough, you know, Timothy Leary was there.

RD: '48 was the time for Charles Olson's *Call Me Ishmael*.

AG: Yeah. In 1948 Gary Snyder in Portland finished his Amerindian anthropology unified field theory honors thesis to graduate, and that morning when he wrote the last words saying sumpin' about consciousness, about primitive consciousness, and then went down to the Willamette River and sat down in dawn silence, kind of exhausted, musing over the silence of nature, just as the sun rose, he heard a rushing of many wings, and thousands and thousands of birds rose up from the trees, and he looked around and his head turned inside out, and he suddenly realized "everything is alive"—the entire universe is alive. Every sentient being is alive, like myself. So that was '48, also. Do you know about that?

RD: No, I didn't know that.

AG: He had a very definite opening of consciousness, then first satori, so to speak, and it's from then that he goes on to—it was from that single experience that he went on to do his sitting [zazen].

3

Kerouac

FICTION CLASS: KENT STATE
April 6, 1971

AG: Most prose writers aren't even aware that the sentence they write has a sound, are not even concerned with sound in prose. In fact I'm not sure what most of them are concerned with. Most prose writers that I grew up with in college were influenced a lot by Hemingway, so one of their main concerns was economy in writing down the facts in journalisticese subjectivity—that is, economy in writing down little insights and perceptions as to how white the dawn was or how cold the icy water was, with the idea in mind of getting a surprising, fresh little short-sentenced, maybe haiku-like image out of it, or at least being accurate as a newspaper—the prose should be as well-written as newspaper prose, at least, in giving the facts—but rarely with the knowledge that it was a sentence which could be spoken aloud, and rarely with the knowledge that it was a sentence which should be in total vernacular spoken aloud, and also rarely with the knowledge that total vernacular spoken aloud has a sound quality. . . . In addition to being pictorial prose, it is also an object of pure sound, and a construction of pure sound, like a mantra, or like with Milton:

> . . . Him the Almighty Power
> Hurl'd headlong flaming from th' Ethereal Sky
> With hideous ruin and combustion down
> To bottomless perdition, there to dwell
> In Adamantine Chains and penal Fire,
> Who durst defy th' Omnipotent to arms.

Kerouac was a regular style prose writer writing in the forms of Thomas Wolfe; that is to say, long, symphonic-sentenced, heavy-voweled periods, a little with echo of Milton. Wolfe had that same Biblical Miltonic prose echo in his sentences, and in a book called *The Town and the City* written in the late forties by Kerouac there are similar lengthily constructed sentences.

So Kerouac was the first writer I ever met who heard his own writing, who listened to his own sentences as if they were musical, rhythmical constructions, and who could follow the sequence of sentences that make up the paragraph as if he were listening to a little jazz riff, a complete chorus, say of "Lady Be Good," by the then-hero of saxophone, Lester Young, or a later hero of alto, Charlie Parker. So he found a rhythmic model, listening to their rhythms, the rhythm of Lester Young's saxophone sentences or paragraphs in his choruses of "Lester Leaps In" or any one of a number of—at that time—celebrated jazz classic records (which are still very listenable, if anybody has the historic ear to know them).

And he would model sentences on the choruses, on the particular squiggly little "dadadadadadaduhdada"—"As I was goin' walkin' down to Larimer" of "Lester Leaps In" is "dadada dadadada dadada, dadadadadadada dadada, dadadadada dada dadada, dadaadadaydyadadda." So it was a definite rhythmical squiggle that he was hearing when he was writing his prose sentences, a funny body rhythm, a breathing rhythm and a speech rhythm that he was conscious of writing when he was writing prose. So he added a dimension to prose which most prosateurs have not yet actually discovered exists or is necessary for epic or historical prose.

Kerouac got to be a great poet on that basis, 'cause he could hear American speech, and he could hear it in musical sequence. He has a book called *Mexico City Blues*—poem choruses, one page apiece, on Buddhist themes, generally, like a little subject rolling from one chorus to the next, one page to another and he would get to funny little rhythmic constructions like

> The Eagle on the Pass,
>   the Wire on the Rail,
>   the High Hot Iron
>   of my heart,
> The Blazing Chickaball
>   Whap-by

Extry special Super
High Job
Ole 169 be
floundering
Down to Kill Roy

Kill Roy (Gilroy, California) being the end of the Southern Pacific line, where the Southern Pacific finishes in the South. "The Blazing Chickaball/ Whap-by/Extry special Super/High Job/Ole 169 be/floundering/ Down to Kill Roy."

And so he would write prose paragraphs and prose sentences that way, in his own speech rhythms, in chosen American speech rhythms. If you don't write your own prose out as part of your own body rhythm, some actual rhythm from real speech, as some really spoken tale as might be spoken by Homer or any old taleteller, you wind up with an impersonal prose, a prose that doesn't proceed from anybody, and thus a kind of bureaucratic prose or a fictional prose that comes from an assignment, an assignment to make money, or a publishing company, or a magazine; you wind up with an hallucination of prose, rather than an actual piece of prose as it issues from the human body.

In other words you can wind up with prose which is a lie, which doesn't represent anything you or anybody else or any human body actually thinks, but only represents a style of prose that is commercially viable or written in a marketplace of plastic political artifacts. All you have to do is look at Nixon's prose style as "prose style" to realize that it does not proceed from his physical body, but proceeds from a composite of information-serving bureaucrats—not personal, not representing any individual human spirit as manifested in a single body.

That's a digression. The main point I was trying to make was that there is a tradition of prose in America, including Thomas Wolfe and going through Kerouac, which is personal, in which the prose sentence is completely personal, comes from the writer's own person—his person defined as his body, his breathing rhythm, his actual talk. And the word *person* there I'm taking from the context of Walt Whitman, who talks about "What we need is large conscious American Persons," as distinct from objects, or citizens, or subjects, or ciphers, or nonentities, or marketing-research digits.

Kerouac then got more and more personal in his prose, and finally decided that he would write big books without even having a plot, but just write what was going on, without like an "impersonally" constructed plot, impersonal to his life. He would just write a book in his own persona, as if he were telling his best friend the story of what they did together in a five-year period of running around the country in automobiles.

So he wrote a long book called *On the Road,* and his project was to sit down, using a single piece of paper, like a teletype roll that he got from the United Press office in New York (which is like hundreds and hundreds of feet) and sit down and type away as fast he could everything he always thought of, going chronologically, about a series of cross-country automobile trips he and a couple buddies took, with all their girls, and the grass they were smokin' in '48-'49-'50 and the peyote they were eating then, and the motel traveling salesmen they met, the small-town redneck gas station attendants they stole gas from, the small-town lonely waitresses they seduced, the confusions they went through, and the visionary benzedrine hallucinations they had from driving a long time on benzedrine, several days, until they began getting visions of shrouded strangers along the road saying "Woe on America," and disappearing, flitting like phantoms.

So what he did was try to write it all out, as fast as it came to his mind, all the associations; the style being as if he were telling a tale, excitedly, all night long, staying up all night with his best friend. The prose style being modeled on two buddies telling each other their most intimate secrets excitedly, the long confessional of everything that happened, with every detail, every cunt-hair in the grass included, every tiny eyeball flick of orange neon flashed past in Chicago by the bus station included—in other words, all the back-of-the brain imagery, which would require, then, sentences that did not necessarily follow exact classic-type syntactical order, but which allowed for interruption with dashes—allowed for the sentences to break in half, take another direction (with parentheses that might go on for paragraphs)—allowed for individual sentences that might not come to their period except after several pages of self-reminiscence, interruption and piling-on of detail, so that what you arrived at was a sort of stream of consciousness, except visioned around a specific subject (the tale of the road being told) and a specific viewpoint, a personal viewpoint, that is, two buddies talking to each other late at night—maybe high on benny or else beer, or just smokin' together—but meeting and recognizing each other like Dostoyevsky characters and telling each other the tale of their childhood or . . .

But then Kerouac finished the book, which was not published for almost a decade after it was finished, and was dissatisfied because he had tied his mind down to fixing it in strictly chronological account. He'd tied his mind down to chronology, and so he was always halting his sentences and stopping to go back to keep it chronological so that if an orange neon light from Chicago intruded on a purple martini glass in neon over a Denver bar ten years earlier, he included the purple neon Denver bar martini glass though he was still trying to keep it up chronologically and tell what happened in Chicago.

So he decided to write another book, which has never been published, his greatest book, called *Visions of Cody,** which deals with the same main character in about five hundred pages. But called *Visions of Cody,* meaning instead of doing it chronologically, do it in sequence, as recollection of the most beautiful, epiphanous moments. Visionary moments being the structure of the novel—in other words each section or chapter being a specific epiphanous heartrending moment no matter where it fell in time, and then going to the center of that moment, the specific physical description of what was happening. One, in particular: two guys taking a piss next to each other in a bar in Denver and having a long conversation and one says to the other "I love you." Which was like one tender moment between them of a real frank meeting of feelings. A second moment being both of them in Mexico and one taking the car leaving the other guy sick, to get home hitchhiking, 'cause there wasn't enough money and Kerouac had to go home and see his mama. So that was the second epiphany. A third epiphany was the main hero with his wife and children in California with his wife yellin' at him, saying that he's a creep, he's always running away, like he's never at home when the wife needs him, when the children need him, that he's always bringing chicks back to fuck in the attic, and he's always smokin' grass and that all the men runnin'

Visions of Cody has now been published by McGraw-Hill (1973), with introduction by AG.

around together are puttin' women down, and so tearing him apart, with neighbor wife girl friends in, all of them finally attacking the guy who was originally the hero of the book. And him going out alone, totally torn down.

But then as he was trying to write out of his present conscious-ness about the epiphany remembered, and as the prose became more and more elongated, he found that after a while his present consciousness of language would obtrude over even the epiphany subject matter: the subject matter itself would begin disappearing, and that he would hear the babble of language in his head, sometimes associated with the epiphany, and some-times taking off from it and going into, like, Bach fugues of language rhythm without any kind of reference, necessarily, just syllable after syllable, "ogmogageddablab, sabadabuv" but still maintaining the same "Whap-by/Extry special" language, "bop-googlemop" part of it, so continuing into one pure syllabic "mop mop mop" after another. So then that novel continues with a hundred pages of pure sound as prose. Then the exact transcrip-tion of taped conversations many nights between him and hero . . . then it goes into a "heavenly imitation" of the tape, then the prose reconstructs itself and comes back to narrative form and describes a scene with the wife yelling at the husband in the end. And that goes on for two hundred pages or so, or a hundred pages, and I think at the end—I haven't read it for many years, I read it in '55—at the end, there's sumpin' that really impressed Robert Duncan, who also saw the novel in the early fifties, 'cause it ends with the hero going out alone, walking past his car by a gas station downtown San Francisco, going out for a pack of beer, I guess, and as he goes out he sees the flash on the highly polished fender of his car of a barber shop mirror, mirrored in the fender of the car, the mirror in the barber shop window mirroring the neon light of a purple martini glass and an orange light from a supermarket across the street, plus a star I guess enters in, or a moon, curved on the fender so making it odd shapes, illusory shapes, and suddenly has like a moment of realization that all nature around him is a total illusory mirror within mirror within mirror, bent out of shape, which he's perceiving, and so Kerouac has a fifty-page description of the contents of the visual imagery on the fender of the automobile. And Duncan, when he saw that, said, like, "He must be a great genius—he's the only one I know who could write fifty pages on what a polished automobile fender looks like, and have it all make sense."

Q: Did you read all of that book as sounds?

AG: Oh yeah, aloud, lot of it. Yeah, it's beautiful. Sound is a physical thing that you can play with, if you're interested in sounds, if you're interested in music.

Q: Why hasn't this book of Kerouac's been published?

AG: Oh, I don't know; there was only one copy of it around. After *On the Road* came out he probably should have published that but his editor, Malcolm Cowley—the great litterateur, friend of Hart Crane and novelists of the twenties and thirties—said "Jack, why don't you write a sort of nice, simple-sentenced book so people can understand your ideas, you know, so it won't be so confusing to people reading it, you know, something for people to appreciate you. You're well-known now, your book will be out, but why don't you write something with short sentences?" So Kerouac took it as a challenge and did write a great little classic called *Dharma Bums,* with short sentences, like haikus, actually.

Thus this longer, more extraordinary piece of prose visions makes the breakthrough for Kerouac's development just as Gertrude Stein's great prose experiment, *The Making of Americans,* stands for her. A thousand pages of insane consciousness babble. I don't know if you know that text. Does anybody know of *The Making of Americans* by Gertrude Stein?* That's actually I think one of the great prose masterpieces of the century. Stein had intentions very similar to those I've ascribed to Kerouac—she was a student of William James at Harvard, a student of consciousness, a psychedelic expert, so to speak, to join it to a familiar reference point for you; she was interested in modalities of consciousness, and she was interested in art as articulation of different modalities of consciousness, and she was interested in prose composition as a form of meditation, like yoga.

And, like yoga, she was interested in the language as pure prayer-meditation, removed perhaps even from its associations.

---

*The only complete version of *The Making of Americans* published in the United States comes from Dick Higgins's Something Else Press (New York: 1966).

To give an example (if this is too abstract and complicated an idea), like Alfred, Lord Tennyson, in order to get himself in an hypnotic state would repeat the name "Alfred Lord Tennyson; Alfred Lord Tennyson; Alfred Lord Tennyson; Alfred Lord Tennyson; Alfred Lord Tennyson; Alfred Lord Tennyson; Alfred Lord Tennyson; Alfred Lord Tennyson; Alfred Lord Tennyson; Alfred Lord Tennyson; Alfred Lord Tennyson; Alfred Lord Tennyson; Alfred Lord Tennyson," until the sounds no longer had any association but were just pure sounds in a spacious physical universe, and he would get into a funny kind of ecstatic egoless state that way.

So Gertrude Stein was interested in using prose in the same way, that it both have a meaning and at the same time be completely removed from meaning and just become pure rhythmic structures pronounceable aloud. If you ever get a chance, you can listen to a record she made on Caedmon reciting some little prose compositions about Matisse and Picasso where she has little things like "Napoleon ate ice cream on Elba. Napoleon ate Elba on ice cream. Napoleon ate ice on Elba cream. Napoleon ate on cream Elba ice. On Napoleon ice ate cream Elba. On Elba ate Napoleon ice cream. Ice cream ate Napoleon on Elba." Little formulas that go round, round the world, which is how she arrived at her famous statement which as you all know is "A rose is a rose is a rose." That's the end of long, long pages of circular prose that exhausts the word *rose* in many different syntactical combinations.

Her great book, *The Making of Americans,* is an examination of the consciousness of one single family. Very few people have read it through, including me—I haven't. I've read, you know, page upon page of it, and read aloud it's really exquisite.

Q: Is that the only way you read fiction—aloud?

AG: No, no, not the *only* way, but what I'm pointing to is that that's a dimension of prose that during a very short period of human history was ignored entirely. In other words, originally, before there was writing, tales, epics, and stories were told aloud. The Australian aborigines, for example, have the most complex system of epics, 'cause they don't have regular writing—it's all mnemonic devices, and they have very, very complicated rituals in their heads which they pronounce aloud, you know. Long things, thousands of pages, if they were measured by pages.

Homer was not written down, originally, remember. The novel never did come out basically until the printing press. And the kind of prose that we're used to now, which is not even spoken aloud but which is read silently by the eye-page mind, is only a McLuhanite excrescence of our immediate civilization, which may not last very long, anyway—they say it's not going to last beyond the next thirty years anyhoo. So if you're preparing immortal, deathless prose you'd better pay attention to the sounds, because it's something that will have to be sounded aloud in memory as well as be able to be printed.

Unless you assume that all that machinery and printing press and electricity is going to survive the century—which it may or may not. But in any case, if it exists within the dimension of sound as well as on the page, you're sure you've got more backbone to it, and you're sure that it's more real.

I'm interested in prose which can be read aloud, which is real speech, speech which is speakable,—not too removed from sumpin' that somebody would say for real.

Q: On these fifty pages, in *Visions of Cody* where it's primarily audible——

AG: Auditory—yes.

Q: Auditory—something like music—is there anything like a Joycean element?

AG: Yes, of course there are themes that emerge. I mean you couldn't possibly write fifty pages of babble without having your obsessional themes emerge anyway. You'd have to be some sort of strange genius like Gertrude Stein to finally remove *all* association from the language. She made experiments in trying to do that; she never could, quite. She got so much into it that she was really trying to refine it to a point where there *was* no association—just like painters, you know, making an abstract painting, so making an abstract sound pattern. It's pretty hard to remove meaning. You'd have to be a super prose yogi to do that—have to practice for years before you could really get rid of the meaning. You can do it superficially, you know, like a jock Greek joke, some little funny composition. Usually if you assign people to write something that has no meaning you'll find that instead they write something which has all sorts of weird *double entendres.*

But no, I think it wasn't that Kerouac couldn't do the same thing with regular meaning prose; it was that he was suddenly aware of the sound of language, and got swimming in the seas of sound, got lost swimming in the seas of sound, and guided his intellect on sound rather than on dictionary associations with the meanings of the sounds. In other words, another kind of intelligence—still consciousness, still reasonable, but another kind of reason, a reason founded on sounds rather than a reason founded on conceptual associations. If you can use the word reason for that. Or a "modality of consciousness."

4

Poetic Breath, and Pound's Usura

MODERN POETRY CLASSES: UNIVERSITY OF WYOMING
Laramie, Wyoming
April 26, 1971

AG: A tendency of nineteenth-century verse forms (as practiced in the twentieth century) was to flatten everything out into metronomic regularity, so you could read a poem almost tonelessly without any affect, without any difference in tone of the voice:

> Tell me not, in mournful numbers,
>   Life is but an empty dream!
> For the soul is dead that slumbers,
>   And things are not what they seem.
> Life is real! Life is earnest!*

You could actually read it out mechanically.

I think Charles Olson's verse allows a certain amount of improvisation but gives you the breathing to start with—the page arrangement tells you where you can breathe. Or gives you a paradigm—the way the poem's laid out on the page is a paradigm for the breathing rhythm. Or at least that's the way I do it. Though I've learned it more from Kerouac than Olson.

The way Olson cuts the line is the way he's waving his finger, breathing, sort of. So that's what I understand of projective verse: the lines are scattered out on the page pretty much the way you would break them up in your own breaths if you were actually

---

*The beginning of Longfellow's "A Psalm of Life."

161

pronouncing them aloud. They were written to be spoken. As if they were actually spoken. You could score the poem on the page to give an indication of what rhythm you'd be using, what phrases would be all in one breath, and what phrases would be in sort breaths; what single words like "O" might be all by themselves in single breaths taking all that weight and time. The breath of the poet ideally is reproduced by the breathing of the reader.

What I mean is, "form is always an extension of content."* Say your content is the emotion "Uuuuh, u^{uu}uh uuuuuuuuuuuuaah," say that was the general content of what you had to say affectively, reducing it to pure affective sigh:

> O!
> That the earth
> Had to be given to you
> This way.

Then how would that be broken up on a page, with what breaths, how many words would you pronounce at one time, in other words in what rhythm would you lay it out? I think it's scored in broken breaths
"O!/ That the earth/ Had to be/ Given to you/ This way."**

Q: Are you suggesting that Olson has been some influence on you?

AG: Oh, yeah, sure, I knew him well—I carried his coffin to the grave! Heavyweight influence, yes.

Q: How do you handle the sound in one of those lines [Olson's]—is there any way to signal a variety of pitch on the page?

AG: No, I don't know of any way to actually do that. Have you ever heard Olson recite live or on tape? He didn't have too much

---

*In his "Projective Verse" essay Olson credits Robert Creeley with the formulation "FORM IS NEVER MORE THAN AN EXTENSION OF CONTENT."
**O that the Earth
   had to be given to you
   this way!
is Olson's arrangement in "The Death of Europe" in *The Distances* (New York: Grove Press, 1960), pp. 70–71.

up-and-down tone; it was more a forward excitement in his voice, as in "By ear, he sd./ But that which matters, that which insists, that which . . ." Sometimes he would get to a kind of almost Shakespearean dramatic emphasis, of "O! O!/ That the earth . . ." And some of his lines were almost wistful: *"This* way." I don't remember much musical tone variation in his attack as I would have in my own, or as Kerouac had very often.

Kerouac has a brief statement on poetry which is in the appendix of Don Allen's book—a whole bunch of statements by different people on how they were writing, how doing their carpentry, so to speak—how they figured they were going about arranging the page. And Kerouac has very good short statements of less than a page which roughly approximate the projective verse practical suggestions for writing and for scoring on the page, published originally in *Evergreen Review*.[11]

Q: Did this come out before Olson's projective verse essay?

AG: No, but I don't think they were mutually influenced; I don't think they even knew each other's work.

Q: Doesn't Kerouac claim in *The Paris Review* that Olson got the projective verse thing from him?[12]

AG: Yeah, I think. But he was drunk. That is, Kerouac was sick of being lumped as a literary poet together with a bunch of other literary poets working in a "projective" verse form. Kerouac felt that he was just like an American cowboy talkin' cowboy talk or railroad talk. He didn't want a big literary stereotype label on him. When critics were writing about poetics in *The New York Times* or other vulgar common sources they'd be lumping him in—"Among other people practicing projective verse is Jack Kerouac." Well Jack Kerouac was a drunken sailor, chanting at the oceanside.

When was "Projective Verse" first published?

Q: I think 1950, *Poetry New York*.[13]

AG: Uh, huh. Tambimuttu's magazine. But I don't think Kerouac even saw that. Though Kerouac was writing spontaneous poetries around 1950 also. So there was like almost a synchronism —everybody began writing open form. Around '48, actually, I would say, is the time. Because I began writing a Williams-like free verse.

Q: At that time?

AG: Consciously, around '49–'50.

Q: Did you ever see a letter or an address that Williams wrote to the National Council of Arts and Sciences I think around 1950 in which he was describing or prescribing what the new American measure was going to be? In which he focused so much attention on a long line with variable feet.

AG: I remember what he said about the variable foot. But I didn't know what he said about the long line part. Anything Williams writes about prosody usually is interesting, 'cause he's so practical and simple-minded that what he writes makes sense on just a very simple level. The projective verse essay of Olson's is very hifalutin', but very useful, actually, because it does have a lot of practical suggestions for use of typewriter key notes, you know, slash bars and dots and things like that, for scoring time, for giving hints to the reader how to suspend his breath, how long to wait, when to stick it, when to take it up again.

Q: I had the impression, though, in that essay, that Olson neglected or minimized certain things, maybe, that Williams was trying to do with the eye. And while you can find so much in that essay that goes back to earlier Williams essays and to Pound's essays, that particular thing, the eye, sight, vision, as it shows up in a kind of geometric prosody in Williams is kind of bypassed by Olson.

AG: You mean the arrangement on the page? Well, I think Olson was more concerned with how you score on the page the equivalent of your varying conversational excited breathing speech.

Q: Yes, but still it's a visual thing. In other words he's trying to use the imprint of the type on the page to signal what you need to do.

AG: With your breath?

Q: Yeah.

AG: Williams arranged his lines very often somewhat arbitrarily, just sort of, you know, to be a little neat on the page.

Q: Do you think it was arbitrary?

AG: Sometimes. In the beginning. Later on he got more and more involved in having each individual line be a separate breath-poem and with the run-on lines that he has at the end—do you know his later poetry where he has the triadic stanza, like in *The Desert Music?*[14] Has anybody seen any of those poems?

Q: Yes. Did he get that from Mayakovsky?

AG: I wonder. Actually, there are translations of Mayakovsky by Jack Marshall and other people that have similar form. Williams met Mayakovsky and heard him read, in the Village in the twenties. But I don't know if he had seen those translations that had that triplet form.

But the way he explained it was as "variable foot," "a relative measure." Does anybody have an idea why he needed a relative measure or a variable foot?

Q: We haven't gotten into that yet.

AG: You see, basically he was listening to himself talk and listening to other people around him talk, and trying to find a way of putting it down on the page so that he'd be able to take advantage of all the beautiful little rhythms of medical office-kitchen-bathroom-street-grocery speech. So that he could get little squiggly tunes out of what he heard his wife say to the grocer on the telephone: "Bringmenothabottamilk."

Or the poem that's the clearest to propose as an example, the one about the mailman:

Why'n't you bring me
a good letter. One with
lots of money in it.
I could make use of that.
Atta boy! Atta boy!*

So he had a little refrain, or song refrain, like "Atta boy! Atta boy!" coming directly from the street ear, which never was used in poetry before—one never thought that it was poetical to say "Atta boy! Atta boy!" or nobody realized its pretty little rhythm, as they do realize it with Shakespeare, like in "With a hey, and a

*"To Greet a Letter-Carrier."

ho, and a hey nonino," or "With heigh! with, heigh! the thrush and the jay," "The white sheet bleaching on the hedge."

And he's got a beautiful little poem, "Turkey in the Straw,"* in which the speaker says he "kissed her while she pissed." What he was interested in was the *sound,* the *rhythmic* sound, 'cause obviously it's a funny line anyway, but beyond its being an oddly funny human line, it's also like that "Atta boy! Atta boy!"—he "kissed her while she pissed." Dadakadadaka—with that kissed/pissed. So it's like a funny little refrain rhyme like out of the most quotidian, most earthly, most daily language. But what he was looking for—like he has an image of Madame Curie looking for traces of radium in *Paterson*[15]—he was looking for little traces of rhythm, little traces of recurrent rhythmic patterns that could be adapted to his poetry from the talk of everyday.

So his ear was very finely tuned, and he suddenly wondered "Gee, how could you put that into iambic pentameter?" and you obviously couldn't, so what kind of prosody would you have to invent out of your own head and ear and ground and place if you were going to include all those exquisite little rhythms that are pure music, but were never counted as music by the prosodic accountants in the academy. Or by the prosodic accountants who were writing

> Meanwhile, we do no harm, for they
>   That with a God have striven,
> Not caring much for what we say,
>   Take what the God has given,
> Though like waves breaking it may be,
> Or like a changed familiar tree,
> Or like a stairway to the sea,
>   Where down the blind are driven.**

So that's Edward Arlington Robinson just a couple decades before Williams was listening to "I'll kick yuh eye," or "Atta boy! Atta boy!" So like two totally different universes of sound are coming through in American poetics: one echoing a tradition of metronomic pulsations, counting of stresses, that's maybe two hundred years old, really, that iambic pattern, or that kind of

---

*"Turkey in the Straw" appeared only in the first edition of W. C. W.'s *Collected Later Poems.*
**The last stanza of "Eros Turannos."

stress prosody—you know what stress prosody is? It's the kind you learn in grammar school for "Hickory Dickory Dock." It's not really very old, I mean it doesn't go back very far as people assume—the vocal singsong part of it doesn't go back far. Those verse measures arose out of sung music—and then when they stopped using music they had to figure another way to hang a stanza together, so they adapted the old Latin notation of long and short vowels, to make out hard and soft accents, applied not to the vowel length but to stress. Do you know about quantitative prosody at all?

Q: Somewhat, yeah.

AG: Or do you have any notion of what quantitative prosody would be as distinct from qualitative or accentual stress prosody? Ever heard of that at all?

Q[Instructor]: Don't say you haven't heard of it, just say you don't remember having heard of it. I've talked about it.

AG: Have you talked about it in relation to Pound at all?

Q: No.

AG: Why don't we talk about that, because that's something I'm interested in. Pound says somewhere in one of his essays what he thinks will happen with American poetry is that its prosody will settle into "an approximation of classical quantity"—approximation, not exactly the same. So what is classical quantity? *(quotes from memory)*

> Malest, Cornifici, tuo Catullo,
> malest, me hercule, et ei laboriose,
> et magis magis in dies et horas
> quem tu, quod minimum facillimumquest,
> qua solatus es allocutione?
> irascor tibi, sic meos amores?
> Paulum quid lubet allocutionis,
> maestius lacrimus Simonideis.*

So. From what I understand, out of Pound, the Romans were listening to length of vowel, and they had an assigned value

---

*Catullus' *Carmen* (XXXVIII).

(length) for each vowel, half-vowels and full vowels, long and short vowels. "Paulum quid lubet"—the "um" would be long and "Pa" would be short, I guess. I mean I don't know the system, I only know the general idea. "Paulum quid lubet al-locutionis." Some of those vowels are short, some of them are long. So you could count four short vowels and two long vowels, which would make a four-long-vowel line—a line including four half-length vowels and two full-length.

Do you know what I mean by half-length, as distinct from full-length? One that takes a longer time to pronounce. Except that the Latins were supposed to have a regular grammatical scheme wherein certain vowels were assigned half- and certain vowels were assigned full-length. We can only make English approximations. The "a" in the word *half* is just a little half-vowel; the "a" in *fall* is long—a full one. So they would compose lines that would be exactly equal in length, made up of say four short and two long, and that would be like a four-vowel length line, and then the next line might have six short and one long, but that would also be a four-long-voweled line. Am I being clear, or am I being confusing?

Q: No, you're clear.

AG: It's a little abstract, but not *that* abstract. So apparently that's the basis of classical quantitative prosody. Now they were measured as long and short, and later on when the English adapted stress prosody and began counting stress, that is, the weight, the emphasis: "This is the forest primeval, The murmuring pines and the . . ."* they weren't counting the length of the vowel, they were counting the sharpness of the accent on the vowel. But they adapted the classical notation of long and short, and the classical foot. One classical foot would include, like, two long and one short; another, one short and one long. So English poets adapted those poetic feet to stress. In other words they simply took the skeleton of the classical count, and adapted it to stress instead of counting quantity, or length.

Pound thought that that transition reduced or homogenized everything in speech consciousness so that you no longer heard musical vowel tone and so no longer counted affect and no

---

*The first line of Longfellow's *Evangeline*.

longer measured feeling, and you no longer paid attention to the tone leading of the vowels, to the musical sound and length of the vowels (as in Greek and Latin prosody), instead of the accent marks. So that Pound finally began writing a poetry which is kind of musical, based on ō all the time, based on the vowel sounds, like the great section on Usura in *The Cantos.* Do you have that here in any form—probably in *Selected Poems. (Is given copy of book.)*

Incidentally there's a really great recording[16] of Pound reading this, made in 1966 at the Spoleto Theater when Pound was sumpin' like 80. Maybe reissued by Douglas Records, I'm not sure. But it's available and worth getting, and he reads this and others of the *Cantos* including some very late ones. Canto XLV:

> With usura hath no man a house of good stone
> each block cut smooth and well fitting

I don't know if you can hear that as vowels—

> each block cut smooth and well fitting
> that design might cover their face,
> with usura
> hath no man a painted paradise on his church wall
> *harpes et luthes*
> or where virgin receiveth message
> and halo projects from incision.

OK now, "or where virgin receiveth message/ and halo projects from incision" is I think "irgin eiveth essage/ ālo rojects incision"—a funny kind of stately music that comes from paying attention to the sequence of vowel lengths that are roughly equivalent, one line to another.

> with usura
> seeth no man Gonzaga his heirs and his concubines
> no picture is made to endure nor to live with
> but it is made to sell and sell quickly
> with usura, sin against nature,

(This is for the macrobiotic conscious folk—you know, with usura, with bread which is made to make money instead of to eat.)

with usura, sin against nature,
is thy bread ever more of stale rags
is thy bread dry as paper
with no mountain wheat, no strong flour

(Just as vowels, it's interesting)

no mountain wheat, no strong flour
with usura the line grows thick
with usura is no clear demarcation

Now if he'd been writing iambic pentameter, he probably would have been trying to fit the words to a preconceived accentual pattern, and he probably would have wound up writing "with usura the line gets thick." Dadadadadadadadada. And certain words in it, like the verb, would have been throwaway words, like "gets," helper words that don't *mean* anything, they're just verbs that show some sort of intransitive action but don't actually portray a picture. Because Pound has his attention focused on the substantiality of each vowel, it means that each vowel *(Allen begins to speak very slowly, as hyphens indicate)* has-to-be-pronounced-as-if-it-hath-meaning. And that means it's got to have meaning, and not be *(pronounces slowly)* bullshit. In other words, if he had said, "with usura the line gets thick," you'd be throwing away *gets*. But he doesn't say that, he says, "with usura the line *grows thick*."

In other words he fills the sound with a meaning because he is paying attention to the fact that the sound is long and real and pronounceable with feeling—therefore it better *mean* something, and can't be just sort of an invisible word like *gets—gets* wouldn't say anything. In that line it's as if he's talking about century after century as people *buy* pictures, as investments, for hanging them, for resale, or paint them for sale rather than paint them for religious purpose, the line becomes less and less delicate, less and less careful, and just becomes, you know, a fast line for a buck: the line *grows thick* as time passes with the growth of the banks, with the growth of capitalism, with the growth of exploitative use of money. This whole usura thing is a summary of his general economic theories and his attack on banks and the abuse of money, an attack which probably makes complete sense to you in other terms—like anybody building a university dormitory in order to make money out of it obviously is going to skimp, and "with usura the walls grow thin, with usura the ceilings grow lower." So he's saying in painting, in mural painting

with usura the line grows thick
with usura is no clear demarcation
and no man can find site for his dwelling.
Stone cutter is kept from his stone
weaver is kept from his loom
WITH USURA
wool comes not to market
sheep bringeth no gain with usura
Usura is a murrain, usura
blunteth the needle in the maid's hand
and stoppeth the spinner's cunning. Pietro Lombardo
came not by usura
Duccio came not by usura
nor Pier della Francesca; Zuan Bellin' not by usura
nor was 'La Calunnia' painted.
Came not by usura Angelico; came not Ambrogio Praedis,
Came no church of cut stone signed: *Adamo me fecit.*
Not by usura St Trophime
Not by usura Saint Hilaire,
Usura rusteth the chisel
It rusteth the craft and the craftsman
It gnaweth the thread in the loom
None learneth to weave gold in her pattern;
Azure hath a canker by usura; cramoisi is unbroidered
Emerald findeth no Memling
Usura slayeth the child in the womb
It stayeth the young man's courting
It hath brought palsey to bed, lyeth
between the young bride and her bridegroom
                    CONTRA NATURAM
They have brought whores for Eleusis
Corpses are set to banquet
at behest of usura.

"Azure hath a canker by usura"—it gives you a lovely stress syncopation. Just as Williams's ear was built on the acute listening to "I'll kick yuh eye," "Atta boy! Atta boy!," (the specifics of his own particular voice-rhythm-and-breathing-vernacular-

Rutherford-New Jersey-talk on which he erected a musical structure in imitation of his own natural music), so Pound shifted his ear, or as he says in the *Cantos*, "to break the pentameter, that was the first heave"[16] of change of consciousness of the century. He was talking of no less than the whole alteration of human consciousness. . . . As Plato wrote, "When the mode [the measure] of music changes, the walls of the city shake." That is, when people's heads change, like with rock, there's a whole change of "body English" and a change in body apprehension, a change in sensory apprehension—and you know, like a sudden realization of the maniacal slant-eyed face of Nixon or something. I mean there's actually a sensory change when there's a rhythmic change . . . a change in apparent sensory phenomena.

"To break the pentameter, that was the first heave." That's somewhere in the *Cantos,* maybe the Pisan Cantos.* I don't know where he got it, entirely, how he got to the study of vowels in music, but he began to study how the medieval minstrels and troubadors arranged their stanzas. They were having the same problem he was: shifting over from the classical language to the vulgar (demotic, or spoken) language. They were shifting from Latin to Provençal French and Spanish local dialects and writing in provincial tongue for the first time, so they had to find a way of measuring the lines in Provençal French. Pound was shifting over from classical English to Provençal American, and trying to write an American language instead of English, as he keeps saying, and Williams especially keeps saying—that it was a shift from English to American. Pound was going through a transition from the old accentual prosody of the last couple hundred years in Britain to something more like idiomatic speech, or as he says, poetry should be at least as well-written as prose.[17] It shouldn't be cornier than prose, as far as being like somebody like oh . . . Walter Benton, or what's that other guy's name?

Q: Rod McKuen.

AG: Rod McKuen, yeah. I mean it shouldn't contain inversions and upside-down vaguenesses. . . .

So. He was going through a transition from one language to another, trying to go from English to American, trying to find

---

*It is a Pisan Canto—LXXXI.

prosody which could actually measure talk so you could get some regular music out of it, and what he settled on, partly from his study of the musicians, originally, was "the tone leading of the vowels." Not merely the length of vowel but also the tone that the vowel was pronounced in. The *tone* that the *vowel* was pronounced in. Because in the Spoleto and Caedmon records of him reading "Usura," there I think is *(varies pitch)* "Usura slayeth the child in the womb," and it's sort of like a musical thing, he's got different notes.

Q: Does he read it pretty much at the tempo you were reading it?

AG: I was exaggerating.

Q: With slowness?

AG: He reads it that slow. It's stately, majestical. There are three recordings that I know of. One is a cranky, splenetic, madhouse version poorly recorded in St. Elizabeth's in the fifties;[18] one is a really great rare recording done at the University of Milan[19] in '57 or '58 just when he'd gotten out of the bughouse and returned, which is absolutely powerful, straight-backed, more like I was reading it; then there's a third reading done in '66 which is the same vowel placement but more whispered, in an old man's voice, like broken Prospero's old man's voice.[20] But the slowness, yeah.

Q: The reason I asked is that the punctuation and the syntax have suggested to me more speed.

AG: No, he reads it slowly. Stately and slow, that's what's so interesting about it.

(A ringing bell brings this class to an end and new students enter while those who can remain. Allen opens with a reference to "With Usura," which leads to discussion of Pound's economic theories.)

AG: In Canto XLV, Pound has just gone through this big exorcism of usury. Now, in the next Canto, he comments and elaborates on it. He goes into incidents and scenes from World War I, people making money on the war; he goes into banking policy in Renaissance Italy. Speaking from the American experience, he says that when a private small group of people get a monopoly on the physical issue of actual money, currency, then corruption enters our *polis*, enters into our government and into the conduct of economic and political affairs.

So he's going back to the old incident we read a little bit about in grammar school and high school, the argument between Jefferson and Hamilton about banks and banking policy. And as I understand it, what he's saying is that banks in America (founded on the policy of the Bank of England defined by Paterson, whom he quotes) control money—instead of the state itself handing out the money, money is actually issued from the banks. It's similar to the oil franchise matter that's being talked about in Alaska now. That oil actually belongs to us, or belongs to Alaska or belongs to the land or to the U.S. or to the Indian state of Alaska. The oil companies give a billion bucks to the state of Alaska to buy a franchise to take the oil out. Now that oil's worth a good deal more than a billion dollars, anyway. So they're paying the politicians of Alaska one billion and getting five–ten billion in return. Sure, they'll have to put in a little more money to get the oil out and hire the technicians, but most of that will be subsidized in another form by the government in any case. So a combine of private hypnotists have manipulated public imagery and contracts and conceptions of public resources for their own benefit.

Now Pound's saying that this happened originally in America with Hamilton and the American banks, and the deal was that Hamilton got together with a claque of people to do the banking and lending money and writing checks and issuing credit, which originally was part of the sovereign power of the federal government—originally only the government had the right to be the bank and to issue money in the form of credit loans, checks, paper.

Now what happened was that Hamilton told all sorts of senators and congressmen that they could be on the boards of trustees of the private monopoly banks if Congress would allow the banks to handle the "difficult" business of issuing credit and money. You know, it was a real *hard job* and it was best for it to be done by people who were specialists in it, and the government was busy doing its own thing, so what they ought to do is to sublet the activity of money lending. So the banks paid the U.S. government at the beginning of the nation a certain amount of money, like a couple million dollars, for the right to form themselves. And they also bribed a whole bunch of people, I think according to Beard, a whole bunch of congressmen and officials—bribed them by putting them on the boards of trustees of the banks. What the banks got in exchange for this outlay was the right to issue (as loans) twenty times as much money in paper as they actually had in real gold backing.

In other words the banks bought the right—they paid a million bucks to the federal government, and they had a million dollars in gold in the basement. By paying that million to the government they bought the right to announce that they actually had a worth of twenty million which they could lend out, and they could even lend it out to the government—which is like the weird part of it.

So what Pound is pointing out is that the whole money system, banking system, is a hallucination, a shell game, and he's explaining the structure of this hallucination and going back historically, because the structure changes from bank reform to bank reform era. It's slightly different now from what it was in Jackson's time, and it was different in Jackson's time from what it was in Hamiltonian times. My conception of it is a general conception, not an exact one, because I don't know how much money was paid to the federal government to buy the franchise.

So the point is the franchise is bought by a group of private monopolists; from then on they own the banking businesses, so in that sense, because they paid the government off one million, and they got a million in the basement, they suddenly, on paper, own eighteen million more than what they started off with. So just like in the twinkling of an eye they've got eighteen million more. I don't have eighteen million more, the government doesn't have eighteen million more, the farmer doesn't have eighteen million more, but this group, this *gang*, this gang of hypnotists has eighteen million dollars.

In what form? They have it in the form that enables them to write a piece of paper saying "I'm as good as money"—a check. In other words I'm a farmer and I need a thousand dollars, so I can go to the bank and get a piece of paper from the bank, a check from the bank worth a thousand dollars. I think that under the federal regulations in the beginning the bank was allowed to keep loaning money out in the ratio of twenty to one—it could loan out in paper twenty times as much as it had in hard gold. And so in a sense it was as if the banks were printing paper money, printing dollars, *because the government backed the bank* and said, "Yes, you've given us this million, therefore you have our government backing, go ahead and do this and lend out money."

That's why you have a quotation from William Paterson on page twenty-seven of the forty-sixth Canto. Paterson founded the Bank of England—the Bank of England was created by the same method of hallucination—and in his prospectus to get money for the initial investment in the bank to pay off the politicians and to have some money in the basement, Paterson said to his prospective investors: the Bank

<u>Hath benefit of interest on all</u>
<u>the moneys which it, the bank, creates out of nothing.</u>

Now this phrase is repeated over and over and over throughout the *Cantos*—is it familiar to those of you who've read them? It mystified me for years; I never really understood what he was talking about, and *why* he thought it was so important, or what it referred to, until I read a book on the Cantos by Clark Emery called *Ideas into Action*,[21] which does explain this whole banking thing.

So that's why Pound keeps saying "Seventeen years on this case," "Nineteen years on this case."* Pound had spent seventeen, nineteen years up to the writing of this Canto—XLVI—in accumulating all the articles and documents and evidence of dirty deals surrounding the original Hamilton deal, and that's why Pound was interested in all the state papers of the Adams family, and why he was particularly interested in Jackson, because Jackson fought the private banks. That was the famous thing about Jackson, being a populist, fighting bankers, and I think trying to take away the bankers' monopoly privileges and return the sovereign power to issue money to the state.

What it boils down to then is that at the present moment, as it stands now, the Federal Reserve System guarantees that any bank presently existing can loan five-to-one. They have an imaginary five times as much money as they actually have, guaranteed or backed or insured by the Federal Reserve System, meaning that actually it's the U.S. government that's really loaning

---

*"Seventeen," "nineteen," or "ninety" "years on this case" appears half a dozen times in Canto XLVI.

that money in the long run, or backing that money. However, the U.S. government, in order to have money to operate when it goes into debt, borrows precisely that same money from the *banks!* And then it also, on top of that, has to pay the banks back in hard money. See, it borrows imaginary money from the banks, which it has allowed the banks to declare "real," and then once the government has it in its hands the bank says "Yup, it's real," and the government has to pay the banks back. But not only pay that imaginary money back in real money but *also* pay interest on it!

5

The Death of Ezra Pound

TALK SHOW: WEBSTER COLLEGE, STATION KDNA
St. Louis, Missouri
November 1, 1972

A conversation revolving on the use of mantra seed syllable AH* being broadcast live on the radio, is interrupted by a professor entering the room to report the death of Ezra Pound.

Q: Have you heard the news?

AG: No.

Q: Ezra Pound died.

AG: AH . . . for Ezra Pound. When did he die?

Q: I don't know. Just heard it on the news—apparently within the last couple of hours.

AG: Rest in peace, Ezra. Beautiful man—he died very peaceful—I'm sure—he died in a state of bodily thinness and grace mentally, I think. He was like Prospero—wise, and a great teacher—and a great guru, and a great silent man at the end. The same silences we had here tonight for a minute he had for days and hours on end, and he wouldn't open his mouth and say anything for the last ten years unless he had sumpin' to say, something sensible and sharp. And then when he opened his mouth he always had something wry, factual.

---

*AH (Tibetan, from Sanskrit) signifies Purification of Speech and Appreciation of Limitless Spaciousness.

179

Q: There's been some dispute recently about an award he received from the American Academy of Arts and Sciences.

AG: It's a bunch of neofascist scholastics attacking Pound—the neoreactionary CIA-mongers attacking Ezra Pound. I----- K------, who's a former editor of *Encounter* magazine when it was being funded by the CIA, and a great advocate of academic law and order, who wrote Harper and Row that they should show their book revealing the CIA involvement with opium traffic in Indochina to the CIA for prior criticism (which must have led to prior restraint before they published it), I----- K------ had the nerve to write *The New York Times* that Pound didn't deserve a prize because he was morally corrupt because he supported fascism. I----- K------ who just signed an ad that he was going to vote for mass murderer Nixon! It's like an immediate karma shot!

Q: What do you think about giving an award to somebody who held the positions that Pound held?

AG: It's irrelevant! If the award is lucky enough to find him, God bless the award. The award needs him—he doesn't need the award. Certainly, give him *all* the awards. It's a shame he didn't get the Nobel and all the other awards at once—he was the greatest poet of the age! Greatest poet of the age . . . Means a great blessing tonight, that he's dead.

Q: What does that mean—greatest poet of the age?

AG: The one poet who heard speech as spoken from the actual body and began to measure it to lines that could be chanted rhythmically without violating human common sense, without going into hysterical fantasy or robotic metronomic repeat, stale-emotioned echo of an earlier culture's forms, the first poet to open up fresh new forms in America after Walt Whitman —certainly the greatest poet since Walt Whitman . . . the man who discovered the manuscripts of Monteverdi in Venetian libraries and brought them out in the twentieth century for us to hear; the man who in his supreme savant investigations of vowels went back to the great musicians of Renaissance times to hear how they heard vowels and set them to music syllable by syllable and so came on the works of Vivaldi also, and brought him forth to public light—

Q: Wrote a book on harmony.

AG: Wrote a book on harmony, wrote an opera on Villon. The book on harmony I don't know.

Q: Well, how about—some Jewish people have reacted very strongly to some of the negative things he said about Jewish people.

AG: Pound told me he felt that the Cantos were "stupidity and ignorance all the way through," and were a failure and a "mess," and that his "greatest stupidity was stupid suburban anti-Semitic prejudice," he thought—as of 1967, when I talked to him. So I told him I thought that since the Cantos were for the first time a single person registering over the course of a lifetime all of his major obsessions and thoughts and the entire rainbow arc of his images and clingings and attachments and discoveries and perceptions, that they were an accurate representation of his mind and so couldn't be thought of in terms of success or failure, but only in terms of the actuality of their representation, and that since for the first time a human being had taken the whole spiritual world of thought through fifty years and followed the thoughts out to the end—so that he built a model of his consciousness over a fifty-year time span—that they were a great human achievement. Mistakes and all, naturally.

Q: Like *Leaves of Grass*, again, isn't it. Like Whitman again, where he did that in making *Leaves of Grass*.

AG: Yes, he did.
  Pound also unmasked or demystified the nature of banks and money and currency; his ideas on the banks and on the hallucinatory role of the banks in distracting everybody from the fact that the money they're issuing as credit really comes from the government because it's backed by the government and the banks couldn't issue it as real credit, paper money, checks—like the government couldn't borrow money from the banks unless the government backed the banks, so the government is borrowing money from its own authority, 'cause the only authority the banks have for lending out money, including money lent to the government, is the fact that the federal government is backing the banks. So Pound demystified that very simple point which has hallucinated people for the last hundred years in America, leading to Abbie Hoffman standing on the balcony overlooking

Wall Street stock market and showering free money down to all these money junkies, matter-habit hookers.

So Pound I think affected many people in many ways, mostly in very revolutionary and charming ways, like Imamu Amiri Baraka probably came a great deal out of Pound with the particularism of his Black revolution. So the net substance and sum of Pound's energy finally comes to mean the liberation of the voice, liberation of the vowel, liberation of conscious attention to language, purification of language, so finally you could say as to Pound's karma, AH.

Q: Do you personally ignore Pound's involvement with fascism, or do you just accept it?

AG: No, I see it as part of character and humour, h-u-m-o-u-r, which is changeable. I think he was, as he pleaded, mentally ill for a while— if you listen to his records, the phonograph records made in St. Elizabeth's, there's a splenetic, irritable voice. Whereas if you listen to the records made by 1958—in Milan, a very rare copy of "With Usura"—and later records at Spoleto in '66, you hear the voice of Prospero himself, whose every third thought is his grave: the fine old man with beautiful manners with the whispering paper-thin voice pronouncing syllable by syllable with great intensity and meaning each thought of the earlier younger man. So he'd come to a resolution of his woes, a rue; like Prospero, he drowned his books and plunged "deeper than did ever plummet sound" his magic wand of Pride, and took unto his counsel silence, broken only by good-humored advisements on rare sensible occasion as when he told me, "Stupidity and ignorance all the way through."

Q: Who was it who said that he was the last American to have lived through the tragedy of Europe?

AG: It sounds like him 'cause after all he died at the age of eighty-six—eighty-seven? And he'd gone to London before World War I and seen the most beautiful men of his generation destroyed by war madness, wrote many elegies about the "Charm, smiling at the good mouth,/Quick eyes gone under earth's lid," so he did remember World War I and he knew stories of the Civil War from his grandfathers in Idaho and Philadelphia, and he was also in Europe during the Second

World War and in between the wars, and then all through the postwar generation.

I had the honor of smoking a stick of grass at his house on his eighty-second birthday and singing Hare Krishna to him with that harmonium I used tonight, and bringing him the first album of *Sergeant Pepper* by the Beatles that he ever heard, and bringing him Dylan—I spent an afternoon playing Dylan and *Sergeant Pepper* and Donovan's "Sunshine Superman."

Q: How'd he like it?

AG: Well, he didn't say anything, he just sat there with a wry smile occasionally playing around his lips. But I asked Olga Rudge what he thought—you know, did he like it—and she said, "Well, if he didn't like it he would have gotten up and left the room!" So he sat through about two hours of Dylan and the Beatles, so he heard that at least. That was nice. Patient man.

I first met him in a theater at Spoleto, at an opera. I came in and he was downstairs seated in the orchestra and I was up in a box in the balcony, so I went downstairs before *The Magic Flute* began and stood by his seat and took his hand and he stood up and stared at me and I stared at him and then we just stood there and stared at each other for a long time, very quietly and calmly, neither of us having to say anything. And then he was still standing there—just standing there—so I put my hand on his neck to ease him down. 'Cause I didn't know if he knew whether to sit down or not and I was unsure of myself so I thought I'd make a gesture, touch him, let him get off his feet again.

Then I went to see him in Rapallo where he'd lived in the twenties with Yeats and came up with the harmonium to a high hilltop where he had a small modest house which overlooked great blasts of blue Mediterranean spaciness and shore, and sat under a tree outside in a wooden chair and sang Hare Krishna mantra to him and Hari Om Namo Shivaye and Gopala Gopala Devaki Nandana Gopala mantras and then we went in to lunch and Olga Rudge—he hadn't said anything—said, "Ezra, why don't you ask Mr. Ginsberg if he wants to wash his hands," so he said, "She says, would you like to wash your hands." And then he didn't say anything more that whole afternoon, except one time, when I talked about a visit with Burroughs in 1958 to Louis Ferdinand Céline, who I thought was the greatest French prose writer. And I'd asked Céline whom he liked among French prosateurs and he said C. F. Ramuz, Swiss writer, and Henri Barbusse, who wrote *Sur le Feu* (*Under Fire*, World War I) and Barbusse, he said, had jazzed up the French language some and so had Paul Morand, whose book name I had forgotten in telling Pound the story, and Olga said, "Ezra, what was the name of that book by Morand you liked so much—you didn't like his later work but you liked that." And he'd been spooning up spaghetti and he lifted his face and said, *"Ouvert la Nuit"* and he finished eating his spaghetti. That book was from 1928 or so—so his mind was very crisp, and funny. And then he didn't say anything more all day. We went off to Portofino and just sat in the sunlight at a café table at the wharf by docks and fishermen's nets and I babbled on and on, whatever I had to say, whenever I thought of sumpin', and then shut up for a while, just keeping silence like meditation silence, and I kept thinking it was like being with Prospero, it was a pleasure. There was no weight in the silence—there was lots of room, there was no need for anxiety about it. It was like silence of the Indian mouni, holy men who have taken a vow of silence, like Meher Baba did—there was a Baba-esque quality to his silence.

And then several months later visited in Venice in Calle San Gregorio where he stayed with Olga Rudge next to the Pensione Cici where he ate maybe every other day and picked up his mail and saw some few people. So I spent three weeks there reading through all the Cantos and a very good book on Pound called *Ideas into Action* by Clark Emery, University of Miami Press, Coral Gables, Florida—the best description of the Cantos that I know. Best analysis, explanations—makes it easy to understand his theories of history and banking.

I used the Pisan Cantos as a guidebook to Venice: "and in the font to the right as you enter/ are all the gold domes of San Marco." So I went to San Marco Church and looked for a font to the right which I found, but there was no water in it and the gold domes of San Marco didn't shine therein. So I went back to him after several days in which he didn't talk at all and said, "I went and couldn't find the gold domes shining in the font to the right." And he suddenly opened his mouth and said, "Ah, that was many years ago. Since then they've put a copper runnel around the baptismal font and filled that with water so there's no longer water in the center to reflect the gold domes." And he didn't say anything more—until I had another specific question: "Where was Salviati's?" "Up the street, the glass manufacturing place." And then the conversation about stupidity and ignorance all the way through and the Cantos being a mess. So actually a quite humble person by then. I told him about acid, and a little about grass, and asked him if I was making sense to him and he said, "Well, you seem to know what you're talking about." I asked him if he'd received Basil Bunting's *Briggflats* and he didn't say anything but a great broad smile passed over his face—he really smiled, like a Crumb cartoon character smiling—and nodded. Basil Bunting being a great fellow poet who lived with him in Rapallo and with Yeats in the twenties and who'd come out of retirement with a great epic long poem, thirty pages, *Briggflats*.

Q: He's a British poet from the north——

AG: Yeah, from Newcastle, Northumbria, who taught Pound the great lesson "Dichten = condensare,"—poetics is condensation, compression of thought. Pound said "Bunting once told me my poetry referred too much and presented too little." So I said, "Well, I saw Bunting last month in New York and he said, 'Read Pound if you want hard, condensed exact precision in language.'"

The difference between presentation and reference is an interesting distinction. Reference—which he does do a good deal—is like referring to the situation without describing it, without presenting the facts—so that a later generation won't be able to figure out what you're talking about. Like, "That man in the White House" or sumpin'—all the abstract hatred laid down on Nixon as on Johnson before him, without the particular form that it attends.

Q: Which of the Cantos stands out in your mind right now?

AG: The last great Canto—

> The scientists are in terror
>   and the European mind stops
> Wyndham Lewis chose blindness
>   rather than have his mind stop. . . .
> When one's friends hate each other
>   how can there be peace in the world?
> Their asperities diverted me in my green time. . . .

Time, space,
    neither life nor death is the answer
And of man seeking good,
      doing evil.
In meiner Heimat
    where the dead walked
      and the living were made of cardboard.

"In meiner Heimat," in my homeland—America—"where the dead walked/ and the living were made of cardboard." The most beautiful piece of his writing, and done in his old age. As he was being constantly attacked.

Q: Beautiful thing, it really is.

AG: Great despairing end, yes. He wrote that I think around 1955 or '60, perhaps. It was published in drafts and fragments of the final Cantos. It's so elegant, though, when he says, "When one's friends hate each other/ how can there be peace in the world?" Very Chinese, probably a paraphrase of Confucius, really. And then there's a very funny leap there for an old man—it's a very abstract line: "Time, space,/ neither life nor death is the answer." So death is not the answer either.

Q: He sounds like Lear, almost.

AG: Well, he sounds like Chuang-Tzu, he sounds like Buddha. He sounds like some Chinese philosopher of the void.

Q: But he constantly rejected the Taoists.

AG: No, he took a Taoist position, basically, or Confucian position. He accepted certain Taoist elements, but he was against religious flattery and incense-burning, I think, against dead ritual. And the incense-burning cult of the eleventh century or so was I think one of his favorite whipping boys. But he was a pragmatic mysticist—he was interested in Eregina, apparently, and Duns Scotus and people like that—Plotinus, I guess. There's a line to Eliot:

"mi-hine eyes hev"
        well yes they *have*
seen a good deal of it
   there is a good deal to be seen
fairly tough and unblastable

It's in the Cantos.

See if I can remember any other incidents of that conversation with Pound. I sang him the St. Francis Canticle of All Creatures which I was trying to figure out how to vocalize 'cause it was a song and St. Francis probably sang it. So I sang it to a C chord, monochordal.

I asked him for a blessing for Sheri Martinelli who was an old girl friend of his when he was in St. Elizabeth's and had suffered many years his absence. And so he finally smiled and nodded, "Yes," which brought tears to Sheri Martinelli's eyes on the Pacific Ocean edge a year later, '68.

Told him that the younger poets all learned from him, all derived from him, and were in a sense developing forms that he opened up. And he said, "That's very flattering, but would be very difficult to prove or substantiate."

NOTES

1. ADVICE TO YOUTH

1. For Allen's most thorough discussion of his Blake epiphanies, see his interview in *Writers at Work: The Paris Review Interviews*, Third Series (New York: The Viking Press), pp. 301–317. See also the "Eternity" chapter of this work.

2. Robert Duncan, *The First Decade* (London, Fulcrum Press, 1968) includes "The Venice Poem" (pp. 81–107) and "Medieval Scenes" (pp. 51–63).

2. EARLY POETIC COMMUNITY

3. Donald M. Allen, ed., *The New American Poetry* (New York: Grove Press, 1960).

4. W. H. Auden included Robert's "The Reaper" and "Hero Song" (pp. 299–301) in *The Criterion Book of Modern American Verse* (New York: Criterion Books, 1956). Published in England as *The Faber Book of Modern American Verse* (London: Faber and Faber Limited, 1956).

5. In *Poetry New York*, 3 (1950), pp. 13–22. Reprinted as separate volume *Projective Verse* (New York: Totem, 1959); included in Robert Creeley, ed., *Selected Writings of Charles Olson* (New York: New Directions, 1966), pp. 15–26, and in Donald M. Allen, ed., *The New American Poetry* (New York: Grove Press, 1960) pp. 386–397.

6. Allen's music to "A Western Ballad" (as well as the entire poem) appears on pp. 12–13 of *The Gates of Wrath* (Bolinas, California: Grey Fox Press, 1972).

7. Kerouac mentions adding "alluvials to the end of your line when all is exhausted but something has to be said for some specified irrational reason" on page 414 of the Don Allen anthology, but specifically lists *"no revisions* (except obvious rational mistakes. . . .)" [his italics] in "Essentials of Spontaneous Prose," *Evergreen Review*, Summer 1958, p. 73.

8. For the charming "The Instruction Manual," see either the Don Allen anthology, or pp. 14–18 of Ashberry's *Some Trees* (New York: Corinth Books, 1970).

9. See pp. 34–63 of Ashberry's *Rivers and Mountains* (New York: Holt, Rinehart and Winston, 1966).

10. "The Venice Poem" can be found on pp. 41–77 of Robert Duncan's *Selected Poems* (San Francisco: City Lights, 1959) as well as in *The First Decade* (note 2).

3. POETIC BREATH, AND POUND'S USURA

11. Kerouac's "Essentials of Spontaneous Prose" appeared in *Evergreen Review*, Summer 1958, pp. 72–73, where on "Method" he writes:

> No methods separating sentence-structures already arbitrarily riddled by false colons and timid usually needless commas—but the vigorous space dash separating rhetorical breathing (as jazz musician drawing breath between outblown phrases)—"measured pauses which are the essentials of our speech"—"divisions of the *sounds* we hear"—"time and how to note it down." (William Carlos Williams)

On page 414 in the "Statements on Poetics" appendix in the Don Allen anthology Kerouac writes:

> The rhythm of how you decide to 'rush' yr statement determines the rhythm of the poem, whether it is a poem in verse-separated lines, or an endless one-line poem called prose. . . .

12. Kerouac says in his interview in *Paris Review* 43, p. 83: "I formulated the theory of breath as measure, in prose and verse, never mind what Olson, Charles Olson says. I formulated that theory in 1953 at the request of Burroughs and Ginsberg."

13. See note 5 ("Early Poetic Community").

14. William Carlos Williams' *The Desert Music and Other Poems* (New York: Random House, 1954).

15. See Part II, Book Four of William Carlos Williams' *Paterson* (New York: New Directions, 1963), pp. 201–213.

16. Canto LXXXI. 1. 53, "The Pisan Cantos," p. 96 in the New Directions 1956 edition.

17. See pp. 96–97 of Ezra Pound's *ABC of Reading* (New York: New Directions, 1960).

18. *Ezra Pound Reading*, Caedmon, 2-vol., TC-1122-A&B; TC-1155-A&B.

19. Pound, Ezra. Canto XLV (con Usura) scrittori su nastro, II, Interfacoltà dell'Università degli Studi di Milano E.P.I.U. 6001333, 1967.

20. C.M.S. 619—*The World's Great Poets Vol. III*, "Ezra Pound reading Cantos III, XVI, XLIX, LXXI, XCII, CVI, CXV." C.M.S. Records, Inc., 14 Warren Street, New York 10007, 1971.

21. Clark Emery, *Ideas into Action* (Coral Gables: University of Miami Press, 1958).

IV

The Scholars of War

What can Poetry do, how flowers survive, how man see
    right mind multitude, hear his heart's music, feel cock-
    joys, taste
ancient natural grain–bread and sweet vegetables, smell his
    own baby body's tender neck skin
when 60% State Money goes to heaven on gas clouds burning
    off War Machine Smokestacks?
—A.G., ''Friday the Thirteenth''

Allen's talk of undercover agents infiltrating the student body in "War and Peace: Vietnam and Kent State" proved to be more than idle speculation or paranoia naturally, as demonstrated by what came to light a year later. "KSU Undercover Agent Freed; Spends Night in Jail on Firearms Charges," headlined the Kent State student paper on April 26, 1972. Brief excerpts from that article are included at the end of this section.[1]

Three weeks after Kent State we were in Davis, California, for Allen's final reading of the tour. The College of Engineering at U.C.-Davis, a large (14,000 student population), traditionally agri-sci school, offers a class in "Science and Technology," which Allen was asked to address on "Myths Associated with Science."

War and Peace: Vietnam and Kent State

1

WAR AND PEACE CLASS: KENT STATE
April 6, 1971

AG: War and Peace. Therefore I'll begin with a text by William Blake on the subject, called "The Grey Monk." You can interpret "Thy father" as Nixon or Johnson or the government and "My brother" as thy brothers, thy militant brothers.... (*Sings "The Grey Monk" with harmonium.*)

Anybody know that text at all? The line "'But vain the Sword & vain the Bow,/ They never can work War's overthrow,'" is famous. Also, "'The iron hand crush'd the Tyrant's head/ And became a Tyrant in his stead.'" He was talking about the French Revolution. Blake was a friend of Thomas Paine, and they had a Jerry Rubin–Abbie Hoffman talk situation among them. Like they'd meet together, I think at William Godwin's house, and plan revolutions, and the fuzz was after Paine and Blake warned Paine to get out of London just before the local cops arrived, and Paine skipped across the channel to France to take part in the French Revolution.

What have you been talking about here?

Q: We're discussing why in 1971 man is still fighting wars and some of the solutions. Also we have a friend who clinks about every second and entertains us. (*Steam pipes knock very harshly every couple of seconds throughout the class.*)

AG: A poltergeist, steam. So what have you arrived at so far? Is there any practical thing you've come to?

Q: Mostly we just rap.

AG: You have an interesting pragmatic situation here at Kent which you can deal with, I think, to the extent that Kent State is in a sense the center of a vortex of anxiety thought-consciousness about the war. Now war itself is magic, or a manifestation of certain fixed ideas, or habit-patterns, or thought-consciousness. To the extent that war is like smoking, like an old pattern constantly repeating itself, here at Kent you could probably do something to apply theory to practice if you could come up with any kind of praxis to break up the pattern.

Q: I think the main problem here is that people don't know how to go about doing anything, and the people that we have who think they are doing something go off onto ego trips.

AG: Well, since I've been here I keep coming back to the problem of war (which you're discussing) as it is incarnated or articulated in your actual practical immediate situation, which is the mind-war here at Kent, the paranoia, the fear, with everybody cooped up in little tiny boxes on the campus in little dorm rooms, all crowded together and with narcs permeating the whole atmosphere so that everybody's afraid to talk to each other, apparently, which seems part of the syndrome; plus the black-white paranoia which apparently has gotten worse this year, or in the last few months.

Though the main fear thing here that I pick up on, just superficially, was running around through people's rooms last night and being really astounded at how small the rooms on campus were, and how crowded together everybody was. 'Cause I got stuck with my friend Gordon in a little guest room that doesn't, like, leave us room to invite anybody in or fuck anybody, really, without beds creaking over each other's heads, or even to talk to anyone. And then if you added to that the fear that anybody you brought in might be a cop—it could drive anyone mad! Apparently this sense of narc and cop paranoia hasn't been the subject of much public discussion in the newspaper, or even approached, has it? Or is it just sort of an underground comment rather than a public discussion?

Q: I haven't been here long enough to discover cops but I'm aware of that problem.

AG: Well, whether or not one discovers actual cops, the thought-consciousness of cops permeates, so it's a paranoia which is unresolved and which has to be dealt with, you know, like brought to front-brain consciousness and talked out publicly and also resolved publicly, I think. 'Cause in other words freshmen and sophomore kids are afraid to make friends, are afraid to turn on with people, afraid to really talk with anybody, to admit people into their confidence. And that inhibits political cellular organization. Because everybody's suspicious of each other, people don't sit around and converse about their political fantasies, and if they can't express their dreams and fantasies in intimate terms they can't come to practical conclusions about what to do. If you're afraid to just sit around a table and talk in a cafeteria, then I don't see how any kind of democracy can operate, if it ever could, ultimately.

But anyway the practical problem about war and peace on the campus is actually articulated to a great extent in the planning for the May Day rallies, April 24th and the first few days of May. It would be interesting to try and focus or particularize or localize theoretical discussion of war and peace on what gestures or actions could actually practically be taken by yourselves physically, or by the school en masse, during those days.

I went to the May Day meeting here yesterday—did anybody else go, was there anybody here who went to that? Yeah. Did you take part in it, too, talk any?

Q: No, I just observed. I don't think anything was accomplished. There aren't any really intelligent people running the coalition.

AG: Rather than badmouthing everybody, rather than complaining about this and that, what would be really interesting is for everybody to use their minds and try to work out an actual scenario for those days, and to make propositions for what could be done that would be interesting enough to involve the entire community.

Q: Part of the problem, I think, is how we define "memorial."

AG: Yeah. Or if you even want to use that word. In other words, it's how do you define "war" and "peace," too, and how do you find the conditions for cutting the Gordian knot? How were you defining memorial, or how was it being defined for you? Or how were you wanting to define it or change it?

Q: I think it's more than just a community thing. You know like every kid in this country, every person in this country, has an idea of what happened here.

AG: Yeah, but what I keep trying to say is that all these discussions are theoretical and have absolutely no meaning unless you can first define the terms of your theater as you want to propose it. You've got to give the scenario first—*then* you can say it's important to other people.

What the cats who are organizing the scenario already have proposed is a pig roast, which is absolutely unimportant to almost everybody, you know, at this point. What it means, literally, is that you're going to have a fire, and somebody's going to be in charge of roasting a pig, and somebody's going to be with some bongo drums on one side, and there's going to be an isolated group that's trying to make love on a blanket on another side, and then there's going to be twelve people standing, shifting from one foot to another under a tree somewhere else saying, "Yeah, man, we're roasting a pig, we're roasting a pig," and you know, "Fuck the pigs," or something; somebody will have a weak mantra like "fuck the pigs" about three blocks away and then say, "Well, man should we go get a Coke?" But as theater, think of it as theater—it's the most decentralizing, uninteresting . . . in fact the only thing interesting about it is the idea of a pig roast!—the interest consists of the words "a pig roast," but not in the actual action being performed. As such, it's like bad poetry, bad theater, bad politics, bad philosophy . . . or not just bad, but just sort of second-rate, like trite, which it is, because it's a hand-me-down idea, it was somebody else's poem a couple of years ago—it's not a newly invented, fresh-minted, fresh-souled idea. So the problem is, what is there to propose?

What I was setting my head to was the same problem for Washington—everybody gets together, yeah, but what for, to do what? So the problem you've got to solve here is the same problem everybody's got to solve everywhere else, and everybody's going to be solving it in different terms, and all solutions should be particular to the locality that they come from—it's like powers rising out of people here, thoughts rising out of people here, peculiar to Kent, which would have to be different from Seattle, which would have to be different from Washington.

The characteristic flavor of a mass meeting, of the ceremony, of the *occasion,* is peculiar to each *tribe,* to each village. Like in Africa, all different tribes with different geographies have different rituals, you know, like they all use drums, yes, they worship certain gods, yes, but then they do it different ways. And their ways differ, depending on whenever the monsoon or the rains come where they are, or when the planting season is. Here you have a very specific occasion, the death of four people. You also have a specific historical circumstance—a ceremonial a year later, when everybody's sick of the war, and when everybody realizes that most of the nation is against the war, too. You also have Calley overshadowing everybody, in everybody's consciousness, so like one thing I thought of was it would be sort of interesting to invite Calley here to give a speech about the war, because he's been saying some weird things. And a ceremonial here inviting somebody like Calley would really blow everybody's mind upside down, even if he wasn't able to come—just the gesture of inviting him. You also have the parallel deaths at Jackson State which should be perhaps memorialized here, of all places, with some sort of ceremony.

Q: Well, they don't do that here.

AG: Well, *"they"* don't do that here unless somebody organizes to do it as part of the theater. In other words, what theater, what scenario, could be written if people actually turned their minds to the creation, the invention, of a real ritual.

This was a ritual for Washington, and it was only a sketch, it wasn't complete: (Reads "Spring 1971 Anti-War Games." AG's extemporaneous discussions of certain portions are given in brackets.)

SPRING 1971 ANTI-WAR GAMES
I
One Million People
Surrounding Capitol and White House
Uttering Simultaneously
The Weapon/Warning
Mantra that Penetrates Material Illusions
Transforming Five Poisons to
Five Virtues

HŪM! HŪM! HŪM!
HŪM! HŪM! HŪM!

An American Sound
Uncanny as at Cosmic Football—
Tantric Cheerleaders

[Like: Johnny get a rat trap bigger than a cat trap bigger than a mouse trap bang! Cannibals cannibals. Sis boom bah! Central High School Rah Rah Rah! Team! Team! Team! Hūm! Hūm! Hūm!]

II

Anti-War Games
All Wear Blue
Symbolizing Pax Wisdom
(Blue Headbands) (Blue Knowledge)
Blue Dresses, Denims, Hats, Handkerchiefs
U.S. Flags in Blue
& Sing the Blues Everyone

MIRRORS

Carried by all in hand
Wisdom

To Ask America to See
Itself in Blue Mirrors
"Blue Grace in Dark Glasses
Getting out of One Hundred White Cars at Once!"
All Over San Francisco

Clairvoyant View of War Maya/Illusion

[That was like stage-prop mirrors; I don't know if it's even practical, but in other words I was thinking what stage props, what scenario, what actual theater is useful.]

& Blacks Sing Equal Blues to Everyone

[Which would mean perhaps—if it were possible—an old-time New Orleans jazz funeral ceremony for the Jackson State people. In other words, formal, old-fashioned ceremonial acknowledgement for the Jackson dead . . . which should perhaps be organized by the black group here.]

& Carry Water, Sap & Honey
To Eat & Fast & Stay

[This was for Washington, though—assuming that they were going to be sitting in on Washington.]

The Five Virtues

[Because I said Hūm! Hūṇ! Hūṃ!—mantra that penetrates material illusions, transforming five poisons to five virtues.]

Right Knowledge
Mirrorlike Wisdom
Equality
Discriminating Wisdom of One
Perseverance & Good Judgement Unerring Action

[No fuck-up actions, no half-assed pig roasts, you know.]

All Sit Together Man, Woman, Black, Brown
Old with Young

[old with young, inviting the old, inviting the square]

Hip and Square [Because]
75% of Population Are Against the War
[Therefore] Sit In

[Representing a majority, not a minority protest—but an articulation of the *majority* antiwar sentiment. Everybody's behaving and thinking as if they're a minority protest, when despite Kent local appearances, it's really a majority that's against the war. So like the role of either Washington or Kent would be to articulate what the actual majority strength opinion is . . . like the real power of the people to articulate it, assuming it to be so . . . you know, perform that magic hypnosis instead of being hypnotized and saying "Free us slaves," it's like "We hereby free." It's a difference of tone, difference of attitude, and therefore a different kind of theater.]

And Stay [there], Except to Visit Congressmen
And Relatives in Bureaucracy
—Delegations to Newspapers & Radio—
Water Sap & Honey
Springtime Flower Power Manifest
III
Organized to Give Blood for War Wounded
(if useful)

A Million War Casualties
North & South
Vietnam

IV

All Gestures Should Be Done on Earth Park

[From earth platform, rather than concrete platform. Sitting in on earth.]

HŪṂ! HŪṂ! HŪṂ!
Blue Flags & Honey Water
Sit-in Meditation

Sit In on Earth—till War Ends—
Equality

V

Vital Heat of Body's Closeness
Sensitivity Sessions Surrounding the Capitol

[beginning the day. Organized, formal sensitivity sessions in order to build the trust of the day for a large mass to be sitting in and acting together as one large group. I think there are people here who are trained to do that—instead of marshals you get people who know how to organize a touching thing. So one touch one, pairs pair off, and build a large crowd out of small cells—pairs pair off, then pairs to pairs, that's four people, and four confronting four make eight, and doubling, eight confronting eight, sixteen, and slowly, over maybe an hour or two hours' time, testing and feeling each other out and touching each other and building a large, huge mass of people who are all interconnected physically. And I don't think that's ever been done as part of a large political demonstration in order to unify the crowd. But it's something that's now developed sufficiently in public consciousness with enough craftsmen of that mode who could actually make use of that as part of a political mass meeting. So thus]

Hold Hands
A Living Circle
Hands Full of Hands Too Full
To Throw Bombs, Bottles, Cans

VI

What Dangers to Face?
The Five Poisons

I   Stupidity (sloth delusion)—think it's OK on the planet, everything's all right, the war's inevitable or it's invisible, who cares anyway.

[Can't see the police, there's no legal evidence that there's fuzz invading the dorms, therefore forget about it until somebody gets busted—instead of like really asking out loud. Hūṃ Hūṃ Hūṃ.]

II   Anger, the hell world—want to bomb the Capitol, bomb North Vietnam, bomb everybody.
III   Egotism (pride, selfishness)—"I don't wanna lose the war, I don't want to be the first President to lose a war"—Nixon

[At this point it seems to me that disunity on the Left is what's, if anything, keeping the war going, because the Left can't get itself together now finally. So I'm talking about the Left's abandoning its egotism and self-righteousness and getting on with the show, with the show as a show.]

IV   Greed & lust for opium, oil, tungsten in Vietnam, attachment to victory or junk
V   Jealousy (of the military titans, the green generals)

[There are all the poisons to be dealt with. Thus the Buddhist divisions of the five poisons: stupidity, anger, egotism, greed-lust, and jealousy. . . . If you dig the reactions to Calley, it all divides into the classical virtues and vices, really.]

Need Sadhana/Ritual
To End War

Include at Dusk
A. One Solid Hour of Prayer
Every Kind
Every Language
Every Priest
Every Mantra
Every God
Every Form of Meditation

B. And One Solid Hour of Silence—
C. One Solid Hour of HŪṂ HŪṂ HŪṂ

HŪṂ: pronounced like Whom for heart, lips touched together vibrate the ending mmmm briefly.

So what I keep coming back to is mass demonstrations in the form of a ritual to end war. *(Allen chooses a few phrases from the end of the text and discusses them.)*

Including at dusk a solid hour of prayer, every kind, every language, every kind of priest represented in the crowd, every mantra, every god, every image of god, every form of meditation, for an hour, limited—Bam! In other words everybody do that free-form thing.

Plus, a solid hour of passing out paper and letters and writing to newspapers, congressmen, president, just like National Rifle Association does to get results—which is very effective. I was in Washington and they told me that really does control Congress-men. Just as you can see with Calley—everybody was writing in and all of a sudden the whole government freaked out.

There's never been organized pro-peace letter-writing inun-dating local newspapers, for instance. The Birch Society and the National Rifle Association do it, but the Left never tries it. So that might be made part of a formal ritual for one hour: write your congressman for fifteen minutes, your President fifteen minutes, your senator, your newspaper.

A solid hour of total silence: so everybody can really cool down and rest and not have anything to do at the middle of the day, or at the most crucial moment of the day. One hour of real peaceful nuthin!

And maybe one solid hour of a single body sound if everybody could get together on one single sound they could make. Lloyd [McNeill], who was here, the musician, was saying that one way of doing it was one hour open forum pray chant body sound, like the ground rule being that everybody start off on his own sound, seeing if at the end out of the mass people could arrive at one single note. You know, it's a gamble—does anarchy-chaos triumph or do we all come together? I had originally thought of Hūm! Hūm! Hūm! as one sound that everybody could make that wasn't too un-American sounding—more like a Major Hoople or W. C. Fields comic strip sound than any other mantra I know of. But whatever. Aah, Aah *(deep resonant sigh)* is one. AH.

Then I was talking with Robert Duncan, and he suggested that in such ceremonies effigies of the dead are usually carried in procession, and that's something I haven't seen proposed. Lit-eral effigies of Allison Krause and the others of papier mâché, which could be prepared in the arts departments here, and would really be weird. Carried in formal processions in four sections. Such ceremonies, historically, are involved with memorizing the names of the dead, so the names of the dead could perhaps be pronounced en masse instead of or as a mantra. Say like one hundred nine times "Allison Krause," then one hundred nine times for each of the other three, and then go through the same ceremony for the Jackson State dead.

There could be like a giant pantomime acting-out of the shooting, with effigies of the Guard and effigies of the victims. If it's felt that demonic forces are there, represent demonic forces in effigy, to make it more than just a big dreary scary thing.

Q: I was thinking, you know, "power to the people." Well, once people possess the power, what do they do with their power, do they use violence? Well, I'm asking for violence to a certain degree, because violence can make changes.

AG: Umhum. Well, General, are you willing to plan your battle right now? I mean we're planning a battle. OK, now violence is a very generalized word. At what specific point in the day do you want to introduce it, can you fantasize it's being introduced and being useful?

Q: I don't know. I just haven't thought of it.

AG: I'm saying if it is time for a specific, violent military action, then concretize the tendency of thought with some specific action that can be taken. Otherwise it remains in the realm of philosophical fantasy and speculation and classroom discussion.

Q: Well, I'm against that.

AG: Well, you're against it, but I'm proposing specific things to do on May 4th, see? In other words what I'm proposing is a kind of classroom exercise in war and peace that's an interesting exercise because it's something that can be done and acted for real. Rather than having generalized discussion, you could propose a theory and act it out, see if it works. So maybe I'm intruding my own personal obsession at this point, but it's also an obsession that involves this specific campus. And as to whether it should be violent or not, well, maybe it should be violent. If you feel it should be violent, then the problem is to articulate it, like a general, Napoleon, or whoever. What is the battle plan?

I don't think violence is useful at this point, in any case.

Q: You don't think violence is useful at this point?

AG: May 4th? No. So what I'm doing is fantasizing a specific program of ideas.

Q: Well, you see, what I think about violence is that it could bring more change; I mean I think you could open someone's mind to say, "Hey, man, what the fuck is going on—someone wants something, someone is doing something. . . ." Like in Detroit in 1967 when the Blacks were rioting and as a result changes started going down, they started hiring people, giving them jobs.

AG: Well now do you think if the majority of people around Kent State did not want a violent thing but wanted another kind of action that it would be appropriate for anyone planning violence to intrude on the main community thing?

Q: Well, like you said, one solution will not solve the whole problem; therefore we must come from different conditions, and what we have at the end will tell. Like if violence doesn't work, it would be set aside, and at the same time, if some nonviolent thing does work, it'll be there at the end. That's the way I'm looking at it now.

AG: Well, it can't be nonviolent and violent simultaneously because the violence will simply drive away the nonviolent, and everybody'll disappear from the scene, period. Because the majority of people don't want a violent scene and won't come if they think it's gonna be violent, or will disappear immediately—they're not gonna fight together with you. Seventy-five percent of the population will not fight together with you. Maybe 5 percent will, or 3 percent will, at most. General, that's my estimate of your troops.

Q: You think that violence will scare them away?

AG: Absolutely. Anyway, we've already had the violence, and it hasn't changed things for us.

Q: What violence? There was no violence here!

Q: National Guard.

Q: Yeah, right, the National Guard had their violence trip!
(Several students speak at once.)

AG: I think the proposition for violence over the last five years has just prolonged the war, all along, 'cause everybody on the Left hasn't been able to get together and will not be able to get together over the violent thing. So I think it's just prolonging the war, prolonging the killing in Vietnam. The Vietnam War, which involved violent resistance to the West, has wound everybody up, including the Vietnamese, in thirty years of war, and hasn't solved their problem. They've got it worse than ever, with more murder than ever from us. Violence hasn't even worked in Vietnam. What if the North Vietnamese had long ago gotten hip and decided to flood South Vietnam with acid, or something like that? I mean why are we limiting our weapons in this battle, why are they limiting their weapons, why is everybody acting out old roles from nineteenth-century battles?

Q: I think there's something you're overlooking. You say you have 75 percent of the people behind you against the war, but you don't have 75 percent of the people against the causes of the war.

AG: That's interesting. We don't know what everybody thinks at this point, and what they're thinking is changeable. And I think a lot of the thinking will be determined by what articulate gestures are made by the Left to clarify things.

In other words the insight is half there, half-formed, half-unformed, and the problem is how do you get the whole insight through, how do you get it all across. How do you articulate what's inarticulate so far, how do you articulate it clearly, how can one of these meetings be like a national teach-in, you know, and get one single idea across: that the war was a mistake because it was capitalist conspicuous consumption cruelty or racism, particularly. The racist nature of the war is something that could be used. One single idea could be brought out in a large massive demonstration, now, particularly, with the Calley thing. If you find the right scenario, the theater of demonstrations could illustrate for the nation that it's a racist war. That Calley's thing was racist, killing gooks.

Q: How are you going to get people to give up their Western thought habits? Like you're bringing up all these Eastern thoughts, these chants——

AG: The chants are just one thing. One alternative would be a Quaker prayer meeting, inviting Nixon. Quaker prayer meeting meaning total silence and then every five minutes out of the silence somebody gets up and says what's on their mind immediately present. And then everybody shuts up for another five minutes; and then Nixon can get up and speak two minutes —which would be more mind-blowing than anything, in terms of actually breaking up consciousness.

Q: I was thinking of some ritual to denounce this whole technology——

AG: OK, so then you have one hour also of ritual concerned with the technology. That means you've got to write it up. And it's gotta be a poem, or an action, in simple form, you know—lift up an auto horn or something.

Q: Yeah, but how do you work it out so that 75 percent of the people are willing to give up some part of this technology?

AG: You're the one that's organizing this public demonstration.

Q: I mean I'm definitely frightened——

AG: It depends how you do it, if you do it clearly enough. Like everybody's sick of car smog, everybody has that in the back of their mind at this point. Everybody's aware of that. I mean you haven't quit riding in automobiles, have you, so why are you talking about other people? What do you talk about other people for? I mean you are sitting here in the middle of the most luxurious booby hatch in the world—talking about curing *other people?*

I mean the question is what gesture can you make in the middle of it—you are the 75 percent—what gesture can you make in the middle of it to clarify it for other people and to suggest then a new and viable technology? What can you do besides pro-testing, besides negatively protesting the old, what can you do to propose a new one, then? And how can you enact it, given the occasion of national publicity, or even just given the occasion of self-education possible on May 4th. What hour's teach-in on life-style change can you propose? Maybe spend an hour forming a car pool so that everybody coming in and out of Kent State for the rest of the year will always have hitch rides. Institutionalize hitchhiking around here, or sumpin, to save gas.

Whatever technologic change you want to propose. Find a form, clarify and articulate it, symbolize, and then propose it there as part of the ritual.

Also, "walking on water wasn't built in a day." What could be done on May 4th? May 4th can't change the entire culture to mass transit overnight, if that were the specific problem. But you can make conscious what people already know unconsciously, conscious and actionable. As in a sense, weakly, the Earth Day did: made conscious the threat to the planet. I think it did some good, because people suddenly realized the whole planet was threatened.

I'm the poet, so I see the role of poetry in terms of a public thing, as trying to invent rituals, poems, trying to clarify the consciousness of occasions like that. That's what it used to be, actually, in the old days—in tribal or ancient Hebrew or American Indian situations the group would get together and a shaman or the spokesman would get up and say what was on everybody's mind. Or the elders of the community would get together and figure out which dances would be danced on the festival day, what songs would be sung on the festival day, and what the songs would say to the entire village—that's what the American Indians would do. It's almost like what's needed here is a tribal council to figure out what dances and songs should be said, sung, performed. And the only thing I've seen working on that is that May Day meeting, but as I say, I think their poem, so to speak, was trite—it wasn't imaginative enough, didn't blow enough minds.

Q: I'm not sure how we go about injecting more creativity.

AG: Realizing you're winning. Acting on the joy of winning instead of on the despair of losing, 'cause I think in the long run ... or in the short run we're winning; in the long run the earth's about ready to fart itself out of creation or sumpin'.

Q: Do you think that the happening at Kent State in May—if it had happened any place else, at another school, that the result would be any different?

AG: No, any school would be confused, and it has happened in other schools, you know, at least other manifestations of heavy police-state acts. Hobart College, for instance, in Geneva, New York, has Tommy the Traveler. They've got the great symbolic police-spy case for all the colleges. I've been out there to raise money for Tommy the Traveler victims. Do you know that story? He was Tommy Tongyai; his father was a Thai military man who used to work for U.S. Army Intelligence in Thailand, and he himself was just an FBI stringer, who was assigned to go around to all the different campuses in that area, Keuka College, and Cornell, representing himself as "SDS from Rochester," urging violence, urging bombs, teaching freshmen.

Everybody was putting him down because he had this raunchy violence, screaming violence, not organized at all, just sort of loud-mouthed, so the only people he actually did influence finally were a couple of freshmen who thought that was the life-style they were supposed to get into. So he got them to blow up the ROTC building on May Day. But not before he himself had gone and tried to get the keys from a secretary, who testified against him. And he took the freshmen to a field outside the college near Lake Geneva and taught them how to use black powder to blow up things. So he taught them how to make the bombs, and provided them with the powder. It's just three or four kids who got burned by him, the dumber high school seniors who just got into college, who were hysteric.*

There was a really interesting guy at Hobart named Rafael Martinez, who's an older Puerto Rican Brown Power pacifist cat who was a friend of Berrigan's. He was the man that Tongyai had originally come to investigate a couple of years ago—he was like the heavy political activist out of the Berrigan civil disobedience line. And so Tommy the Traveler was originally assigned to check out the Berrigan influence in that area of New York State, and as part of it he also dealt dope a little bit, or encouraged people to deal dope, and finally led the local sheriff on a dope bust in the dorms.

So Hobart has its thing, and Stony Brook has the first mass dope bust thing—every college has its own. Jackson and Kent State have maybe the best you know, death theater, and should

---

Chicago Sun-Times, Dec. 7, 1973: "FBI HARASSMENT OF NEW LEFT DETAILED —The FBI marshaled a three-year nationwide counterintelligence program 'to expose, disrupt and otherwise neutralize' the 'New Left' movement, according to two internal agency memos made public Thursday. The FBI refused to discuss details of the program implemented in 1968. But an informed Justice Department source said the operation involved the use of agents-provocateurs to infiltrate New Left groups and stir up possibly violent activity."
—AG, Dec. 20, 1973

use it, I think, should work with it as their karma and do something really interesting, something actual. Blake says there's no art except in "minute particulars," in actual concrete details. Or William Carlos Williams says "no ideas but in things"—no general philosophical concepts but in particular actions that you can actually perform or do, tangible things that you can program.

I guess everybody is scared of trying to plan sumpin heroic. But just because everyone is scared, if you plan something that's of a pacific nature to begin with, that immediately removes the paranoia and you can go ahead into it. And then you'd wind up getting the whole community out. It might ultimately turn out to have been a false community—a false, scared gang of cowards willing to settle for sumpin pacific, whatever they can get, just so they can get together—but I think the net effect of actually being able to bring everybody together in a single community with a radical purpose, ending the war, would be stronger than the "enemy," whoever the enemy is, can resist. Even funnier, like, to invite Nixon to declare the war over here. You know, he's going to declare it over pretty soon, maybe, I don't know, or maybe that's one of the wavering things in his head, so tell him, OK, we'll give him safety here if he'll declare the war over.

I have to go. Thank you for your time.

Myths Associated With Science

2

CLASS: UNIVERSITY OF CALIFORNIA AT DAVIS

April 27, 1971

AG: I wonder to what extent does the science that we have, that runs the country, reflect scientific method? To what extent is it an absolute, inevitable product of its own presuppositions, independent research and pure fact? And to what extent is it actually just the neurotic spin-off of Laird's willfulness or MacNamara's willfulness or Richard Helms's obsessions or Nixon's obsessions or McGeorge Bundy's obsessions—or for that matter, all the liberals' obsessions of 1961 when Kennedy read Mao Tse-tung and Che Guevara and decided that what was necessary for America was hip counterinsurgency Green Beret development, and therefore a technology was developed to accompany that hip counterinsurgency guerrilla warfare which he thought so romantic and *macho*—backed by Schlesinger, backed by Robert Kennedy, backed by McGeorge Bundy; an ideology which created the heavy scene that we're into in the Vietnam War's saturation bombing and model village Orwellian concentration camps and Green Beret terrorism and counterterrorism. Ideology created Helios and STOLS (that is, Short Take-off and Landing planes), specialized infrared sensory equipment to smell the heat of human bodies underneath green leaves—a whole technical scientific apparatus exfoliated out of Kennedy's liberal hipness.

So to what extent does the science that we have reflect our own insanities or our own obsessions, or to what extent is it, as *Fortune* magazine-type "scientific" metaphysicians would have us believe, the development of hardheaded, hard-thinking, practical, inevitable, necessary human resourcefulness going in the only evolutionary direction possible given the dangerous world we live in?

The thing that strikes me most clearly, since I live on a nineteenth-century-technologized farm in Upstate New York, is the paucity of research and development of solar power, decentralized power sources, the primitiveness of wind-power technology. We have on our farm a wind-charger (which is like a propellor linked to a generator linked to golf cart batteries linked to a solid-state inverter with wires under the ground to carry a little bit of electricity to a plug in the house which can be switched on and off by remote control). The actual propellor-generator is the same model that was used on the same farm fifty years ago—there's been no technical development in half a century in getting independent power out of the wind for remote farms. Which is really astounding, when you consider that everybody now agrees that it's like total insanity to be despoiling Persia of its oils to bring them to Maine or New York—that people go to so much trouble to fuck up the earth rather than make use of the available possibilities of their own environment, solar, wind, or ocean.

There was a long letter[1] in *The New York Times* about three weeks ago from Buckminster Fuller to Senator Muskie, a long poem saying that there was enough power in the tides of the Bay of Fundy—which I think has a 50-foot tide, off the coast of Maine—enough power there to actually supply all of the world's power needs, if it were harnessed properly, like making use of tidal flow to push wheels to pull chains to crank up springs to set a giant watch in motion. Actually, there was a patent on a similar thing—a platform on the ocean which would be raised and lowered by tides, and a chain would pull and crank springs —taken out mutually by M.I.T. and Takis, a sculptor who taught at M.I.T. In other words nobody had ever thought of it before because nobody was thinking in those terms, because nobody's mythology went in those terms, of solar power or tidal power or natural power rather than unnatural scratch-the-earth rape mother nature power.

To what extent are the obsessions of the metal freaks or the electronics freaks not actually the obsessions of the scientist or the technologist but the obsessions of the banks, businessmen, managers, and money speculators who are hiring them? And as Pound[2] pointed out in his Cantos half a century ago also, beware usury, the use of money to make money. The bank will loan you money to build a weird plane that the Defense Department will use because the bank knows it can make some fast money on it and get a high rate of interest because the government is going to, like, pay cost-plus, or anyway spend a lot of money and so it's a sure loan and you know you're not going to lose on it. The bank's usuriously attempting to make money on money. High rates of interest make money flow in the direction, at present, of a technology which is shoddy and half-assed, in the sense that it doesn't take into account its own feedback waste pollution, that it doesn't account for its own shit, so to speak—jerry-built real estate speculation type technology. Bank loans and money do *not* flow in the direction of earth-preserving, durable living technique. The problem of what is going on with science is more political than "scientific."

Fuller's letter to Muskie was really crucial. Did anybody here see that letter or hear of it? Well the East Coast heard of it because it took up three-quarters of the page opposite the editorial in *The New York Times.* There was in F. D. Roosevelt's time a Passamaquoddy power project of similar nature to Fuller's proposal for the Bay of Fundy which was abandoned, they said back then for technical reasons—you couldn't carry electric over that kind of wire two hundred and fifty miles, or sumpin'. Fuller, writing Muskie, said that the Passamaquoddy project was knifed not for scientific reasons but because of opposition from the local power and oil and banking interests in Maine at the time. And that present projects to bring Persian oil all the way to Maine were on the face of it total insanity. That is, to puncture a hole in the earth and bring all the gluck over to Maine, when they could get power right there in Maine cleaner, was carrying coals to Newcastle, but worse that that, was like messing up Newcastle, messing up Maine. That if Muskie wanted to be President *(laughter from class)* this was the major present and future political, social, and economic problem he would have to solve; that is to say, power sources. That there was not really a population problem, because wherever there was lots of electricity the population went down, so that by the year 2,000, given proper derivation of power, clean power, there would be no population bomb explosion.

So, Fuller was saying, in order to contain the population ex-plosion you needed unlimited supply of ocean power. That's the major political crisis of the latter half of this century, and the resolution to this crisis was available on sample basis in Senator Muskie's own home state. According to Fuller the allocation of energy wasn't a "technical" problem. It was a question of whether money and investment green was going to go into the Bay of Fundy's clean power or into the Kennebunk, Maine, dirty money oil refinery, bringing oil from Persia or down from Alaska.

Three-quarters of a page in *The Times*. It was a direct chal-lenge, it was fantastic, because it zeroed the entire world's prob-lems right onto Muskie, looking to be President, and said OK, if you're going to solve the problems without suicide of the earth, here is your opportunity and here are the *terms*. Here are the *terms* of twentieth-century technological solution, if there's going to be a technological solution. If we don't return to neolithic as Gary Snyder and David Brower of Friends of Earth suggest.

I think Muskie replied in poem form also, but I haven't seen it yet. A short thing saying he sort of agreed in general, but I don't know if he laid out any programmatic political response.

Q: A lot of people in this room are probably engineering students or hard scientists, but if so much of what controls them is political or economic what can they do to use their knowledge for sci-ence?

AG: Paul Goodman has lots of homilies, lectures, and analyses of that problem, calling on professionals to *be* professional, to stay true to the knowledge within their actual profession and not sell their bodies and minds out as pollutive wage slaves to banks and real estate speculators. In other words even if you include tech-nology in your personal metaphysics and be, you know, long- or short-haired engineer or chemist or biologist or agronomist or geologist, you are still confronted with the same horrific twentieth-century choice that any freak-out acidhead hippie is confronted with, which is how to make a living without further polluting the earth, and without consuming more than your share of material goods. Your share being, well, no more than what the average Chinese or Indian consumes. Yet apparently the statistics are that one American wastes forth into fresh waters and oceans one thousand times more than any African or Asian

Which means that like we are earth's cancer. We are precisely a cancerous cell growth, skin cancer, I guess you'd call it, on the surface of the planet, a cell which has lost certain sensitive information that relates it to the other cells around it and grows egotistically, or just unrestrainedly, consuming all the other nourishments and substances around it, finally poisoning and killing the host. And it may be that the cure, if there is a cure, would be the same as for individual cancer. Just as you have cobalt treatment for cancer, the cobalt bomb mythically leaves buildings intact but destroys the individual cells, the human beings; that might well be the therapy for this particular disease. . . .

So what does someone who's working in technology do? You would have to be omniscient, like a good technologist, you really would have to examine the corporation you're working for and the consequences your work will produce. Which means that you really will be stuck with a political problem no matter what technology you're into—you'll still have to examine where it's going to lead you, or lead others. In the medical field and psychiatric and legal fields, there are now alternative societies, like the Medical Committee on Human Rights, or Health Pac (Dr. Howard Levy), or with the lawyers there's an experimental model in William Kunstler's law commune. There probably are already the beginnings of cooperative technological groups. Does anybody know anything about that?—because I don't.

Q: There's some, but the one I think of as really active right now is Computer People for Peace in New York.

AG: Well, obviously the growth of decentralized societies within societies, sort of hip electrical societies, would be desirable. And you can't really say our talk about the politicization of science comes from an anarchist bias, because science is already politicized. The whole direction of science has been politicized by the fact that it's been bought by the government, already, if its not bought by the Mafia. Imagine what complex electronic mechanisms must go in to Las Vegas!

We don't yet have any development of some kind of independent social organization among the technologists who understand the potentialities of their own field, and also understand the limitations of science. I went on a wildflower walk on Mt. Tamalpais with Sterling Bunnell, who's a biologist and psychiatrist, and Michael McClure, who's a poet interested in biology, and we were into these particular points: Is the earth going to survive, what kind of social organization is *possible* and/or desirable, and is technology going to be part of that survival?

Now Gary Snyder basically says that there is no possible survival outside of neolithic, total back-to-earth integration with plants, flowers, bees—that's a technology, actually, understanding the functions of nature right around you. The California Indians had a contact with nature that was not just Wordsworthian romantic but was very precise, and the terms of that knowledge, the details of that knowledge, are all in the early 1900s Smithsonian Institution *Handbook of the California Indians*[3] —does anybody know of that? It's like a fantastic big thick book put out in 1915–1920 giving the name of like every edible wildflower and herb and root, what the California Indians used to weave baskets, what stems were tripartite (you could split them in three and then use them to weave), how to build houses out of local materials, how to make "Kotex" out of the fluff of certain flowers; that is, an entire living technology. There's probably nobody now that's got all that technology in his head. It exists, though, in books, and could be studied in the field, too.

Well, Snyder says that's the only kind of technology that actually integrates man with nature, or integrates us with what's really around us, besides ourselves. And the Other technology, capital Other, wastes every other sentient being and sucks all energy forms up for use as our own inanimate extension, burns life out. Snyder's opinion is that only neolithic culture is perdurable, defining "neolithic" as living closer to the ground, as the old, viable, stable form of social intercourse with nature that's lasted since the Magdalenian cave paintings—that's what, twenty-thirty-forty thousand years?

Our present "What is this?" is perhaps twenty-thirty-forty-fifty years old, out of these thousands of years. The earth absolutely cannot sustain this kind of despoliation and wasting for very long. In fact we already have a date given for the irreversible degeneration of the cancer we're into, which is the year 2000, by which time all of the oceans will have been deadened, like Lake Erie, according to J. Y. Cousteau, who pointed out that in the last twenty years 40 percent of the oceans' life has been destroyed; 40 percent of the fish and the flora of the world's oceans have disappeared in the last twenty years! Do you know that figure? I got it out of *Time* magazine,[4] quoting J. Y. Cousteau, and then I saw it repeated several other times and then finally I saw it emerge in the first paragraph of a *New York Times* editorial as a "legitimate," "distinguished" estimate of what really has happened to the planet. So we have Year 2000 as a terminal date for our cancer.

The alternative that Sterling Bunnell was suggesting was an economy of life style—a change of consciousness, obviously—of simplicity of consumption rather than complication of consumption. In other words, the less you consume the hipper you are, the less you consume, the less you desire, the more satisfied you'll be, which corresponds to Buddhist theory—the less activity you involve yourself in that consumes other organic and inorganic material, the less dependent you'll be. Like you can look at a junkie and say "Listen, if you were off your habit you'd be a lot more peaceful, you know, you wouldn't have to be running away from the cops and you wouldn't have to be scoring every day." Well, Bunnell's proposing for human society that we get off our matter habit, because we very definitely do have a matter habit. To put it in a metaphor, we're "shooting gasoline electric speed"—burning down the veins of the earth ... it's going to lead to a giant bust sooner or later, like a blue light flash.[5]

To cut down on consumption and make a virtue of conservation in terms of personal use would mean, as it does now, like, if you have Levis you sew little American flags over the holes instead of buying new Levis, using bicycles rather than oil-burning, fossil-fuel-burning machines, hitchhiking more, and picking up hitchhikers more, instead of making hitchhiking illegal. Well, there's the whole spectrum of value changes which you already know and have read about.

Imagine a technological reorganization of the planet of such an infinitely delicate and at the same time vast nature! Buckminster Fuller proposes to tap the Bay of Fundy and set up a power grid network that'll stretch from the U.S. all through Canada all through Alaska through the Siberian power grid down through China and including India and stretching over to Europe. He proposes a unification of all the world's power grids, too. That kind of organization, said Dr. Bunnell, would preclude the anarchy so desired by the Goldwater longhairs—by Goldwater and the longhairs who've said they were anarchists and wanted to do their own thing and didn't want to be linked up with a universal world power grid because that would mean centralized technical leadership with all the dangers that it proposes. However, Bunnell also thought that the self-discipline and awareness —that is, self-discipline in the sense of cross-legged meditation type psychedelic awareness—necessary for everybody to collaborate on such a universal technological toy world project, would preclude its becoming a totalitarian rigidly functioning bureaucracy.

Whether that's so or not is the question that's open to everybody and was actually brought up, right up in front of the eyes of those who marched on April 24th in San Francisco. You had this very superaware mob, 100,000 people out there, an articulate populace representing 75 percent of the country's opinion, that the war should be over. (The experience of the march itself was exquisite—I mean even if there were no war such a march would be a beautiful thing, like what May Day was—a great bacchanal festival. The only thing missing was the May pole and fucking in the bushes, which used to be the traditional end of May Day. On *Walpurgis Nacht*, the night before, the ancient celebrants used to gather flowers to lay on the doorsteps of the townsfolk at May Day dawn.) But what happened up on this week's stage was a centralized revolutionary leadership and everybody saw that it auto-destructed in two hours. The stage itself auto-destructed.*

So we haven't apparently, on a political or on a social level, among ourselves, literally among ourselves, or among yourselves, among the younger generation, developed common leadership, organization, or dictatorship, or authoritarian forms, whatever, adequate even to keep the stage together! Which may be a good thing, but if we are going to use a highly sophisticated technology, a total system like an organism in which all the parts are interconnected with intelligence, sensitive to each other's balance, there will have to be a centralized network of some sort where each cell feeds back into each other cell. That kind of

---

*Members of several different militant groups, some of whom had pushed a rock band off the stage in the middle of their performance to harangue the 100,000 assembled at Golden Gate Park for enjoying themselves, appeared on stage simultaneously in a fight for the microphone. The electricity failed, and with the extra weight the stage collapsed, leaving at sunset a few bleakly silhouetted figures shouting, hands cupped to mouths, at large groups of fellow citizens peaceably departing.

science may theoretically be possible; I don't know if it is, it's up to you. People haven't really begun thinking very clearly in this area; the only people who have machinery for such vast analysis are in the Pentagon, where they've developed some sort of rudimentary system for trying to impose their will on Indochina and are doing it finally by sheer robot force and blood-bone-mashing hammer destruction. Not, obviously, taking into account all the information, operating on totally fucked-up information, in fact.

Which brings us to Herman Kahn and systems analysts and think tanks and manipulators of scientific mythology. Kahn told me two years ago that in 1965 he had applied to the Department of Interior for funds for ecological systems analysis for his Hudson Institute, and the Department told him there was no funding available for such research, and so he had to return to the Pentagon for more military money to maintain the Institute in essentially planet-destroying research.

So I said, "Yeah, OK, so why not say 'All Power to the Pentagon,' you know—let the Pentagon fight the enemy with all the money they want, and say that the enemy henceforth is earth pollution, not the Communists—a real enemy! You don't have to argue about it, don't have to imagine it, don't have to create FBI's to invent it—a REAL ENEMY, at last!—Go out and fight it!"

And Kahn said "No, no, no, no. That would be the worst thing imaginable—just look at what a mess they've made of the war in Vietnam!"

And as you know, the Army Corps of Engineers, who are supposed to be building dams and taking care of conservation with the Department of Interior, has the worst, the most notorious record of screwing up the landscape. At this point the Army Engineers' dams have so messed up the Columbia River that news stories in the last week have prophesied 90 percent of the returning salmon dying prematurely. That's like the entire salmon universe may be ending, on account of the Army Engineers Corps' ecological reconstruction of the Columbia River. Has anybody seen those stories in the papers lately? Some total horror story about the great salmon industry that everybody dug so much, from the Jews of New York adoring smoked salmon lox to the dried salmon freaks among the Kwakiutl, for whom salmon finally became a god—Salmon, like the god Coyote, is apparently being destroyed.

Anyway, Kahn and I were taping a show with Bill Buckley at the same time back in '68, and he said on the air that the majority of the people in South Vietnam *wanted us there,* which was astounding then to hear anybody say. So I asked him, "How do you get that?" and he said, "Well, let's see now. I was there in 1962 and we made a study, and it was one-third of the Bao Dai wanted us there, so that was two hundred thousand people, and then there were the Christians, and they wanted us there, and that was what—7 percent of the population—and then there were three different Buddhist sects and one-third of one Buddhist sect wanted us there, and three-thirds of another Buddhist sect wanted us there, and the Mahayana Buddhists didn't want us there, but they were only a minority group that were fighting among themselves, so if you totaled it all up on a great big blackboard and did a systems analysis on it, they wanted us there."

But *anybody* who walked around the streets of Saigon from like 1955 knew they didn't want us there. In fact Eisenhower knew it, you know, from the seat of his pants when he said that 80 percent of the people would have voted for Ho Chi Minh, and that's why we betrayed the Geneva Convention, and that's why we didn't abide by elections in the mid-fifties.

So the data observed by scientists—or social scientists in this case—or by people who'll go around yakking about scientific hardheaded realism, and nobody is more representative of that mythology than someone like Herman Kahn—the data they observe is all pure magic, finally. This is an admittedly shoddy example because it's a social science rather than electronics, but what I would have gone on to say if I had another six hours, is that science itself finally is pure magic, really, and it's just pure wish-fulfillment, whichever direction it goes.

I had one other thing in mind to say before I came here, if you'll give me just one more minute. I think, scientifically speaking, the most important project that we have is the investigation of inner space—the exploration of our subjective universe, the exploration of consciousness, the alterations of consciousness, the capacities of consciousness, functions of consciousness, seats of consciousness. The one area where you can do a certain amount of reproducible experimentation is with LSD and the psychedelics. The one single professor in America who knew most about it and who is the most scientific practitioner, who formulated the best language for dealing with it, is in exile from the country for practicing his science: Leary.

And I would say that's actually the state of science in America now. That the most important scientific investigator in the most important field—at the moment—is in criminal status and is in exile.* And I would like to leave you with that thought.

---

*See note pp. 7–9, "Identity Gossip."

NOTES

1. WAR AND PEACE: VIETNAM AND KENT STATE

1. Just one year later an undercover police agent was arrested at Kent:

KSU Undercover Agent Freed; Spends
Night in Jail on Firearms Charges

Reinhold Mohr, a KSU junior and undercover agent for the KSU police, was released at 12:30 P.M. yesterday after charges filed against him for illegal possession of firearms were dropped. . . . [Federal agents claimed the arms were inoperable.]

He was carrying a Russian-made AK-47 submachine gun and a Chinese-made rocket-propelled grenade launcher wrapped in a beach towel.

. . . the VVAW has known Mohr, a VVAW member, to be an undercover agent for several months. Johnson [Ken Johnson, President of KSU VVAW] called Mohr an "agent provocateur," saying Mohr had planned on planting the weapons with leaders of the VVAW so they would be arrested.

. . . [Spokesmen for the VVAW] claim to have sworn testimony from members "that Mohr said the AK-47 was good to kill 'pigs' with."

—from the Kent State student paper, *The Daily Kent Stater*,
April 26, 1972

2. MYTHS ASSOCIATED WITH SCIENCE

1. Fuller's poem-letter-telegram appeared in *The New York Times* on March 27, 1971, p. 29.

2. See pp. 173–177 of this book, and Pound's Cantos XLV and XLVI.

3. A. L. Kroeber's *Handbook of the Indians of California* (Washington: U.S. Government Printing Office, 1925).

4. "The Dying Oceans," *Time*, September 28, 1970, p. 64.

5. "How long this Addict government support our oil-burner matter habit
shooting gasoline electric speed before the blue light blast & eternal Police-roar
Mankind's utter bust?"

—from "Friday the Thirteenth" (written March 13, 1970), *The Fall of America* (San Francisco: City Lights, 1972), p. 144.

Epilogue

This book has presented a slice of life, not a whole life, in offering informal lectures transcribed and edited, tapping in on one season, ending now with an epilogue and followed by a poem from a period two years later than most of this material. A major prose presentation of the development of Allen's thought over a long period, Essays Interviews and Manifestos 1955—Present, *is under preparation and will appear within a couple of years.*

In the time intervening between spring '71 and spring '73 Allen recorded a second album of music he'd written to Blake poetry, and assembled Complete Poetry Vocalized, *a 16-volume L.P. record set, explored blues forms and improvisation and recorded an as-yet unissued selection of original songs with Bob Dylan; deepened his practice of Buddhist meditation and took Refuges and Vows with Tibetan teachers and fellow poets Gary Snyder and Philip Whalen; and continued his political involvement by campaigning for George McGovern throughout the election season and participating in Miami passive resistance demonstrations against Nixon and his bombing, for which he and many others–850 on the same occasion–were jailed.*

At the farm in January 1973 Allen slipped on the ice on his way to the barn and suffered two spiral breaks in his right leg which required him to remain in a cast to his hip until summer. Immobile during his virtual seclusion at the farm for most of the winter, he continued to write poetry and music, and also found more time, more occasion than ever before for meditation. This conversation concerns that winter's thoughts.

GB: Basically I'd like some commentary on events discussed in the book which have developed further since—not just transient political events but also Pound's death and Kerouac's and the attention Kerouac has received since. But to start with politics, I'm perplexed by the course of Alfred McCoy's book, *The Politics of Heroin in Southeast Asia,* beginning with the CIA's request for the manuscript and Harper and Row's compliance —and McCoy's congressional testimony. After all the prepublication notice, it seems there's been no follow-up on the information in the book by anyone in the press or government.

AG: In the course of composing that book McCoy used my files and the files and research of many other people as well as his own research, and he went around the world and actually interviewed some of the people that I was talking and gossiping about in these conversations. What I figured out and was attempting to expound was just on the basis of a very careful between-the-lines reading of newspapers and putting two and two together and having practical experience in the junk world, and a paranoically judicious stoical eye on government pronunciations, plus a lot of interviewing of CIA people later on the basis of my first perceptions derived from newspapers. So what I'm trying to point out is that the material that I presented in the spring of 1971 was more or less validated by further, more extensive research, and what few statements were awry were corrected by later research. But most of the generalizations I made more or less made sense.

Now my interest and intention, and McCoy's, was to help break the back of the war by pointing out how corrupt it was —corrupt unto the point of the government being involved with dope dealing and dope transmission. I think that scandal did actually have some effect in sort of disillusioning young people who were already disillusioned but without clear reason, and on some older people in Washington, like some of the news people. It didn't scandalize the public sufficiently to explode the mythology of the war and the mythology of our moral superiority. The crucial point was that the governments that we were allied with were dealing in dope, including the Thieu government, which I said at one point in all of this material, and which McCoy proved at great length. And the question of the U.S. maintenance of the Thieu government was like a primary question of the continuation of the war even after the peace.

So obviously Thieu's involvement in dope dealing made no dent in public consciousness, but on the other hand there never was like a full-scale, all-out fourth-estate acknowledgment of that situation. There were specialized articles which did get to the front page of *The Times* alluding to the situation, walking around the situation, but there was never any direct research by AP or UPI or *Life* or *Time* outside of McCoy's work, or everything that was published was on the basis of McCoy's work. There was never a full-scale investigation like with the Watergate case. So apparently the public at this point is so weary and confused and punch-drunk that it'll accept any variety of mass-murder, My Lai, giant bombing (as right after the election of '72) without flinching, and still attempt to maintain the United States' ego intact, no matter how much poisonous material or poisonous motivation or activity comes to its attention as part of that ego structure. So it seems like the nationalistic ego is almost impervious to any kind of disillusionment except physical catastrophe.

If we can put up with mass murder then what's a little dope dealing? On the other hand, everybody did get so bugged with the whole Vietnam situation that it was absolutely necessary to stop the war, or to officially try to stop the war, or to appear to have stopped the war, and it's still likely that if the war isn't stopped physically there will be a revolt in Congress—or it's taken for granted that there's now more weight possible to end the war, and I think the revelation of the government's complicity in the international heroin trade is part of that weight that is slowly dragging the war to a stop and forcing America to get out.

I don't think we can calculate the effects of the propaganda imagery produced in this kind of dope research.

GB: Well, we do have government announcements encouraging tribesmen to change from raising opium to growing corn—that kind of effort—implying that at least the U.S. knows its allies grow opium.

AG: Well, that's always been government policy from the very beginning in certain agencies. But in other agencies, like the military (which supports Thieu) there's a totally different policy. In other words, some bureaucrats in AID might be trying to tell young AID people to teach tribesmen to switch crops, whereas the CIA or Air America or military generals and liaison people might be at the same time buying up the Meo opium tribe crop.

GB: The point is we have those pronouncements [about efforts to change crops] but we don't really know what's going on. We know what's said officially——

AG: Well, yeah, we do know something, because Jack Anderson has still been reporting, and there has been a lot more information coming out. We do know what is happening in the sense that the corruption in regard to opium dealing is just as bad. Anderson had a story in February '73 about the entire Thai government being involved in opium dealing. He got ahold of a whole pile of State Department and CIA secret reports analyzing the opium situation and bearing out everything that we said. . . . He's had I think at least a dozen columns—a dozen very incisive columns—covering Laos, covering corruption in the South Vietnamese government, covering the Thai government. And when I was there [Washington] this time I went to his office, and he had a whole dossier of secret documents, or semisecret documents, which he showed me, and offered Xeroxes. What he has is a collection of documents of the last five years covering late last-minute panic investigations of the corruption of our allies which say yes, there's corruption everywhere—Thailand, Laos, South Vietnam—just as described in the McCoy book.

Though the thing I've found is that the government documents—that is, the papers circulated around for reading, which are summaries of raw information and stringers' reports (CIA or State Department stringers), are always couched in great generalizations. They don't have the juicy details that McCoy has or that you could find even in the newspapers. Instead they have generalizations like (I'm paraphrasing), "Yes, it is true that we are having great difficulty in straightening out the drug problem; we've talked with the leaders of this country or that, and they say that they're doing their best about it, but our information is that they're not doing the best they can about it and are very lax about it, and the people associated with the government, including several of the in-laws, are making a great deal of money, so it's a long-continuing problem which we're still working on." They talk about it like that. They generalize it over and make it sound like a working problem rather than a scandal, and they don't name names and give particulars. The people that know the actual details are the on-the-spot CIA men and newsmen and State Department people who know the actual arguments back and forth and the personalities involved, and by the time they write down their reports and they get boiled down to be "papers" on the situation in Turkey, "papers" on the situation in Laos, it's like five pages of generalizations with a recommendation for action like, "It is not recommended that we withhold military aid because that would be too extreme and might offend; however, the ambassador intends to have high level conversations in an attempt to impress on the premier the high importance which America has and the difficulty we'll have getting money out of Congress if this policy of laxness in illegal opiate trade continues." That kind of terminology is used. That's why the high bureaucrats really don't know what they're doing, even. It's all on such a level of abstraction because everybody's so distant from the scene.

The other thing of interest is that since the days when I was piecing together reports by David Burnham from *The Times* about collusion in the dope traffic by New York cops and by local police everywhere, the Knapp Commission report* has come out publicly on the subject, and there has been more and more acknowledgment of the complicity of the police and the corruption of the narcotics police in that area, climaxed with the revelation of the whole "French connection" dope loss, the theft from Police Department storage, by police, of several million dollars' worth of heroin.

I was interested in demystifying the cruel, authoritarian, totalitarian police-state facade, and pointing out the essential corruption of public junk policy in regard to two points: that the police were peddling and that high levels of government were involved in the junk traffic, wittingly or unwittingly, as part of the general neurotic syndrome of authoritarian strong-arm government. So those are now out front, clear, proven publicly, whereas they were only private supposition or private knowledge or gossip before. I knew all that through Huncke, say, or through talking with junkies. And now it's all been on the front

---

*See Appendix, pp. 260–262, for excerpts from text of Knapp Commission report.

page, so in a sense I feel that my research there is finished. Or the essential point I started with is finished—I could go on to some other lifetime task. I think I'll just shift over to meditation. All that can happen is that you prove the same point over and over again.

One might now go into Rockefeller's history to find why is Rockefeller getting so invertedly het-up, why is he refusing to face the facts and making all these ridiculous statements on drugs and beating the wrong end of the horse. I've kept thinking over the years he's displayed such stupidity on the problem since '63 when he introduced the stop-and-frisk laws against junkies, followed by the idea in '65 or '66 to put them all in jail hospitals without having any money to build the hospitals —enforced incarceration, followed by his breaking of strength in '68, '69 when he said, "Oh, it's a federal problem" and now, the ridiculous freak-out anger speech to the union people saying to put 'em all in jail forever. In a speech the other day to the AFL-CIO convention they all got up and applauded him when he called for the death penalty or life imprisonment.

That kind of stupidity and obtuseness couldn't be accidental over so long a period of time—he couldn't be making the same wrong moves in the wrong direction, in a strong-arm direction, every time, year after year, for a whole decade now accidentally. If he'd wanted to solve the problem he could've years ago, by simply legalizing heroin and letting doctors prescribe it and being done with the whole scene, like in England. And that's the one thing they've always refused here—they've been willing to put junkies to death rather than let them kill themselves with junk, a stupidly exaggerated stereotype anyway.

GB: Junk ordinarily is deadly only because of police regulations—that is, because of government-pronounced illegality, one can't be sure of a substance's strength or even its identity, like whether it's smack or rat poison.

AG: Yeah. So at this moment the whole situation's in chaos, total chaos, with different branches of the government and different advisers of the government pulling in different directions, the whole public mind split down the middle. Simultaneous with the recognition of junk as a medical problem and of the practicality of maintenance, as with methadone, and of the culpability of the police as one of the most corrupt elements in the society, there's this opposite desire to persecute and punish the local junkies, hard-line, pitiless, "without pity," as Nixon says, death penalty or life imprisonment for peddlers who are just fulfilling the function of serving a black market along with the police. So there's both a hard line and a soft line going on simultaneously, and so I guess you could say it just indicates a splitting-in-two of the government mind—different minds, different bureaucracies. Recognition of the corruption of the police is open and aboveboard, printed in *The Times,* acknowledged in the news, acknowledged by everybody except the cops and those who push the death penalty for drug peddlers, including even hashish and LSD dealers in Rockefeller's terminology—in his original statement people peddling hashish and LSD were to be included with the hard-drug people.

GB: Did he retract that?

AG: He didn't retract it; he simply restated it without mentioning those two. But his original speech to the legislature included that.

GB: Did you react to him directly after either of his last two speeches?

AG: No. I haven't done anything. I haven't done anything but take note of all that, 'cause I went around talking for so long I made my point as well as I could. I'm at the moment more interested in meditation—'cause apparently I was making my point with anger, or my *upaya* or skillful means were lacking 'cause I wasn't able to penetrate. So it requires maybe a calmer-balanced objective impersonal egoless cast of mind to point out the contradictions of samsara.

It's like the catastrophes have occurred and rape has occurred over and over again and everybody's now so inured to rape and catastrophe it's like a fatigue: nobody can take it in any more, nobody cares. Intellectually people care but it seems like America is so sunk in scandal and debauchery and corruption and disillusionment it's like a great wave of horror that nobody can fight against—everybody's just floating on the tide, waiting for the wave to crash. 'Cause people tend, I think, to put more and more out of mind the ecological wave we're riding which is bound to crash.

Yet the original pre-apocalypse conditions still prevail, and the actual apocalypse conditions have arrived to some people, even in the United States, like the junkies—or to the Indochinese. In those pockets of America where the apocalypse has not touched except spiritually (in the sense of the deprivation and emptiness of soul and desensitization and hypnosis of airwaves by television) there still is a feeling of security and comfort, there still are "no threat" conditions.

GB: "Don't rock the boat."

AG: Yeah, well, partly it's 'cause people have nowhere to go and I don't have anywhere to go and nobody has anywhere to go; we're all sustained in this electric air-conditioned nightmare. Turn off the air conditioning and half the old people in America will die. All over Florida there's a lot of people whose lives depend on air conditioning.

Where is everybody gonna go? I'm still using a car. I vowed not to get on planes this year, and I'm gonna wind up on a plane I'm sure. I'm still getting and spending in a world too much with me. If I can't control myself I don't see how the mass of people are able to control themselves without ever having the conscious perceptions that I do of the disastrousness of my behavior. So the only way out I see at this point is altering my own behavior. Generalizations about the junkie-like behavior of the American populace make no sense unless one can begin with oneself and dredge one's own harbors.

GB: Yeah, but again it's like going further and further to prove one's point again and again, because it's not like you spend your evenings drinking beer and watching TV.

AG: But unless one can pose the problem and find a way out for oneself at least, or for the whole society, there's no point in proposing it angrily or getting mad in spirit at the society. In other words I've been indulging myself in superior criticisms, but I haven't been able to get out of the syndrome that I'm criticizing.

So I guess that's what one must work on—finding a path for oneself and by example a path for others. . . . It's very difficult in so complex and mechanized a society for anybody to get out, get out on their own and do anything healthy. Nonetheless that's the necessity, that's the teaching, that's the path. I'm sure there are a

lot of squares I've met that realize the problem almost as much as
me or maybe more than me but who don't change because they
don't have any path either, any answer either—they don't know
how, and are stuck in their roles. So how to get really unstuck
from our roles is sumpin'.

Well, Peter [Orlovsky], the organic farmer, sets a certain
example—of personal sacrifice or change, physical change.
Nanao Sakaki* sets an example, Gary Snyder and his friends set
an example of positive actions in a communal way to reduce
conspicuous consumption. I do less so because I do less physical
work. So I think I'll have to just go out and change my life a little.
I'd like to get rid of a lot of my possessions and unload a lot of
things like archives and whatnot, collections of clippings from
The New York Times that drive me to maintain an establishment
with lights and electric and research facilities.

What else we gotta cover?

GB: Pound, for one—most of one chapter is devoted to him and
he's died within the last year.

AG: Oddly enough, I have a tape. I was at Webster College, St.
Louis, giving a reading, and then afterwards talking with students on the radio, and someone came in, a professor came in,
and said that Pound was dead. And so I have a tape** of the
conversation that followed, including a chanting of the Praj-
naparamita for him and a lot of comments.

GB: Kerouac had died a year and a half before most of the material presented in this book was recorded, and this year one
biography has already come out and another is expected.

AG: I keep thinking that Kerouac proposed—like Whitman—a
sort of noble ideal American open-mind sensibility, open road,
open energy, with some flaws in it, and some contradictions, but
nothing unresolvable with common sense; the direction
America took was toward a military hardheartedness and mass
murder that even he disapproved of, so the openhearted sensibility, the sensibility of "the happy nut," that Kerouac was prais-
ing, the openhearted sensibility that he proposed, was rejected

---

*Zen Buddhist poet-singer, pioneer of communal living, and mountain climber.
**See pp. 179–187 ("The Death of Ezra Pound").

by the nation, so his soul and his sense of soul was rejected, and his art was also rejected for that reason—not only by the hard-hearted people, but also by, say, literate people who doubted the reality of soul, finally, seeing around them the great mechanical robot monster of the nation, thinking that force has to be met by force. So the radical left rejected Kerouac's open heart, the middle-class hippie book reviewers of *The Times* rejected Kerouac's open heart, the pseudo-bohemians wanted sumpin' smarter and more degenerate and terrible; the weekly news magazines thought it was naive in the face of the giant holocaust the military mind created and perpetuated; so Kerouac's art was never really appreciated or understood or accepted, though it was the right medicine for the nation. So his whole sensibility was rejected, and I think that crushed him in the sense of making him pessimistic, making him realize how really unrelievedly awful American destiny was, and I think he just took the hint and retired from the scene, in a sense, seeing that the condition of America was hopeless. It's like what Gregory says in his elegy for Kerouac: if Kerouac was the nation's singer, or prophet, or the man who sings for the nation, and if the nation itself dies, how can the singer live? He gave himself to the nation as its singer, and the nation rejected him.

GB: The nation as a whole does not seem to have followed your prescriptions either, but your reaction has been different from Kerouac's.

AG: Well, I know, but my development was much slower, my maturity was much slower than Jack's. Jack was already mature around 1950, '51, and had a complete visionary conception by '53, not only visionary but complete metaphysical and visionary and Buddhist conception of the open road, being on the road, and the ghosts on the road and everything, and already had produced like his great art work; it took me till years later to slowly learn from him. He went into the chaos ahead of other people and saw ahead of other people and was perhaps more lonely, and was wounded.

GB: Do you think the longer time you spent before assuming something like a nation singer role might have made a difference?

AG: Except that the time has in a sense perhaps inured me to the social lie and made me part of the large social lie of hope. Kerouac was essentially hopeless, finally, saw no hope. And having accepted that he could, you know, like drink himself to death. I still maintain this perhaps false hope. Don't wanna be moved out of my comforts, out of my comfortable body. I don't know. I think it's unanswerable. But the very simple, tiny point I wanna make is, as Gregory said,* as the nation fell, so did its singer, to the extent that he was the original singer of open heart open road for that generation, of the fifties, so it must make him most raw and most vulnerable to the poisoning of the body politic.

It's his own role so what can he do, and in a nation which is itself so messed up, what is he going to be—a happy singer? Happy, healthy singer of a dying, decadent destructive world? Happy joker?

And I keep thinking I'm too comfortable in this chamber of horrors, so my own future I think will probably be more meditative and ascetic.

---

* See Gregory Corso's "Elegiac Feelings American (for the dear memory of John Kerouac)," pp. 3–12, in *Elegiac Feelings American* (New York: New Directions, 1970).

Note from AG September, 1973: Mass public assembly for redress of grievances is still beautiful and crucial as manifestation of public subconscious: and such meetings can be in the form of million-mass meditations, totally silent, for days. And complete change of the system—monopoly capitalist avaricious money-as-commodity usury—is urgent, since otherwise everyone remains trapped in exploitation habit till death.

"What Would You Do If You Lost It?"

said Rinpoche Chögyam Trungpa Tulku in the marble glittering
    apartment lobby
looking at my black hand-box full of Art, "Better Prepare for
    Death."
The harmonium, that's Peter's
the scarf that's Krishna's, the bell and brass lightningbolt Phil
    Whalen selected in Japan
a tattered copy of Blake, with chord notations, black books from
    City Lights,
Australian Aborigine song sticks, incense, Tibetan precious-metal
    finger cymbals—
A broken leg a week later enough reminder, lay in bed and after
    few days' pain begin to weep
no reason, thinking a little of Rabbi Schacter, a little of father
    Louis, a little
of everything that must be abandoned,
snow abandoned,
empty dog barks after the dogs have disappeared
meals eaten passed thru to nourish tomatoes and corn,
The wooden bowl from Haiti too huge for my salad,
Teachings, Tantras, Haggadahs, Zohar, Revelations, poetries,
    Koans
forgotten with the snowy world, forgotten
with generations of icicles crashing to white gullies by roadside,
Dharmakaya forgot, Nirmanakaya shoved in coffins, Sambhoga-
    kaya eclipsed in candlelight snuffed by the playful cat—
Good-bye my own treasures, bodies adored to the nipple,
old souls worshipped flower-eye or imaginary auditory panoramic
    skull—
good-bye old socks washed over & over, blue boxer shorts,
    subzero longies,

new Ball Boots black hiplength ready for snowdrifts near the farm
    mailbox,
good-bye to my room full of books, all wisdoms I never studied, all
    the Campion, Creeley, Anacreon, Blake I never read through,
blankets farewell, orange diamonded trunked from Mexico for old
    tearful age, himalayan sheepwool lugged down from Almora
    days with Lama Govinda and Peter trying to eat tough
    stubborn half-cooked chicken.
Paintings on wall, Maitreya, Sakyamuni & Padmasambhava, Dr.
    Samedi with Haitian spats & cane whiskey,
Bhaktivedanta Swami at desk staring sad eye Krishna at my
    hopeless Void self-consciousness,
Attic full of toys, desk full of old checks, files on N.Y. police & CIA
    peddling Heroin,
Files on Leary, files on Police State, files on ecosystems all faded
    & brown,
notebooks untranscribed, hundreds of little poems & prose my
    own hand,
newspaper interviews, assemblaged archives, useless
    paperworks surrounding me imperfectly chronologic
    humorous later in eternity, reflective
    of Cities' particular streets and studios and boudoirs—
good-bye poetry books, I dont have to take you along any more
    on a chain to Deux Magots like a red lobster
thru Paris, Moscow, Prague, Milan, New York, Calcutta, Bangkok
    holy Benares, yea Rishikesh & Brindaban may yr prāna lift
    you over the roof of the world—
my own breath slower now, silent waiting & watching—
Downstairs pump-organs, musics, rags and blues, homemade
    Blake hymns, mantras to raise the skull of America,
good-bye C chord, F chord, G chord, good-bye all the chords of
    the House of the Rising Sun
good-bye farmhouse, city apartment, garbage subways Empire
    State, Museum of Modern Art where I wandered thru
    puberty dazzled by Van Gogh's raw-brained star-systems
    pasted on blue thick skyey Suchness—
Good-bye again Naomi, good-bye old painful legged poet Louis,
    good-bye Paterson the 69 between Joe Bozzo & Harry Haines
    that outlasted childhood & poisoned the air o'er Passaic
    Valley,
Good-bye Broadway, give my regards to the great falls & boys
    staring marijuana'd in wonder at the nearby roar of Godfather
    Williams' speech

Good-bye old poets of Century that taught fixed eye & sharp
    tongue from Pound with silent Mouni heart to Tom Veitch
    weeping in Stinson Beach,
good-bye to my brothers who write poetry & play the violin, my
    nephews who blow tuba & stroke bass viol, whistle flute or
    smile & sing in blue rhythm
good-bye shades of dead and living loves, bodies weeping bodies
    broken bodies aging, bodies turned to wax doll or cinder
Good-bye America you hope you prayer you tenderness, you IBM
    135-35 Electronic Automated Battlefield Igloo White
    Dragon-tooth Fuel-Air Bomb over Indochina
Good-bye Heaven, farewell Nirvana, sad Paradise adieu, adios all
    angels and archangels, devas & devakis, Bodhisattvas,
    Buddhas, rings of Seraphim, Constellations of elect souls
    weeping singing in the golden Bhumi Rungs, good-bye High
    Throne, High Central Place, Alleluiah Light beyond Light, a
    wave of the hand to Thee Central Golden Rose,
Om Ah Hūṃ A La La Ho Sophia, Soham Tara Ma, Om Phat Svaha
    Padmasambhava Marpa Mila's Gampopa Karmapa
    Trungpaye! Namastaji Bramha, Ave atque vale Eros, Jupiter,
    Zeus, Apollo, Surya, Indra
Bom Bom! Shivaye! Ram Nam Satyahey! Om Ganipatti, Om
    Saraswati Hrih Sowha, Ardinarishvara Radha Harekrishna
    faretheewell forevermore!
None left standing! No tears left for eyes, no eyes for weeping, no
    mouth for singing, no song for the hearer, no more words for
    any mind.

February 1, 1973

William Blake
Tuned By
Allen Ginsberg

On his return from the 1968 Chicago Democratic Convention Allen began composing music, starting with poems from William Blake's Songs of Innocence and Songs of Experience. Less than a year later he recorded twenty-one Blake songs which were issued by MGM as Allen Ginsberg/William Blake: Songs of Innocence and of Experience by William Blake, tuned by Allen Ginsberg (ETS-3083). At this time (August 1973) he has put to music nearly all of Blake's songs and recorded a second Blake album.

The four songs following have been selected from the dozen or so Allen used frequently during the spring of 1971. Two of them, "The Lamb" and "The Chimney Sweeper," can be heard on the first Blake album.

Little Lamb, I'll tell thee, Little Lamb, I'll tell thee:

He is called by thy name, For he calls himself a Lamb:

He is meek, & he is mild, He became a little child.

I a child, & thou a lamb, We are called by his name.

Little Lamb, God bless thee! Little Lamb, God bless thee!

C Poetry music

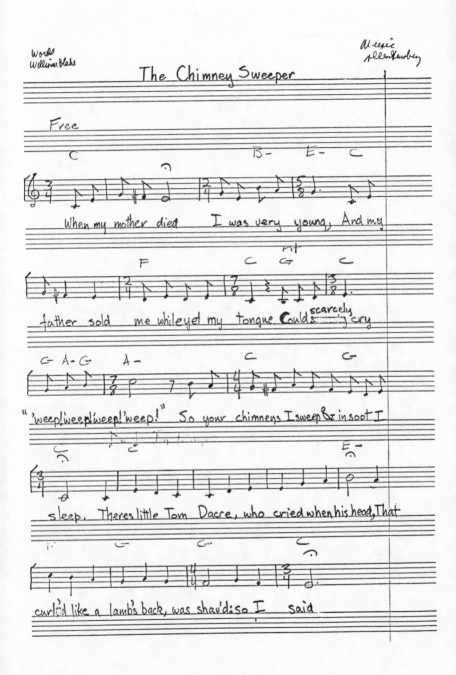

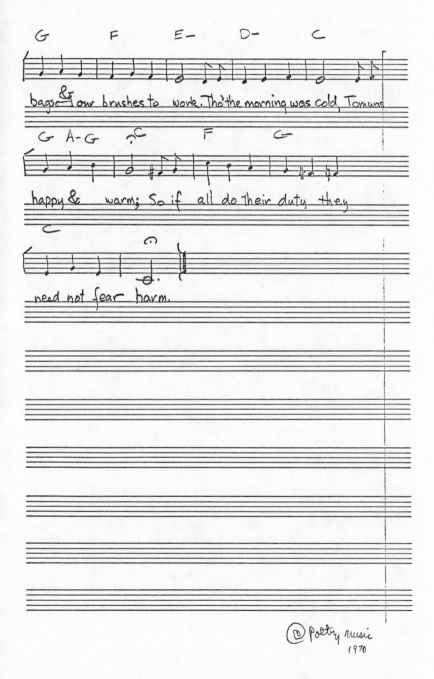

G   F   E-   D-   C

bags & our brushes to work. Tho' the morning was cold, Tom was

G A-G   C   F   G

happy & warm; So if all do their duty they

C

need not fear harm.

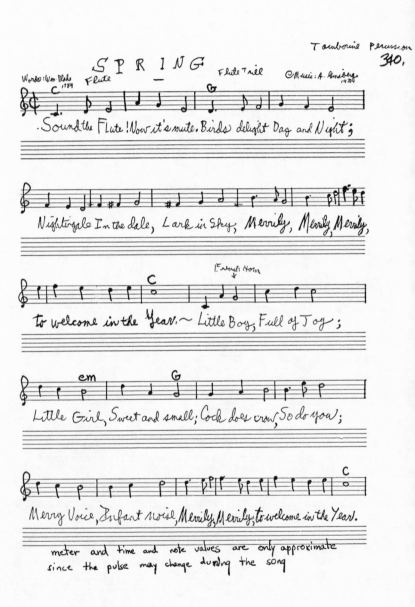

Little Lamb, Here I am; Come and lick My white neck;

Let me pull Your soft Wool; Let me kiss Your soft face:

Merrily, Merrily, we welcome in the Year. Merrily, Merrily

we welcome in the Year. Merrily, Merrily, we welcome in the Year.

Merrily, Merrily, we welcome in the Year. Merrily, Merrily,

We welcome in the year, etc.

© Poetry Music

Appendix

Gists of Other Sources and Cases Supplementary to Text

ADDICTION POLITICS 1922–1970

1. "Derelictions of the Medical Profession Concerning Narcotic Addiction," opinions and views by Robert C. Stokes, M.D., *Texas State Journal of Medicine,* September, 1963, Vol. 59, pp. 839–842. (Includes excellent reading list.)

> Society has accepted for 40 years the idea that the word "dope" existed to modify the word "fiend." . . . The Harrison Narcotic Act of 1914 was passed as a Tax Measure and its intent and purpose was to bring under control and force into legal channels the flow of narcotic drugs. . . . No one suspected . . . a federal police bureau dictating the terms under which a doctor can prescribe a narcotic drug for a patient. . . . The driving force in the big "takeover" has been Harry J. Anslinger, who was the first commissioner of the Bureau of Narcotics and the only commissioner from 1930, when the Bureau was established, until his retirement in 1962. . . . Rufus King suggests that the Bureau of Narcotics has "succeeded in creating a very large criminal class for itself to police (i.e., the whole doctor-patient-addict-peddler community) instead of the very small one that Congress had intended (the smuggler and peddler)."

The quote in the above from L. Kolb, *Drug Addiction: A Medical Problem,* Springfield, Ill., Charles C. Thomas, 1962.

2. *The New York Times,* May 26, 1970, O'DWYER CALLS FOR GIVING FREE NARCOTICS TO ADDICTS. By Clayton Knowles.

> "Simply put," Mr. O'Dwyer said of his proposal, "the results must be the end of profit for the gangster and the pusher, and thus the end of the pusher salesman, and, therefore, a vast reduction in new young addicts. . . . The cost of Administration by a government agency would be much less than the cost of any one of the major law-enforcement bodies now involved in the attempt to suppress addiction."

3. *Report to the United Nations* by Her Majesty's Government in the United Kingdom of Great Britain and Northern Ireland on the working of the International Treaties for Narcotic Drugs for 1968.

> [Contains statistics on containment of addict population and analysis of paper rise in new addict statistics] partly attributable

to the operation of two new factors: (1) The system of compulsory notification of addicts by physicians brought to notice addict patients who might otherwise have remained undetected by the Central Authority. (2) The system of allowing only specially licensed physicians to prescribe heroin for addicts, and the consequent reduction in the amounts individually prescribed, forced a number of undetected addicts to present themselves for treatment instead of continuing to rely for their supplies of heroin on other addicts. . . .

4. *Report to the United Nations,* 1969:

These statistics give ground for cautious optimism [on registered addict statistics leveling out].

5. *The New York Times,* April 29, 1969 (Bradford, England):

. . . according to C. G. Jeffrey, the Home Office's chief inspector for narcotics. . . . "A certain amount of overprescribing goes on. . . but if anything it is better than under-prescribing, which could lead to an illicit market."

CRIME IN THE STREETS CAUSED BY ADDICTION POLITICS

1. Letter to *The New York Times,* March 30, 1968, George D. Cannon, M.D., Secretary, Board of Directors, NAACP Legal Defense and Educational Fund.

Adopt the recommendations of the New York Academy of Medicine given long ago, to stop drug addiction. Protect the law-abiding inhabitants from that 85 percent of the crime they are having inflicted on them by their fellow residents. I raise voice to seek protection for the black masses who are unable or who are too terrorized to speak. . . . Free us from violence.

2. *The New York Times,* February 9, 1968.

Britain regards her addicts not as criminals but as sick people.

There is no accurate count on the number of addicts here, but one estimate is that the figure has tripled in the last five years. The Government's last official estimate of the total of known addicts was more than 1,400. But officials concede that the real figure is several times that.

3. *New York Daily News,* July 20, 1970, SEYMOUR HINTS HE'D OK LEGALIZED DRUGS, p. 3. By Paul Meskil.

Calling narcotics "the single most important element in terms of the breakdown of criminal justice," [U.S. Attorney Whitney North] Seymour [Jr.] said addicts are responsible for at least half of the major crimes in the metropolitan area. . . . Only about 10% of the estimated 62,000 addicts in the metropolitan area have any contact with the various treatment programs. . . ."

4. *The New York Times,* August 28, 1970, COURT OFFICIAL SEES IMPENDING CRISIS IN CASE BACKLOGS.

[Justice Saul S. Streit] warned yesterday of "an impending crisis in the administration of justice" because of huge backlogs of civil and criminal cases. . . . The report gave striking evidence of the association of narcotics with felony crimes of all types. Justice Streit said a study by the Probation Department of the 3,196 persons convicted last year in Manhattan of major crimes showed that at least 60 per cent "were in one way or another involved with narcotics."

A Few Cases Not Mentioned in the Text of NARCOTICS AGENTS PEDDLING DRUGS

1. *The New York Times,* December 15, 1967, $2,783 THEFT FROM SUSPECT CHARGED TO NARCOTICS DETECTIVE. By David Bird.

2. *The New York Times,* January 25, 1968, COURT TOLD NARCOTICS UNIT SOUGHT BRIBE. By David Bird.

3. *The New York Times,* June 10, 1969, ACCUSER OF POLICE TELLS OF THREATS.

> ... incident in which Mr. Vidal's establishment ... was badly vandalized and Mr. Vidal arrested on narcotics charges ... dismissed ...

4. *The New York Times,* May 17, 1970, INDICTMENTS NAME 6 CITY DETECTIVES—"Narcotics Extortion charged—2 Accused of Seeking a $250 Weekly Payoff." By David Burnham.

5. *The New York Times,* May 19, 1970, POLICEMAN SEIZED AS EXTORTIONIST—"Victim was Allegedly Target of Narcotics Arrest Threat."

> A plainclothes policeman was arrested in Brooklyn yesterday on a charge of extorting money from a cab driver by threatening to accuse him of selling narcotics.

6. *The New York Times,* September 19, 1970, JUDGE SAYS POLICE FREQUENTLY LIE IN DRUG CASES. By Lesley Oelsner.

> ... frequent lying in court to conceal violations of the Fourth Amendment ban on illegal search and seizure...

EPILOGUE

Pages 91–94 of the *Knapp Commission Report on Police Corruption* (New York: George Braziller, 1973) confirm and reveal that:

> corruption in narcotics law enforcement has grown in recent years to the point where high-ranking police officials acknowledge it to be the most serious problem facing the Department. In the course of its investigation, the Commission became familiar with ... corrupt patterns, including:
>
> > Keeping money and/or narcotics confiscated at the time of an arrest or raid.

Selling narcotics to addict-informants in exchange for stolen goods.

Passing on confiscated drugs to police informants for sale to addicts.

"Flaking," or planting narcotics on an arrested person in order to have evidence of a law violation.

"Padding," or adding to the quantity of narcotics found on an arrested person in order to upgrade an arrest.

Storing narcotics, needles and other drug paraphernalia in police lockers.

Illegally tapping suspects' telephones to obtain incriminating evidence to be used either in making cases against the suspects, or to blackmail them.

Purporting to guarantee freedom from police wiretaps for a monthly service charge.

Accepting money or narcotics from suspected narcotics law violators as payment for the disclosure of official information.

Accepting money for registering as police informants persons who were in fact giving no information and falsely attributing leads and arrests to them, so that their "cooperation" with the police may win them amnesty for prior misconduct.

Financing heroin transactions.

In addition to these typical patterns, the Commission learned of numerous individual instances of narcotics-related corrupt conduct on the part of police officers, such as:

Determining the purity and strength of unfamiliar drugs they had seized by giving small quantities to addict-informants to test on themselves.

Introducing potential customers to narcotics pushers.

Revealing the identity of a government informant to narcotics criminals.

Kidnapping critical witnesses at the time of trial to prevent them from testifying.

Providing armed protection for narcotics dealers.

Offering to obtain "hit men" to kill potential witnesses.

At the time of the investigation, the [narcotics] division was a separate unit within the Detective Bureau, and had a complement of 782 men divided into two main groups, each with a different level of responsibility . . .

. . . [One] main unit of the Narcotics Division was the Special Investigation Unit (SIU), to which approximately seventy-five officers were assigned. SIU's responsibility was to initiate long-term investigations of narcotics wholesalers in an effort to apprehend those responsible for high-level drug distribution in the City.

In 1968, allegations of irregularities in the Narcotics Division led to an investigation by the Department's Internal Affairs Division. As a result of this investigation, many members of the Division, including almost the entire staff of SIU, were gradually transferred out of the Division. However, three years later, this Commission's study of narcotics-related corruption revealed that both sectors of the Narcotics Division were still pervaded by corruption. Within the past year, there has been a nearly one hundred percent turnover in Narcotics Division personnel, but as the present commander of the Division recently told the Commission, the problem of corruption remains.

INDEX